The Scholarship of Creative Writing Practice

The Scholarship of Creative Writing Practice

Beyond Craft, Pedagogy, and the Academy

Edited by
Marshall Moore and Sam Meekings

BLOOMSBURY ACADEMIC
LONDON • NEW YORK • OXFORD • NEW DELHI • SYDNEY

BLOOMSBURY ACADEMIC

Bloomsbury Publishing Plc, 50 Bedford Square, London, WC1B 3DP, UK
Bloomsbury Publishing Inc, 1385 Broadway, New York, NY 10018, USA
Bloomsbury Publishing Ireland, 29 Earlsfort Terrace, Dublin 2, D02 AY28, Ireland

BLOOMSBURY, BLOOMSBURY ACADEMIC and the Diana logo are trademarks of
Bloomsbury Publishing Plc

First published in Great Britain 2024
This paperback edition published 2025

Copyright © Marshall Moore, Sam Meekings, and Contributors, 2024

Marshall Moore, Sam Meekings, and Contributors have asserted their right under the
Copyright, Designs and Patents Act, 1988, to be identified as authors of this work.

Cover design and illustration by Rebecca Heselton

All rights reserved. No part of this publication may be: i) reproduced or transmitted in any form, electronic or mechanical, including photocopying, recording or by means of any information storage or retrieval system without prior permission in writing from the publishers; or ii) used or reproduced in any way for the training, development or operation of artificial intelligence (AI) technologies, including generative AI technologies. The rights holders expressly reserve this publication from the text and data mining exception as per Article 4(3) of the Digital Single Market Directive (EU) 2019/790.

Bloomsbury Publishing Plc does not have any control over, or responsibility for, any third-party websites referred to or in this book. All internet addresses given in this book were correct at the time of going to press. The author and publisher regret any inconvenience caused if addresses have changed or sites have ceased to exist, but can accept no responsibility for any such changes.

The author and publisher gratefully acknowledge the permission granted to reproduce copyrighted material in this book. The third-party copyrighted material displayed in the pages of this book is done so on the basis of fair use for the purposes of teaching, criticism, scholarship or research only in accordance with international copyright laws, and is not intended to infringe upon the ownership rights of the original owners.

A catalogue record for this book is available from the British Library.

Library of Congress Cataloging-in-Publication Data
Names: Moore, Marshall, 1970- editor. | Meekings, Sam, editor.
Title: The scholarship of creative writing and practice : beyond craft, pedagogy, and the academy /
edited by Marshall Moore and Sam Meekings.
Description: London ; New York, NY : Bloomsbury Academic, 2024. | Includes bibliographical references and index.
Identifiers: LCCN 2023025525 (print) | LCCN 2023025526 (ebook) | ISBN 9781350290990 (hardback) |
ISBN 9781350291034 (paperback) | ISBN 9781350291003 (pdf) | ISBN 9781350291010 (epub)
Subjects: LCSH: Creative writing (Higher education) | College teaching--Methodology. | Authorship--
Vocational guidance. | Authorship--Moral and ethical aspects.
Classification: LCC PE1404 .S355 2024 (print) | LCC PE1404 (ebook) | DDC 808.0420711--dc23/
eng/20231107
LC record available at https://lccn.loc.gov/2023025525
LC ebook record available at https://lccn.loc.gov/2023025526

ISBN: HB: 978-1-3502-9099-0
PB: 978-1-3502-9103-4
ePDF: 978-1-3502-9100-3
eBook: 978-1-3502-9101-0

Typeset by RefineCatch Limited, Bungay, Suffolk

For product safety related questions contact productsafety@bloomsbury.com.

To find out more about our authors and books visit www.bloomsbury.com
and sign up for our newsletters.

Contents

List of Contributors		vii
Introduction *Marshall Moore and Sam Meekings*		1
1	Three New Myths for Inspiration *Kim Wilkins*	9
2	On the Plurality of Practices *Andrew David King*	23
3	Travel Guide to the Unconscious Practices of Creative Writers *Jason Wirtz*	35
4	Faculty Creative Writing as Nationally/Notionally Funded University Research *Darryl Whetter*	47
5	Write a Novel in Twelve ~~Easy~~ Steps *Lania Knight*	63
6	The Writer as Citizen: Creative Writing, Social Action, and Political Responsibility *Jen Webb*	77
7	But What about the Imagination? Representation, Other People's Stories, and Fiction Writing *Tresa LeClerc*	89
8	Drafting, Revision, and an Author's Duty of Care: My Novel 'Housework of Desire' and the Near-Destruction of a Thirty-Year Friendship *Shady Cosgrove*	103
9	A New Vision of Beauty in Creative Writing Practice *Belinda Hopper*	117

10	In Pursuit of the Writer's Life: Despite the Academy *Xu Xi 許素細, with support by research associate Grace Keith*	129
11	Writing and Anxiety: What Are Writers When They're Not Writing? *Sam Meekings*	143
12	The Value in Authors' Writing Self-Reports: Helping Student-Writers Learn the Practice of Writing from Those Who Practice *Tamara Girardi*	153
13	Author Platform and the Boundaries of Creative Practice *Marshall Moore*	165
14	Navigating Academia as a Couple, as Parents, as Writers *Stephanie and John Vanderslice*	179

Contributors

Kyle Allan is a writer, musician, researcher, actualist, lecturer, and currently a PhD candidate in English Studies at the University of KwaZulu-Natal, South Africa. He is affiliated as a lecturer, Academic Writing Consultant and Research Associate at the School of Humanities and Social Sciences, Varsity College, Independent Institute of Education, Pietermaritzburg, as well as a lecturer in English Studies at the University of KwaZulu-Natal, Pietermaritzburg campus. He has published three books of poetry: *House Without Walls* (2016), *The Space Between Us* (2018), and *Remote Harbour* (2022), and is the editor of *New Coin*, the 57-year-old Rhodes University affiliated journal of poetry.

Shady Cosgrove is an Associate Professor and teaches creative writing at the University of Wollongong, Australia, on Dharawal Country. Her work includes 'Flight' (2022), *What the Ground Can't Hold*, and *She Played Elvis*. Her short works have appeared in *Best Australian Stories*, *Cordite*, *Overland*, *Antipodes*, *Southerly*, *Island*, *takahe*, *Eunoia Review* and various Spineless Wonders collections. She has received the Varuna Eleanor Dark Flagship Fellowship, as well as residencies with the Australian National University's Humanities Research Centre and Bundanon Trust.

Tamara Girardi is an Associate Professor of English at HACC, Central Pennsylvania's Community College, USA. Dr Tamara Girardi is an editor for the Digital and Multimedia/Multimodal section of the *Journal of Creative Writing Studies* and co-edited the essay collection, *Theories and Strategies for Teaching Creative Writing Online*. In addition to her academic research and writing, she also writes books for children and teens. Her award-winning debut young adult novel, *Gridiron Girl*, tells the story of Julia Medina who quits her high school volleyball team to compete against her boyfriend for the starting quarterback position on the football team. Three additional sports novels in the Iron Valley Vikings series followed in 2022. *Above the Fold* is the first book in Tamara's second series, all about teens exploring their dreams and their true selves through exhibits at a popular, mardi-gras-esque hotspot called Carnivalesque. *Above the Fold* released in January of 2023, and its sequel, *Behind the Mask* followed in

February, both from Wise Wolf Books. Tamara's debut board book, *Why, Daddy? Why?* was named a 2022 Editor's Pick by Amazon and is being followed by *Why, Mommy? Why?* in the spring of 2025.

Belinda Hopper is a sessional academic at Macquarie University, Australia. Her undergraduate degree was in Communication, majoring in professional writing, from Western Sydney University. She graduated with a Master of Creative Arts from the University of the Sunshine Coast and was awarded a scholarship for her PhD at Macquarie University. Hopper was the 2018 Don Bank Writer in Residence through North Sydney Council and has been a guest lecturer at Stanton Library for five years. Her research interests lie at the intersection of creative writing and religious thought.

Andrew David King is a PhD student in the English Department at UC Berkeley, USA, where they work on issues of disability, medicine, class, and poetics in Anglophone literatures of the long 20th century. They hold an MFA from the Iowa Writers' Workshop, where they served as a Teaching-Writing Fellow and, later, as Provost's Visiting Writer at the University of Iowa's English Department and Research Assistant at the Walt Whitman Archive. Prior to joining the English Department at Berkeley, they earned an MA in Philosophy from Central European University. Since 2022, they have served as the Director of the Disabled Students Advocacy Project with Berkeley's Graduate Assembly, and in 2023 they taught creative writing to incarcerated youth in Contra Costa County, CA, through a New Literary Project Simpson Fellowship. They are a sub-editor of the open-access *International Journal of Disability and Social Justice*, based at the University of Leeds, and their critical and creative work has appeared in numerous publications, ranging from *The Routledge Handbook of Ecofeminism and Literature* to the Fine Press Book Association's journal *Parenthesis*.

Lania Knight lives in the UK and lectures in Creative Writing at The Open University, UK. She holds a BSc in Plant Science and Environmental Conservation from the University of New Hampshire, and an MA and PhD in English Literature and Creative Writing from the University of Missouri. Her first novel, *Three Cubic Feet*, was shortlisted for the Lambda Literary Award in Debut Fiction. A poem, 'Susurration,' was shortlisted for the Rattle Poetry Prize. Her most recent book is a collection of personal essays, *There Is Fire Here*, from Signal 8 Press. Read more about her at www.laniaknight.com.

Tresa LeClerc holds a PhD in Media and Communication from RMIT University, and an MA in Teaching English to Speakers of Other Languages from the University of Melbourne, Australia. She is currently a Lecturer in Professional Writing in the Media and Communications program at the University of Melbourne. Previously, she was a lecturer at the University of California, San Diego in the Synthesis Writing Program at Seventh College. Her research interests include cultural appropriation in the literary industry and far-right ideology in food discourse. Her writing has appeared in *Djed, Overland, The Conversation, A Voz Limpia, Wild Tongue Zine, Essay Daily*, and *TEXT Journal*.

Sam Meekings is an Associate Professor of Creative Writing at Northwestern University, Qatar. He is the co-editor of *The Place and the Writer: International Intersections of Teacher Lore and Creative Writing Pedagogy* (Bloomsbury 2021), and *Creative Writing Scholars on the Publishing Trade: Practice, Praxis, Print* (2021). He is the author of *Under Fishbone Clouds* (called 'a poetic evocation of the country and its people' by the *New York Times*), *The Book of Crows*, and *The Afterlives of Dr Gachet*. He has a PhD in Creative Writing from Lancaster University and has taught writing at NYU and the University of Chichester in the UK. His website is www.sammeekings.com

Marshall Moore is Course Leader and Senior Lecturer in the School of Communication at Falmouth University, UK. A native of eastern North Carolina, he lived and worked in Hong Kong and South Korea for 15 years before relocating to the UK in 2020. He holds an MA in applied linguistics from the University of New England (Australia) and a PhD in creative writing from Aberystwyth University. Recent books include the short story collection *Love Is a Poisonous Color* (2023) and the memoir *I Wouldn't Normally Do This Kind of Thing* (2022). His essays and short fiction have appeared in *The Southern Review, Pithead Chapel, Eclectica, Asia Literary Review, Quarterly Literary Review Singapore, trampset*, and many other magazines and journals. With Sam Meekings, he has co-edited two previous books on the subject of creative writing and publishing pedagogy. To follow him online, visit linktr.ee/marshallsmoore.

John Vanderslice teaches creative writing at the University of Central Arkansas, USA. A native of muggy and rural southern Maryland, USA, he has spent virtually his entire life below the infamous Mason-Dixon line, a fact that both astounds and strengthens him. His short fiction has appeared in journals in both the United States and Europe, including *Sou'wester, Seattle Review, Crazyhorse, Notre Dame Review, Versal*, and *New Writing*. His books include the child abduction novel *Nous Nous* (2021), the historical novel *The Last Days of Oscar Wilde* (2018), and the linked story collection *Island Fog* (2014). When he isn't writing, reading, or teaching, he can be found cooking, exercising, discussing the university life with his wife Stephanie, hanging out with their animals, or dreaming of France.

Stephanie Vanderslice is Professor of Creative Writing and Director of the Arkansas Writers MFA Workshop at the University of Central Arkansas, USA. She is the author, most recently, of the novel *The Lost Son*, *The Geek's Guide to the Writing Life* (Bloomsbury), and the forthcoming *Teaching Creative Writing Reflectively: A Guide and Sourcebook* (Bloomsbury). She has edited or authored several additional books and dozens of articles, all with the aim of promoting the idea that creative writing can be taught and that we have an obligation as writers/teachers to teach it well. She has had the privilege of being a board member of the Association of Writers and Writing Programs (AWP) and the Creative Writing Studies Organization, of which she was the founding chair.

Jen Webb is Distinguished Professor of Creative Practice, and Interim Executive Dean of the Faculty of Arts and Design at the University of Canberra, Australia. Publications include *Art and Human Rights: Contemporary Asian Contexts* (2016); *Gender and the Creative Labour Market* (2022); and the poetry collections *Moving Targets* (2018) and *Flight Mode* (with Shé Hawke, 2020). She is co-editor of the literary journal *Meniscus* and the scholarly journal *Axon: Creative Explorations*. Her scholarly work focuses on the ethics of representation, and on the field of creative practice; her poetry focuses on material poetics and questions of seeing and being.

Darryl Whetter is the author of ten books of fiction, poetry and creative nonfiction. His most recent books are the climate-crisis novel *Our Sands* (2020), and *Teaching Creative Writing in Asia* (2022). His writing has been selected to various anthologies, including *Best Canadian Stories*, *Best Canadian Essays*, and *Best Asian Short Stories*. His essays have been published by *The Globe and Mail*, *The Detroit Times*, *The Brooklyn Rail*, *THIS Magazine* and several other prestigious presses. He has been a festival or campus author in Bali, Singapore, London, Penang, Swansea, Perth, Sydney, and throughout his native Canada. He holds a PhD in literature and was recently the inaugural director of the first graduate creative writing degree in Singapore, in a degree conferred by Goldsmiths, University of London. His forthcoming books include the 2023 poetry collection *#Travelsend: Poems at Travel's End* and *Teaching Creative Writing in Canada* (2024).

Kim Wilkins is a Professor of Writing at The University of Queensland, Australia. She is a recognised expert on creative practice, popular literature, and the publishing industry. She is the author of more than 30 full-length works of fantasy and historical fiction, and her work is translated into more than 20 languages globally. Her scholarly research centres on creative communities, such as writing groups and fan cultures. She is most recently the author of *Writing Bestsellers: Love, Money, and Creative Practice* (2021) with Lisa Bennett; and *Genre Worlds: Popular Fiction and 21st-Century Book Culture* (2022) with Beth Driscoll and Lisa Fletcher.

Jason Wirtz has been obsessed with the writing process ever since a visiting writer in his MFA program talked about hearing voices while writing a novel. After completing his MFA in fiction, Jason went on to earn a doctorate in Rhetoric & Writing from Michigan State University where questions about the creative writing process continued to fuel his research and eventual dissertation. Jason has been teaching at Hunter College, City University of New York, for the past fifteen years pursing this line of inquiry using interview and, most recently, eye tracking technology. His book, *The Write Mind for Every Classroom*, makes connections between brain research, writing practice, and the teaching of writing. He lives in New York City with his wife, two children, and a 20-year-old cat. He welcomes questions or comments at jwirtz@Hunter.CUNY.edu.

Xu Xi 許素細 (b. 1954) is an Indonesian-Chinese novelist, fiction writer and essayist from Hong Kong who became a US citizen. Author of sixteen books—five novels, nine collections of fiction and essays, one memoir and one co-authored textbook—she also edited or co-edited four anthologies of Hong Kong literature in English. Recent titles include *Monkey in Residence and Other Speculations* (2022), *This Fish Is Fowl: Essays of Being* (2019), *Dear Hong Kong: An Elegy for a City* (2017), the novel *That Man in Our Lives* (2016), and *The Art and Craft of Asian Stories* (Bloomsbury 2021). She was writer-in-residence at Arizona State University, the City University of Hong Kong, the University of Iowa, among others, and directed two international MFA programs in creative writing and literary translation. Earlier, she held management positions in Asia and the US at the Asian Wall Street Journal, Federal Express, and Pinkerton's. Co-founder of Authors at Large, she is currently William H. P. Jenks Chair in Contemporary Letters at the College of the Holy Cross in Massachusetts. A diehard transnational, she now splits life between New York and the rest of the world. Follow her at @xuxiwriter or online at xuxiwriter.com.

Introduction

Marshall Moore
Falmouth University, UK
Sam Meekings
Northwestern University in Qatar

In 'One Simple Word: From Creative Writing to Creative Writing Studies', Tim Mayers argues that creative writing within the academy has bifurcated into two strands, one being more focused on craft and the other on research (2009). Creative Writing, as Mayers puts it, is the 'academic enterprise of hiring successful writers … to teach college-level creative writing courses', whereas creative writing studies 'is a field of scholarly inquiry and research'. He goes on to point out that the former is considerably more developed than the latter, which has largely concerned itself with questions of pedagogy. As editors, we tend to agree with this assessment; in fact, if anything this bifurcation may have become more entrenched, at least in the scholarship. Current practitioners who entered the discipline via the traditional workshop route will have been introduced to pedagogy in that context, and developed their craft there; and they are likely to have furthered their knowledge via the abundant scholarship that exists on the subject. However, discussions on creative practice itself – the work habits as well as the habits of mind; the relationship with reading; the orientation toward publication and the publishing industry – largely continue to rely on the writings of authors past and present. To the extent that this is discussed in academic contexts, it tends to be as anecdotes presented in the service of whatever is being argued. R. Lyle Skains has noted that there is little scholarly research being done on creative practice itself, and points out that '[a]s creative practice expands as a field of academic research, there is a need to establish an ongoing discourse on and resource for appropriate practice-based methodologies' (2018). In the same paper, he goes on to identify various approaches within the realm of practice-based research, while suggesting that Creative Writing scholarship has not yet fully engaged with such discussions.

In a book on practice-based research, Linda Candy defines the term 'creative practice' as

> ... the act of creating something novel with the necessary processes and techniques belonging to a given field of endeavour, whether art, music, design, engineering or science. In the life of an individual person, it involves conceiving ideas and realis[ing] them in some form as artefacts, installations, compositions, designs, or performances. It can be an everyday or intermittent activity and a life's work, during which there are many transformations in thought and works. Practice that is creative is not only characterised by a focus on creating something new, but also by the way that the making process itself leads to a transformation in the ideas, which in turn leads to new works ...
>
> 2011: 33

Candy goes on to contrast research with creative practice by stating that the difference lies in intent: unlike practice, which as mentioned above is done for the sake of creation, research is conducted for the purpose of adding to existing knowledge. Although that knowledge-making may take place in the hopes of creating something 'new', even the term 'new' is problematic and arguably a matter of 'gatekeeping' (2011). This situation has already been recognised in the field of filmmaking and production, as well. For instance, Agnieszka Piotrowsa writes in her edited volume *Creative Practice Research in the Age of Neoliberal Hopelessness* that the guiding idea behind much contemporary film scholarship on creative practice research 'is the notion of reclaiming the subjective, and at times the deeply personal, as the legitimate site of knowledge, particularly in creative practice research in which a personal undertaking, reflection and commitment to work carried out defines the knowledge it produces' (2020: 6). She notes that much feminist scholarship has engaged in deconstructing the problematic prioritisation of 'objective' research in the academy, and in shifting the focus to knowledges that are subjective, personal, and embodied (11). Scholarship on practice-led research in the visual arts has drawn similar conclusions, albeit with caveats about the prioritisation of traditional forms of research in institutional funding structures (Biggs 2002: 2003; Durling, Friedman, and Gutherson 2002; Niedderer 2005). This is consistent with Mayers's observations, suggesting that 'creative practice' is for all intents and purposes an academic term that exists alongside and within the framework of research, and therefore subject to the whims and imperatives of budgets and committees. In fact, one might even conclude that the term exists because there is a need for something that sounds academic enough to justify the presence of creative work in educational institutions. Fortunately, we aren't that cynical – not yet, at least.

Although we think the definition of the term 'creative practice' is fraught because of its relationship to the academy (it isn't widely used in lay society), to research, and to funding, none of this changes the lack of scholarly discussion about what writers *do*.

In this volume, we aim to bridge that gap by asking creative writing scholars to reflect upon the practice of writing – and in doing so, to keep discussions of the workshop and pedagogy to a necessary minimum. An idea Stephanie Vanderslice explores in her book *Rethinking Creative Writing* (2021) and we (Meekings and Moore) extend in our collection *Creative Writing Scholars on the Publishing Trade: Practice, Praxis, Print* (2021) is that academic creative writing programs have begun to adopt a more pragmatic, industry-facing stance toward pedagogy: today, students of writing need and expect to complete their degrees at least somewhat prepared to monetise the skills they have learned. However, a paradox exists in this configuration: if the workshop teaches craft but the academy is at last beginning to embrace outcomes pertaining to the trade, and if the scholarship is still perhaps overly concerned with pedagogy, where does that leave examinations of creative practice itself? To put it another way, how does the creative work actually get done? What are the conditions in which it takes place? What are the contexts that most affect it? What is its origin? What do practitioners then do with it?

Even if, as Mayers posits, academic creative writing is 'a *de facto* employment program for writers who are unable to earn a living simply by writing', the subtext in this statement is that these writers have managed to maintain some version of a creative practice at least up until the completion of their academic credentials and, one hopes, beyond. Given that a creative commentary or exegesis is a required component of the PhD in creative writing, many practicing academics will have already done some degree of scholarly reflection on their own work. However, though this speaks to the development and importance of reflexive writing within the field, such reflection frequently prioritises the product of writing (by examining, for instance, the literary influences and the genre conventions of the text that has been created) rather than the process and practices that lead to its creation. This may be one reason why there seems to be so little about creative practice in the academic journals. Moreover, this leads to several other important questions over and above the ones already mentioned. How beholden are scholars of creative writing to myth and superstition, despite the best efforts of the academy to dispel these? How anxious are they about time management, workload and demands to spend more time marketing their work than actually producing it? How has social media influenced their practice, particularly in light of prevailing social movements such as #metoo, #publishingpaidme, and #BlackLivesMatter? If Twitter collapses, as seemed likely at the time of this writing, how will that affect the trajectory of these trends? We believe a focused, scholarly reflection on the topic of creative practice is both urgently necessary and long overdue, hence this book.

Before we introduce the chapters in this collection, let us take a moment to offer some context by introducing ourselves. We both came to the academy via similar routes: first as published writers with experience in the publishing industry, then going on to do PhDs in Creative Writing (Moore at Aberystwyth, Meekings at Lancaster) before finding the positions we currently hold. Both have also adapted practice to changing environments (China, Hong Kong, Qatar, Greece, the UK) and to the changing nature of industry practices and institutional expectations. Among other effects, our diverse international experiences have provided us both with a critical distance from which to reflect on the different approaches to writing practices and approaches that we have witnessed in classes, communities, and institutions around the world.

If our earlier collection *The Place and the Writer: International Intersections of Teacher Lore and Creative Writing Pedagogy* (Bloomsbury, 2021) foregrounded how a diverse and localised approach to lore and pedagogy reinvigorates thinking about place and writing, then this collection extends our investigations of how we might conceptualise and discuss the fundamental issues of creative practice in changing environments. In our previous edited volume, *Creative Writers on the Publishing Trade: Practice, Praxis, Print* (2021), Peter Anderson reflected on portfolio practice: namely the modern reality of a writer having to build a diverse and wide-ranging portfolio of jobs, writing skills, and marketing strategies in order to survive in the modern world. He marked the growth of this trend as a reflection of 'the way that so much work within the creative fields requires an understanding not just of creative practice, the craft of writing, but also the infrastructural and operational conditions within which practice is embedded – the organisational and business side of creative work' (2021: 94). The chapters in this book expand on this concept by examining the lived realities of these intersections of craft, practice, and the contexts in which they operate.

Several themes, including some we did not anticipate, emerge in the chapters that follow. As such, we have arranged the chapters into three distinct sections: on the act of writing and its attendant challenges; on the ethics of creative practice; and on career, practice, and identity.

In the first section, a group of writers look at the act of writing itself, scrutinising it in terms of its attendant issues and challenges. Full disclosure: this was the topic we had expected to attract the most attention, not career-related concerns. Yet one underlying theme that emerges in many of the discussions of practice in this book are strategies for and articulations of *writing against the odds*. Financial, career, family, social, and time constraints do indeed emerge as barriers to writing processes, as anticipated, and yet these chapters present a multitude of approaches to responding to such pressures in building adaptive and creative approaches to both conceptualising and actualising practice. There are mythology and philosophy, but there are also precarity, income and time management, among discussions of aesthetics, values, and reflexivity. Darryl Whetter unpicks the complex relationship between economics and creativity: in Canada, government funding initiatives play a significant role in which books get written and which ones never make it past the proposal stage, a conundrum likely to be relevant far and wide. Lania Knight reflects upon the dynamics of trauma, education, and research that led to the genesis of a novel. Kim Wilkins, Andy King, and Jason Wirtz all analyse and investigate the ontology of creativity, thereby suggesting new ways of conceptualising the nature of creative practice.

One area of overlap between many of these chapters (in particular those of Jen Webb, Shady Cosgrove, and Belinda Hopper) was a consideration of the ethical dimension of practice. This therefore is the focus of the book's second section. A number of authors argue for the necessity of considering craft as a means of engagement with the world, and thereby conceptualise practice as a means towards achieving this. Through this lens, the processes of research, planning, and revision (not to mention the pedagogy of these) are analysed as vehicles for interaction and nexuses of interactivity. Practice is, in this way, a means of generating new knowledge both about writing and about the world(s) in which it takes place. Case in point: Tresa LeClerc explores the important issue of (mis)representation and the ethical and practical limits of ethnography and imagination in constructing 'the other' within fictional worlds, and calls for direct and specific action from the publishing industry. We are proud to share such new knowledges and approaches in this volume, and we believe they offer ways into new debates about how we discuss and research practice both in the academy and beyond its walls.

Finally, the third important theme was the focus on career, creative practice, and identity. These three items coexist and overlap, interpellated for many of the contributors to the point where it would be difficult to find the boundaries. Quite a few of the writers examined this trifecta, albeit from various angles: for example, Xu Xi examines the discrepancies between the mythology of the writing life and its professional realities, finding the views of the writers she surveyed more varied than one might expect; while Meekings looks at how outcomes and publishing affect the ways in which we consider practice. Indeed, the effects of the uncertainty and precarity of the writing life in the 21st century emerge as an important factor influencing the ways in which writers approach and conceptualise their writing. Moore interrogates the uncomfortable relationship between what has traditionally been regarded as the 'creative' work and the industry-driven mandate to spend more time marketing it than writing it. Tamara Girardi examines the value of writers' own self-reports in providing a clear and specific framework for ways in which students and developing writers can both consider and act on their own cognitive, social, and expressive encounters with writing. Finally, John and Stephanie Vanderslice reflect upon their lives as writers and academics, sharing a very personal account of the choices – and, often, sacrifices – they made in order to balance their creative lives with the demands of jobs and families.

Before we draw this introduction to a close, we would like to add two disclaimers. One is what might appear to be a contradiction or paradox in the subtitle of this book: *Beyond Craft, Pedagogy, and the Academy* might at first glance suggest that there will be no discussion of these topics whatsoever, when the opposite was always our intention. We have maintained since our first co-edited book that the scholarship of creative writing tends to be siloed into discussions/interrogations of pedagogy (mainly the workshop, plus what we might call the Vanderslice Question) and social justice. Indeed, the conversations arising in response to recent pedagogical works such as Felicia Rose Chavez's *The Anti-Racist Writing Workshop* (2021) attest to the importance and urgency of such discussions. However, while foundational, these are not the only topics pertinent to the field. In fact, what emerges herein is the point mentioned earlier: as practitioners, we do not necessarily draw boundary lines between our written work and the contexts in which we create it. Does that mean, to reconfigure an old American joke, you can take the writer out of the university but you can't take the university out of the writer after they have worked in one? We suspect this is true.

The second disclaimer is that reflection on creative practice is, by nature, personal. Over the centuries countless writers have discussed the process of writing, as evidenced by the existence of books such as *Writers on Writing: A Book of Quotations* (Alysoun Owen, 2021); *Writers on Writing: Collected Essays from the New York Times* (John Darnton, 2001); *Writers on Writing: Inside the Lives of 55 Distinguished Writers and Editors* (Chip Scanlan, Kathleen Fair, et al, 2021); and Margaret Atwood's *On Writers and Writing* (2015). While instructive, volumes such as these are generally intended to be pithy, compelling, and marketable, with writers expounding upon or lamenting about the struggles that accompany their craft. Mythology often rears its translucent, shaggy head. What these books are not, however, is rigorous, systematised, and academic. Hence the lacuna in which this collection appears. Since the outset of this project, we have become aware of one other title in the academic realm – the estimable Graeme Harper is working on it – but there is still little else out there to draw from when researching creative practice. This is why as editors, we made the executive decision not to require the contributors to adhere strictly to the conventions of scholarly writing. This is partly an acknowledgment of the growing body of work that challenges those conventions: scholars such as Candace Spiegelman have argued in favour of treating personal reflection as relevant in the academic realm. We also feel strongly that the boundaries of research in creative writing are still rather confining due to the newness of the discipline. There are too many subjects that require active, innovative approaches to knowledge-making for us to be convinced it would be useful to limit ourselves and the work we are doing here to gleanings from an emerging field.

In conclusion, this volume maps the varied landscape of the ways that writers, scholars and instructors conceptualise creative practice. Despite the foundational reference to scholarship in the title and in the approach of these chapters, the consensus that emerges is clear: practice means thinking beyond the academy and interrogating the ways in which creative habits, researches, processes, careers, and craft intersect and engage with the changing world in which we are writing.

References

Anderson, P. (2021), Beyond the Double Life of Writers: Creative Writing as Portfolio Practice. In S. Meeking and M. Moore (eds) *Creative Writing Scholars on the Publishing Trade: Practice, Praxis, Print*. Routledge: Abingdon, 84–98.

Biggs, M. (2002). 'The Rôle of the Artefact in Art and Design Research', *International Journal of Design Sciences and Technology*, 10(2), 19–24.

Biggs, M. (2003), *The Rôle of 'the Work' in Research*. PARIP 2003 National Conference. Retrieved January 2006, from http://www.bris.ac.uk/parip/biggs.htm.

Candy, L. (2011), 'Research and Creative Practice'. In L. Candy and E. A. Edmonds (eds) *Interacting: Art, Research and the Creative Practitioner*. Farringdon, UK: Libri Publishing Ltd, 33–59.

Chavez, F. R. (2021), *The Anti-Racist Writing Workshop: How To Decolonize the Creative Classroom*. Chicago: Haymarket Books.

Durling, D., Friedman, K., and Gutherson, P. (2002), 'Editorial: Debating the Practice-Based PhD', *International Journal of Design Science and Technology,* 10(2), 7–18.

Mayers, T. (2009), 'One Simple Word: From Creative Writing to Creative Writing Studies', *College English,* 71(3), 217–228.

Meekings, S. and Moore, M. (2021), *Creative Writing Scholars on the Publishing Trade: Practice, Praxis, Print.* London: Routledge.

Niedderer, K. (2005), 'How Much Theory Do We Need to Ride a Bicycle: Or How Useful Is Research for Practice?' In P. Rogers, L. Brodhurst, and D. Hepburn (eds) *Crossing Design Boundaries.* London: Taylor and Francis: 9–14.

Piotrowsa, A. (2020), *Creative Practice Research in the Age of Neoliberal Hopelessness.* Edinburgh: Edinburgh University Press.

Skains, R. L. (2018), 'Creative Practice as Research: Discourse on Methodology'. *Media Practice and Education,* 19(1): 82–97, DOI: 10.1080/14682753.2017.1362175.

Vanderslice, S. (2011), *Rethinking Creative Writing.* The Professional and Higher Education Partnership, London: Frontinus.

1

Three New Myths for Inspiration

Kim Wilkins
University of Queensland

Those Romantic myths about how creative writing happens are hard to shake. The Western popular imagination still cleaves strongly to the idea of the special individual, the emphasis on exclusivity and disconnection, the notion that 'real' art should be effortless and sublime. In fact, these ideas are so firmly embedded that when artists are asked about their creative processes, they 'repeat creativity myths, even though scientific studies of those same individuals later find that it didn't actually happen that way' (Sawyer 2006: 18). I have written elsewhere about creative myths, noting that while they can sometimes be counterproductive and are often if not mostly untrue, 'less is said about how productive inventing and musing on these too-good-to-be-true narratives can be too. Creativity, like dreaming, is something ordinary that seems out of the ordinary. We attach stories to it because it gives us pleasure to do so and this pleasure is not trivial' (Wilkins and Bennett 2021: 64). That is, one does not need to believe the myths of creative practice to garner benefits from them. If a dreamed story idea fuels enthusiasm, or a writer manages thousands of words while writing on retreat near the sea, myths can be seen to have an enabling function.

However, what if there were other pleasurable and inspiring stories writers told themselves about creative writing that were closer to material experience, and thus did not seduce writers into perfectionism and self-doubt? What if these stories were achievable, able to be folded into our daily lives, and did not require us to be white men with puffy sleeves taking opium in lonely farmhouses?

In this chapter I will foreground the pleasures of the creative process. This perspective is developed from my experience and is thus deeply subjective, though supported with evidence where it can be. Certainly, there are pleasures in creative outcomes, and in the early years of my career my pride in publications was immense. However, it did not take long for me to realise that publications (and good reviews, the occasional award, or seeing somebody reading my book on the bus) could not sustain me as a creative writer; the only thing that ever has sustained me (and inspired me) is the practice of writing itself. I have chosen three of my favourite perspectives on the creative writing process to elaborate below: the importance of making art that is not even close to perfect, the value of community in our practice, and the satisfaction of slogging it out. I do not mean to imply that wilful craft blindness, writerly social relationships, or difficult labour are always positive, but my focus is on how pleasure may be generative, so my examples help build out those stories – those new myths – that may inspire writers to write.

Make 'Bad' Art

Cultural institutions are obsessed with good art, including good literary art. Reviews are written, prizes are given, canon is established. Those starting out as writers cannot fail to see the goal posts in the distance, and feel themselves small and far away. Literary value remains text-centric. The object of review or study must be a 'good' text, one that offers a rich reading or evidences novelty and beauty. Not a great deal of scholarship is interested in the idea of bad writing. Those who do examine bad art still maintain a text-centric model. For example, Dyck and Johnson write about artworks 'which we enjoy *just for* their bad artistic features', and this they call 'good-bad art' (2017: 279). Good-bad art, they argue, is work that has aesthetic value even if it does not have artistic value (281). I am far less interested in classifying individual texts as either good or so-bad-they're-good; instead, I want to look beyond the texts to the pleasures of creation, regardless of artistic outcome. That is, if we locate the value of art in its production rather than its reception (while not altogether excluding its reception), what stories about humans and art may we be able to tell?

Dyck and Johnson suggest that cultural institutions and the individuals who shape them are 'relatively agnostic about what makes for artistic badness', though they assume that it involves 'failed artistic intentions' (282). I challenge the idea of both failure and of intention. Drunk friends in a karaoke booth singing 'Bohemian Rhapsody' are likely producing bad art, but there are no failed artistic intentions here. Instead, there is kindred and community, love for a classic song, and the sheer joy of using the body as a musical instrument. Conversely, a teenage fan of a young adult fantasy series may devote great care and attention to the fan fiction she writes about the characters, but the results will always be derivative by definition and that is her intention. Further, not only does she derive pleasure from the craft and purpose of writing, but thousands of other fans may enjoy reading her work just as much; so it cannot be considered failure. As Louis Tay and James Pawelski note, there are intrinsic benefits to art, including 'personal enjoyment, individual and societal growth, and meaning-making' (2022: 5); and in particular self-expression is a 'a deep and rich way for people to bring out their ideas, feelings, and perspectives' (8). There is no reason so-called bad art cannot still be a valued aspect of creative practice. In fact, if writers valued the pleasurable dimensions of process it may encourage them to keep creating, when idealism about the quality of finished products would otherwise stop them. This section explores three of those pleasurable dimensions: flow, lingering, and passionate investment.

The concept of flow was developed by psychologist Mihaly Csikszentmihalyi to describe the pleasurable sense of immersion in practising art, based on interviews with both professional artists and serious amateurs. Flow is 'an almost automatic, effortless, yet highly focussed state of consciousness' (1996: 110) where 'action and awareness are merged', 'distractions are excluded from consciousness', and 'the sense of time becomes distorted' (111–113). Csikszentmihalyi went on to position flow as one of the pillars of his work on positive psychology, developing it from a concept about creative practice to one about immersion and intrinsic motivation more generally, noting with Jeanne Nakamura that 'a good life is characterised by complete absorption in what one does' (2020: 279).

One aspect of flow that is often noted is the way that it changes the perception of time: 'clock time no longer marks equal lengths of experienced time; our sense of how much time passes depends on what we are doing' (Csikszentmihalyi 1996: 113). I explored this aspect of flow in previous research, and my interviews with creative writers revealed the intense pleasure associated with the flow state in creative practice:

> Forsyth calls this asynchrony 'that miraculous space of being outside time'. . . . Her use of the word miraculous is typical of the kind of effusive reaction writers have when talking about time's distortion: when I asked Carmody about it, for example, she paused for nearly ten seconds, eyes closed, in rapture.
>
> Wilkins 2017, np

In conducting my interviews, this question about time and the flow state was evidently my interviewees' favourite question, demonstrating the enormous creative value derived from the process of writing, rather than in its output or outcome. Being in flow while writing is what makes it feel like art to the writer;

whether that art is considered good or bad at the end cannot diminish this material experience.

My interviewees were all professional writers, and certainly not creators of what might be called bad art. But amateur expressions of art – those least likely to be valued by critics or make their way into canon – also have a unique relationship with time. Rita Felski has theorised the way that time may be experienced differently by different social groups, and one temporality she writes of is 'life time'; or the narrative that 'encompasses and connects the random segments of daily experience' (Felski 2000: 17). When applied to professional writers such as those cited above, life time might encompass how a professional identity is forged over time through a series of projects, deadlines and outputs; that is how they order their work to 'make sense of [their] identities by endowing them with a temporal Gestalt' (Felski 2000: 17). This identity is a version of what Dinshaw calls 'the modern expert' who emerges out of 'time-as-measurement hitched to Western European concepts of progress toward a singular goal'. By contrast, amateurism is 'everything the professional leaves behind on the modern train of forward progress' (Dinshaw 2012, 21–22). Amateur creative expression does not 'follow a predestined career path' and so 'starts and stops at will; tinkerers and dabblers can linger at moments of pleasure when the professionals must soldier duly onward' (22). This freedom from professionalism – arguably the very thing that distinguishes their art from good art – allows for a unique and liberated personal investment; 'all over the map or minutely focused – or both – depending on particular interests' (22). If writers saw the value of their work not in its reception by others, but in the investment of their own time and joy, then all art is good and no time writing is wasted. This perspective also disempowers gatekeepers, especially those who espouse elitist views that may be based in class, gender and race. As Dinshaw notes, amateurs shift 'the boundaries of knowledge production' and therefore display the potential to shift the 'whole system of credentializing, of judging who gets to make knowledge and how' (2012: 24).

Centring passionate engagement as the marker of art that is good (fulfilling, pleasurable, expressive and so on), allows connection with others who share that view of art. More and more, digital tools allow such art to be shared. The disintermediation of the publishing industry has not been greeted with open arms by those invested in its traditions. Widespread grumbling about e-books may have subsided, but dichotomies between traditional publishing and independent publishing (only recently liberated from the label 'vanity publishing') persist. But, as Arthi Vadde notes, 'Whether a cause of chagrin or excitement, the digital domain of publishing culture is definitively changing the ways in which contemporary writers, artists, and audiences conceive of their creative works and creative selves' (27). Vadde locates pleasure – both as an experience in itself, and as an experience 'enhanced by dialogue' with others – in amateur expression (28). Nowhere is the dialogue with others more apparent than in fan fiction communities, communities that function as safe spaces for 'bad' writing. In her essay about One Direction fan fiction, Ksenia Korobkova (2018) writes of how fans who may be embarrassed about how much they love the band use Wattpad as a place to 'geek out' and connect this enthusiasm to their creative writing aspirations (67).

Mythic stories about writing are all here for the taking: writing can feel wonderful, especially if freed from expectations about its reception; lingering, loving, being present in process are all real possibilities for writers, both professional and amateur. That this joy can also be shared with others is the next new myth for inspiration I will turn to.

Share the Joy

The solitary individual myth of creativity is one that is hard to shake. It remains in everything from the existence of writing retreats to the continued use of the word 'gifted' to describe creative people. Creativity, in this view, thrives on being tucked away from the world and the demands of others, and is something an individual is born with. An inspiring counter-story to this myth, however, is that of the value of creative communities in developing craft, and getting words on to the page and into the world. My research on genre communities has proven over and over that writers write best among and with other writers (Wilkins, Driscoll, and Fletcher: 2022). What if we not only acknowledged it, but celebrated it as a way to reach our full creative potential?

Howard Becker (1984), a cultural sociologist and a jazz pianist, argues that every work of art (including works of creative writing) materialises not solely through the labour of creative individuals, but through 'radiating networks' who perform 'cooperative activity'; that is, everything that the writer does not do 'must be done by someone else' (35). In terms of creative writing, this can be industrial personnel – everyone from acquiring publishers to warehouse foremen – but the social dimension of an 'art world', as Becker calls it, cannot be underestimated. Becker holds that wherever a 'cooperative link' exist, there is influence to some degree (25). While his theory is not too concerned with the value of social and community affect in these radiating networks; to understand creativity it is vital to understand the enormous influence of pleasurable social links among creative writers. They might appear in direct and formal settings, in collaborations, or even in informal friendships.

First, we might consider aspects of direct influence via the social. By direct influence I refer to social activity that is deliberately aimed at producing creative writing. Writing courses have long been staples of community arts organisations, and have grown rapidly through the late twentieth and early twenty-first century at universities. A large part of the structure of writing courses is the 'workshop' or a formalised process by which writers have their writing assessed by their peers.

In a book I co-wrote with Beth Driscoll and Lisa Fletcher (2022), we examined the way that genre communities (what we called 'genre worlds', after Becker's 'art worlds') routinely operate to share knowledge. The example par excellence is the 'con', or convention, where formal learning experiences between people who share a love of genre exist, such as the training opportunities available at the Romance Writers of America events held annually in the United States. Craft development in this instance goes hand in hand with a sense of cohort (in this case, writers who share a love of romance writing), intensifying the social complexion of learning craft (105–107). This kind of craft development can happen in online spaces too. On a simple level, workshops and knowledge transfer can be replicated virtually, especially post-pandemic when the use of conferencing technology has become pervasive. But native online applications for creative writing such as Wattpad have built-in functionality for gaining feedback from readers. According to Wattpad, nearly 90 percent of its 250 million stories are serialised:

> When writers serialize on Wattpad, a push notification brings their audience back every time they update a chapter. Audience feedback also helps writers gauge how cliffhangers, one-liners, and epic passages are received. Inline comments on Wattpad stories reveal the words that spur the most reaction from readers ... Audience feedback, along with tools like writer analytics, helps writers tweak chapters where they see reader drop-off, or improve upon scenes that got the most comments. The positive comments from passionate fans are also something that many Wattpad Stars credit as inspiration.
>
> 2016

This is a view of inspiration that eschews Muses and solitary genius, and embraces connected and invested communities.

While the examples so far may seem to pertain to the work of amateur or emerging writers, professional writers benefit from them too. Many professional writers rely on 'crit groups' (groups of other writers who offer feedback on ideas) and 'beta readers' (writing peers who will read early versions of a manuscript) to help them shape their works (Wilkins et al. 2022: 119). While such critical and creative relationships have been researched and theorised, quite simply we know these social relationships exist and matter because acknowledgements pages tell us they do. Writers, for the most part, need other writers.

Romantic accounts of creativity, invested as they are in the idea of the individual, rarely if ever endorse the idea of collaboration. And yet, collaboration can be a story of immense appeal. Moreover, collaboration is common for writers. Cassandra Clare and Holly Black, for example, share a close friendship and collaborate on writing projects where they write 'side-by-side sharing a laptop' (Wilkins et al. 2022: 125). While there are other kinds of collaborations – for example the highly mediated collaborations between megaseller James Patterson and authors with smaller profiles – the idea of a writing collaboration coloured by the pleasure and delight of friendship is a story with the power to inspire.

Children's authors Holly Goldberg Sloan and Meg Wolitzer tell their 'strange and delightful' story of a creative friendship. After meeting at a conference:

> we were drinking wine in a hotel bar and discovering that we had so many life similarities. We're both writers married to writers. We both have two sons. We are born nine months apart. We both want to laugh more than anything. Over the course of the next few years, as we sent each other email and text messages, we decided we wanted to write something together.
>
> 2019

As Wolitzer notes,

> I usually think of writing as such a solitary act, but that wasn't true here. I took a lot of pleasure and comfort in the fact that when I had written a page and sent it off to [Sloan, she] would respond and write more. Usually when I write a page, my only reward is to have to write another one.

For Wolitzer and Sloan mutually reinforcing delight is apparent. The friendship inspired them to be creative, and the creativity reinforced their friendship. As Sloan says, 'my favorite thing about the past two years of working on this book was that our friendship grew'. Again, this is a story of inspiring connection, highlighted in words such as 'pleasure', 'comfort', and 'favourite'. Wolitzer's account of their similarities even takes on a mythic quality, finding destiny in coincidence ('We both have two sons. We are born nine months apart').

But social influence goes beyond writers actively seeking feedback on writing projects or collaborating, among both amateur and professional writers. Put simply, writers often form friendships with other writers. As with most friendships, they are formed between writers who are similar in other ways (beyond writing). Two of my closest friends, with whom I am in daily if not hourly contact over iMessage, are also academics who write speculative fiction. Some writers even marry other writers (though that isn't a prospect I would relish). Nonetheless, these friendships provide a range of paratextual benefits that support writers through their lives and thus have an indirect influence on their writing.

Friendships provide perspective. In running my problems past my friends, that is what I always seek primarily: 'help me see this anew'. Luckily, writers (as with most creative people) are good at finding new perspectives. Decisions about which book to write next, what to do with troublesome publishing industry relationships, how to find time to meet deadlines: all of these may indirectly influence what I write, and my friendships have material impact on how I answer those questions.

Nowhere has friendship given me more perspective as a writer than in dealing with tumultuous life changes, particularly those attendant on having children. for me writing requires deep thought on a regular schedule and babies are not quiet or predictable. Michael Chabon (2018) tells of a 'great man' writer who approached him early in his career to say 'You can write great books, or you can have kids', subscribing to the oft-cited musing of Cyril Connolly that there is 'no more sombre enemy of good art than the pram in the hall' (1938: 116). Managing a deadline and a new baby is terrifically challenging, but a common enough proposition among writers. For my sixth novel *Giants of the Frost*, I credit its completion as much to the writer friend who took my son and babysat him for an hour while I wrote every day, as to the writer friend who simply handed me noise-cancelling headphones so I didn't hear him cry for those agonising fifteen minutes before he went to sleep each naptime. As my children grew, I was both the recipient and the imparter of knowledge around how to write as a parent: from advice about getting to school pick-up half an hour early to write (and also score the best parking spot), to how to have conversations with publishers about deadlines, to knowing when to put projects down and focus on family. These networks of knowledge are rarely given attention when we think about how creative writing happens.

What I write of above, of course, is the value of shared experience and knowledge. These friendships function as what Paul Gee (2005) would call 'affinity spaces', where social interactions can determine 'the (changing) universe of possible (and emergently routine) ways in which people can think about, value, act and interact about those interests' (228). Social relationships, then, 'support the development of shared interests' (Wilkins et al. 2022: 99). The activities in the affinity space do not need to directly be writing activities: they only need to be affinity-building between writers to work. Sharing a meme, creating an in-joke, complaining about a mutual colleague: these things cause friendships to deepen over time thus deepening influence. Without ever having read another's work, being 'not alone' in a writer's life enhances, perhaps even inspires, creative productivity.

All of these examples of social relationships have the capacity to shape what gets written: the solitary (white male) writer on the moors does not find much of a foothold in this account of creative sociality. Instead, the inspiring story here is one of shared enthusiasm, playfully batting creative ideas back and forth, supporting each other through thorny problems, and ultimately – after the hard work – celebrating successes together. It is to the topic of hard work that I now turn.

Find the Romance in Labour

Many myths of creativity are underpinned by an idea that 'real' creativity must be effortless: from Milton's invocation of the Muse in the opening of *Paradise Lost*, to Coleridge's account of dreaming hundreds of lines of poetry while isolated on Exmoor. The unfortunate and common corollary of this is writers who refuse to write unless they feel inspired. Of course, there are sayings that mitigate against this passivity in artists; for example, Thomas Edison's 'Genius is one percent inspiration and 99 percent perspiration'. But this saying lacks much mythic resonance and allows perspiration (or work) to remain dull and mundane. What I seek to express here is the way that non-effortless writing can be romanticised enough to be inspiring, as it is to me. I need to be very clear, though, that I am not referring to the myth of 'suffering for your art': that is actually a story about the damage people have already suffered and how it drives them to make art. All too often, this idea forms part of the 'great man' myth that sits at the centre of so many other myths of creativity (Glăveanu 2014: 9). Suffering seems to me to be universal, and those whose suffering is most often mythologised are often the people who cannot claim a true lack of privilege; they merely have a platform to talk about it.

This section is the most subjective part of the essay; not only because it draws on my experiential knowledge, but also because it is assembled from my personal history, from deeply held convictions that feel innate, and from ancient philosophies that I have not theorised or problematised. The common thread through all is the idea that work has its own Romantic qualities, that labour is sweet, and that the love of *doing* is self-inspiring: to love it inspires one to do it, and to do it enhances the love in a virtuous cycle.

When I was ten, I read a book that would affect me profoundly. It was Gladys Malvern's *The Dancing Star*, an account of the life of Anna Pavlova written for children, first published in 1944. Like many little girls, I dreamed of being a ballet dancer but unfortunately I was, and remain, graceless and didn't progress beyond the one disastrous Christmas concert. Nonetheless, I was less attached to my dreams of dancing than I was to the way hard physical work was portrayed in the book. Anna Pavlova, according to Malvern, was obsessed with dancing. She practised and practised until her toes were mangled, until her teacher told her 'You wanted to be a dancer, didn't you? Then you must learn not to be afraid of pain!' (Malvern 1944: 39). This notion, that one could love something so much that they would push through barriers of extreme discomfort, took hold of my imagination. From that moment on, I understood the incredible romance of work: diligent hours spent on something that mattered, to make an outcome appear in the world.

The inspirational view of pushing through discomfort already exists in the world of sports, which is likely why the Romantic image of a ballerina's bleeding toes is widely viewed this way: dance is physical as much as artistic. A much-shared meme is emblematic of this tension between the 'gifted' view of art and the hard-work view of art, and how they are integrated into the mythology of dance. The photograph is of a dancer's feet, one in a pale pink satin ballet shoe with ribbons, the other bare but for bloody bandages around the toes. The caption reads 'Everyone wants to be successful, until they see what it actually takes'. Here, the creative artist is special not because they have been divinely chosen, but because they work harder than everyone else.

What this perspective reminds us is that creative work is embodied and material. As Hvidtfeldt and Tanggaard (2019) argue, 'when working creatively, irrespective of level and domain, we involve ourselves in a physical, embodied sense; we are always positioned somewhere in a tangible space, surrounded by physical objects with various "affordances" … things suggest specific actions' (546). Even for writers, these affordances and limits include aspects of the physical body: as my peers and I age, we have become all too aware of the material impact of writing careers on our bodies, particularly our backs, shoulders, and wrists. But the material and physical labour of writing is also registered in the physical weariness that can arise from the restless frustration of a bad writing day, or the energetic exuberance that fills the body after a good writing day. Writing is not magical or effortless; people do it with their bodies. It comes from them, not from outside of them, and it imbues them with agency and purpose.

I was raised an atheist, which means my philosophy of causality, particularly around reward, lacked any blush of religious thought: I did nothing for or to God, and God did nothing for or to me. God and I have a completely neutral relationship. For me, growing up with an alcoholic and abusive father in an economically depressed outer suburb taught me that circumstances were beyond my control. Thus, when I encountered Germanic heathenism in early mediaeval literature and thought, I felt immediate resonance. In short, while these heathen religions recognised gods, their gods 'did not create the Universe and were themselves only one aspect of it' (Pearson 2019: 288). The events in a person's life were not decided by the will of a monotheistic God, but were just what happened: they were a person's *wyrd*, a word derived from the Anglo-Saxon *weorthan*: to become (related to modern German's *werden*). While *wyrd* has been later translated as fate, as a heathen concept it cannot be translated into a Christian worldview with an intentional creator God. It is, instead, a 'concept of impersonal causality' (289). In the face of *wyrd*, nothing was to be done but 'striving courageously' in order to win fame and honour that could be passed down to future generations (287). That is, one was not determined by fate, but by deeds. A commonly used metaphor to explain this dynamic is the loom: *wyrd* is the warp, the long threads that attach from bottom to top and are there as the given starting point; deeds are the weft, the thread, the pattern, the skill.

Importantly, the people who believed this perceived an 'irresistible grandeur' in the causal forces that shaped their lives (Pearson 2019: 291). *Wyrd* was beautiful, and glory was derived by anyone willing to work with and around those forces. Not in the same sense as the Catholic idea of good works, or Weber's concept of the Protestant work ethic, both of which had the ultimate aim of expressing grace. Rather, to achieve something for self and family and descendants. Earthly, rather than heavenly.

Perhaps the reason such ideas appeal to me so much is related to my working-class upbringing. Unlike my own children, whose lives have been shaped by the benefits of my current middle-class lifestyle, I grew up understanding that aspiration and class mobility are only available to those who take action and work hard. Even then, nothing is guaranteed. Class mobility has not been evenly spread across my childhood friends, despite lives of labour. To misquote Bennett Miller's film *Capote*, many grew up in the same house; but they went out the back door, while I went out the front.

Work, I understood, afforded me dignity, independence, and opportunity. I had always written, finding moments tucked away in cubbies or in the early-morning light of my bedroom. As an adult, bending my writing labour around a day job was the sweetest joy to me. When I teach writing, I am often asked how I fit it in: students ask this because they see writing as one more obligation in a day of obligations. I tell them that writing is the place I go to restore after my day of obligations; that the work is the only thing that matters and if one loves it enough, they will make the time and expend the effort. To me, writing is not just work it is *special* work. The history of women's literature has always told stories about women having to find time and space to write. Unlike Coleridge traipsing around on Exmoor while his wife Sarah looked after their child, the Brontë sisters all wrote at the same table after dinner. These ideas might usefully be romanticised. They might also remind us of other marginalised groups who might have different ways of knowing, being, and doing around creativity. Glăveanu (2014) underscores how the chosen or special creator myth has been typically gendered male by calling the Romantic paradigm the 'He-paradigm'. The 'great man' myth has performed the work of excluding marginalised people and their voices (9). Those great men of Romantic myth are often what Bernard Lahire (2010) identifies as *rentiers*; their freedom to create only when the mood takes them is due to their economic freedom, linked to social determinants rather than creative ability (448). To my mind, there is very little to inspire in a story about a privileged person rehearsing their privilege in the field of literature; and so much to inspire in a story about writers who work intently and persistently despite their distance from the literary centres of power.

And so work has become for me the most inspiring of my beliefs. Work in the early morning hours when the family is asleep. Work until late when the words are flowing. Work on a freshly printed manuscript with a brand new pen while it rains outside. Work when it all seems too hard and your metaphorical toes are bleeding and you have to push through the pain. Work on something you care about so passionately that, like a new lover, you can't leave it alone. Art, when viewed in this light, is not a divine bolt from above, but the sweet, constant labour of real human beings manifesting things with their feet in the soil. And there is no idea about art more pleasing to me than that.

Conclusion

In this chapter, I have explored what I perceive to be three areas of writing practice that may be usefully 'mythologised' to inspire writers. Many of our cultural myths about creativity date back to the Romantic period and can exert influence that can be an obstruction for writers achieving their goals. Instead, I have suggested that we celebrate the inherent romance of creative writing derived across three aspects of practice. Writers should express more fully the pleasure in process as a ward against overemphasis on outcome, the value of which is often decided by gatekeepers who seem neutral to process. Writers should also seek further inspiring links between people, rather than see genius as only existing in solitary individuals; such links have evident positive influence on art and enrich the lives of writers. Finally, writers should lean harder into the notion that writing is achieved through purposeful striving in a material, embodied way. Art matters because we are humans connecting with other humans; I suggest we restore that human (not divine) complexion to our stories of how creative writing gets done.

References

Becker, H. S. (1984), *Art Worlds*, Berkeley, CA: University of California Press.

Capote (2005), [Film] Dir. Bennett Miller, USA: Sony Classics.

Chabon, M. (2018), 'Are Kids the Enemy of Writing?' *GQ*, 27 April. Available online: https://www.gq.com/story/michael-chabon-are-kids-the-enemy-of-writing (accessed 30 September 2022).

Connolly, C. (1938), *Enemies of Promise*, London: Routledge.

Csikszentmihalyi, M. (1996), *Creativity: The Psychology of Discovery and Invention*, London and New York: Harper Perennial.

Dinshaw, C. (2012), *How Soon Is Now? Medieval Texts, Amateur Readers, and the Queerness of Time*, Durham NC: Duke University Press.

Dyck, J. and Johnson, M. (2017), 'Appreciating Bad Art', *The Journal of Value Inquiry*, 51: 279–292.

Felski, R. (2000), *Doing Time: Feminist Theory and Postmodern Culture*, New York: New York University Press.

Gee, J. P. (2005), 'Semiotic Social Spaces and Affinity Spaces', in D. Barton and K. Tusting (eds) *Beyond Communities of Practice: Language, Power and Social Context*, Cambridge: Cambridge University Press, 214–232.

Glăveanu, V. P. (2014), *Distributed Creativity: Thinking Outside the Box of the Creative Individual*, Cham, Switzerland: Springer.

Hvidtfeldt, D. and Tanggaard, L. (2019), 'Creativity as a Meaningful, Socio-(im)material Practice: The Emergence of Roskilde Festival', *Culture and Psychology*, 25(4): 544–558.

Korobkova, K. (2018), '1d on Wattpad', in M. Ito et al. (eds), *Affinity Online: How Connection and Shared Interest Fuel Learning*, New York: NYU Press, 66–72.

Lahire, B. (2010), 'The Double Life of Writers', G. Wells (trans), *New Literary History*, 14(2), 443–465.

Malvern, G. (1944), *The Dancing Star*, London: Collins.

Nakamura, J. and Csikszentmihalyi, M. (2020), 'The Experience of Flow: Theory and Research', in C. R. Snyder et al. (eds) *The Oxford Handbook of Positive Psychology*, 3rd edn, Oxford: Oxford University Press.

Pearson, R. (2019), 'The Roots of Science: Wyrd and Causality versus Providence', *The Journal of Social, Political, and Economic Studies*, 43(3–4): 285–293.

Sawyer, K. (2006). *Explaining Creativity*, Oxford: Oxford University Press.

Sloan, H. and Wolitzer, M. (2019), 'In Conversation', *Publishers Weekly*, 15 January. Available online: https://www.publishersweekly.com/pw/by-topic/childrens/childrens-authors/article/79009-in-conversation-holly-goldberg-sloan-and-meg-wolitzer.html (accessed 19 September 2022).

Tay, L. and Pawelski, J. O. (2022), 'Introduction: The Role of the Arts and Humanities in Human Flourishing', in L. Tay and J. O. Pawelski (eds) *The Oxford Handbook of the Positive Humanities*, Oxford: Oxford University Press, 1–15.

Vadde, A. (2017), 'Amateur Creativity: Contemporary Literature and the Digital Publishing Scene', *New Literary History*, 48(1): 27–51.

Wattpad (2016), 'Almost 90% of Wattpad's 250 Million Stories are Serialized; Find out Why', *Wattpad*, 18 May. Available online: https://company.wattpad.com/archives/2016-05-18-almost-90-of-wattpads-250-million-stories-are-serialized-find-out-why (accessed 16 September 2022).

Wilkins, K. (2017), 'Writing Time: Coleridge, Creativity, and Commerce', *TEXT*, 21: 1–13.

Wilkins, K. and Bennett, L. (2021), *Writing Bestsellers: Love, Money and Creative Practice*, Cambridge: Cambridge University Press.

Wilkins, K., Driscoll, B., and Fletcher, L. (2022), *Genre Worlds: Popular Fiction and Twenty-First-Century Book Culture*, Boston: University of Massachusetts Press.

2

On the Plurality of Practices

Andrew David King
University of California, Berkeley

Introduction: Worlds and Practices

My title is a riff on the philosopher David Lewis's book *On the Plurality of Worlds*, a defence of a stunning thesis in analytic philosophy that riffed, in turn, on the title of Bernard le Bovier de Fontenelle's 1686 *Entretiens sur la pluralité des mondes* (Lewis 1986; Fontenelle 1990). Stunning and seemingly unbelievable: Lewis wrote of how his proposal was often met with what he called, in a turn both hilarious and a little sad, 'the incredulous stare' (Lewis 1986: 133). Lewis sought to explain how statements about possibility and necessity could be true – a problem vexing metaphysicians ever since they first fired up their enterprise. He suggested an explanation that to many seemed, well, necessarily impossible: these kinds of statements are made true by their corresponding in some way to spatiotemporally isolated worlds in which the things in question obtain – worlds that really exist, though they aren't accessible to us. Without getting bogged down in the details, the idea is that, if I say 'It's possible that I could be reading a poem right now, rather than writing this essay', and this is true, then it's true because there exists a world, separated from ours in space and time, in which I *am* reading a poem right now.

I have less earth to shake than Lewis. But I will be saying what I take to be some controversial things about creative writing pedagogy. Not about how creative writing should be taught in the finer details, but about how the whole endeavour of creative writing pedagogy should be *thought*: about the relation of the plurality of actual writing practices to the aspirations of creative writing as a formalised academic discipline. What I have to offer is less a prescription than a diagnosis; I'm trying to both create and discover the language for what I want to point out; and I have often met myself with my own incredulous stare. But it's helpful, I remind myself, to remember that Lewis' defence of his thesis rested on its purported explanatory power. When I consider the 'field' of creative writing, that meadow to which I'm often permitted to return, I'm struck by the sense that something there cries out for explanation. What unifies this field, if anything, besides contingent institutional and cultural histories (Bennett 2015)? What conjoins all its curricular goals, and the pedagogical strategies devised to help students reach those goals, under the heading of 'creative writing' besides a series of individual and collective decisions to so group them?

The explanation I want to pursue deflates certain rationales for the teaching of creative writing in contemporary universities, namely those that ground creative writing's value *qua* discipline in its providing students with skills that enable them to produce a specific 'product' (Sikelianos 2010). What it offers in exchange is movement towards an understanding of academic creative writing as a discipline that preserves its contact with its non-academic wellsprings – to writerly practices that may never be assimilated, whether for practical or principled reasons, into the academy. I want to suggest that we imagine creative writing as the sum, not the average, of the disparate practices and aesthetic protocols to which 'creative writing' is used to refer. The anti-essentialist kernel of my idea involves a refusal to designate any of these practices, or any set of them, as *the* practice of creative writing (and hence what should be taught in universities), preferring instead that a thousand flowers bloom. In this respect, it's similar to Sam Thorne's proposal that we think of art criticism as 'a number of related practices with different goals rather than a uniform field of activity', the 'untidiness' of which 'could be a virtue' (Thorne 2012). This conception of creative writing offers at least two benefits. First, as I'll argue, it's a more accurate description of the diversity of actual practices than what one might infer from the ways in which some of those practices have been incorporated into the academy. Second, it helps students and teachers of creative writing retain a grasp on what the standardisations of academic pedagogy, however useful they may be, can't capture: the worlds of creative practice that exist beyond the academy's walls.

Divided by a Common Language

One could tell a story about the evolution of creative writing as an academically-sanctioned practice: a story that begins with rejection and ostracisation, proceeds through toleration, and ends with celebration, or at least the hope of profit. It could be usefully preceded by or adjoined to a story about how the practice of criticism, now an undertaking of professors in many major English departments, snuck into the academy in the twentieth century despite the protestations of older generations of scholars, such as those who lambasted Yvor Winters's critical proclivities at Stanford (Winters 1957: 13). Another kind of story one could tell would be about pedagogical outcomes given the use of this or that strategy – another worthwhile type of undertaking. My account is neither kind of story. My view is *in medias res* and synchronic, and to that extent polemically ahistorical. I suspect that a description of appearances is worthwhile even if it leaves the underlying phenomena untouched. In this case, however, I don't think what I have to say leaves those phenomena wholly untouched, because, at the very least, I know my own experiences as a writer and teacher first-hand. While these may be idiosyncratic, they constitute part of the dataset I wish to argue from and about.

To argue that the teaching of creative writing is tied to a plurality of practices, not all of which the university can digest, risks cleaving academic creative writing apart not just from other humanistic, let alone scientific, disciplines, but from the other fine arts. Because creative writing is distinct in ways I'll explain, it resists the standardising pressures that would render it fully legible to the academy. This is not to say that creative writing resists internal standards – to the contrary. But it is to suggest that the very terms used to formulate a conception of creative writing *qua* field are often in dispute even when they appear to be shared. The fact that creative writing pedagogies, let alone practices, appear so multifariously is belied by the singularity and ease with which the phrase 'creative writing', uttered within the context of the modern university, seems to refer. Not only 'creative writing', but 'text', 'poem', 'story', and 'workshop', are not uncontested terms; the polemical character of their use in academic discourse is concealed by the appearance, itself institutionally generated, of a stable referent.

The simple but neglected idea that 'creative writing' refers not to one clearly defined phenomenon but many ramifies both backwards and forwards from the creative writing classroom. It cues us to look backwards to the organic variety of practices that predate and parallel creative writing's inauguration as a discipline and to which it bears an integral, rather than incidental, relationship. And it connects forwards, or inwards, to our own conceptions of what it is we're doing when we teach creative writing – challenging us to impart a sense of the plurality of these possibilities for practice to our students. Having taught and taken workshops and creative writing classes for around a decade and a half, it seems safe to say that there are as many ideas about how to teach creative writing as there are ideas about what creative writing is or should be – and that, as a corollary, the teaching of literature is likewise flooded with competing methodologies (Galin, Haviland, and Johnson 2003; Middleton and Marsh 2010). As things stand now, however, it seems to me that we, the teachers of academic creative writing, have both grown complacent about the terms of our pedagogy and practice and have strategically effaced the complexity of these terms for our own institutional survival.

The Absent Centre of Academic Creative Writing Pedagogy

One reaction to the preceding might be that I've flagged a non-problem. Scholars in other disciplines have all sorts of ways of working – practices, let's call them. Witness a Prussian spy's report on Karl Marx's working habits: 'He often stays up all night, and then lies down fully clothed on the sofa at midday and sleeps till evening, untroubled by the comings and goings of the whole world' (Wheen 1999: 170). Nonetheless, these scholars aim to produce work that conform to shared standards. Creative writers, despite their numerous ways of working – with respect to which a Prussian spy might be less surprised – may still produce work that centres around a shared standard, even if that standard is more contestable or less obvious. The appearance of a problem here, one might suggest, is due more to academic creative writing's still being, if not in its infancy, in its toddler or teenage phase; more convergence is to be expected in the future. Furthermore, one might also argue, the lack of an analogue to scholarly consensus in other disciplines follows from the theoretical and practical diversity surrounding *any* art.

Much in this line of thought is plausible. But I dispute a key premise: that the teachers of creative writing in the academy share standards in a way akin to teachers in other academic disciplines, even those of other fine arts. I remember being told, while attending a poetry fellowship one summer, that a prominent poet had described the work of one of my closest poetic mentors as 'not poetry'. Another charming tale comes to mind, that of Denise Levertov telling David Antin that what he was writing was not poetry (Antin 2014). No doubt practitioners of other disciplines claim that their opponents' work is 'not really' the thing it purports to be; and no doubt, also, that the distillation of American poetics into camps and coteries is aided by contingencies of geography and institutional affiliation. But all this aside, the diversity of what falls under the rubric of 'poetry' – and, by extension, 'creative writing' – in the twenty-first century is so remarkable that it renders the second premise implausible: I deal it the incredulous stare. What do Simone White's *or, on being the other woman*, Dana Gioia's *Pity the Beautiful*, Mary Hickman's *Rayfish*, Kenneth Patchen's doodles, Robert Grenier's poem-drawings, and Christian Bök's genomic poetics have in common (Patchen 1957; Gioia 2012; Ackerman 2013; Hickman 2017; Vaidyanathan 2017; White 2022)? One might say, following Wittgenstein's lead, that they have some sort of family resemblance. But what could that possibly be? (If one is tempted to point to line breaks, that's ruled out by *Rayfish*, a book of prose poems.)

I'm certainly not attempting, in the space of a paragraph, to defend an anti-definition of poetry. The point is rather that this rancorous debate – even if its volleys are sometimes only embodied in the books poets publish, rather than in critical skirmishes – is an indispensable feature of the terrain of contemporary writing practices. That debate may also extend into the academy, but the academy's standardising, normalising forces inevitably tend towards the forging of another image: that of a consensus-based discipline offering its trainees a path towards forms of mastery, if not employment. My worry is that when the teachers of an academic discipline, especially an artistic discipline, fail to attend to the ways in which it, *qua* institutional entity, differs from what it purports to study, it becomes harder for them to claim that they're conveying is something other than a set of merely contingent attitudes and operations. Some may not find contingency, in and of itself, too troublesome; but even the as-yet-unrankled should be concerned about the possibility that academic teachers of creative writing may lose altogether the ability to articulate the distinctions between versions of creative-writing-as-academic-practice and versions of creative-writing-as-non-academic-practice.

Perhaps most crucially, what the plurality of actual practices suggests is not just that the academic image of creative writing is contingent or false or both. The depth and breadth of this plurality also suggest that there is no discernible basis for the selection of a shared standard towards which differing creative writing pedagogies could proceed – which raises the question of what sense in which academic creative writing pedagogy is pedagogy at all. In W. H. Auden's terms, in poetry, 'the most provincial of the arts', there can't be 'an "International Style"', (Auden 1979) something for which he thought we should be grateful. There is no single terminus at which, say, all poetry courses aim; in this sense, they remain distinct from composition courses, which, despite their variety, all shepherd students towards the production of written work legible across academic contexts. Flannery O'Connor, participating in a symposium in the literary journal *Four Quarters* in 1961, hazarded that creative writing courses could be valuable if led 'by an intelligent teacher who is not interested in impressing his own image on the writing of his students …' (O'Connor 1961). O'Connor's thinking is consonant with my own: one natural response to the issues I'm raising is to reconceive of the creative writing teacher as primarily one who guides students along on their own journeys, who helps them towards a personal destination that neither perceives clearly at the outset. But then the creative writing teacher is already, and even more obviously, a different kind of 'teacher' than the teacher of physics, philosophy, or dance, and the 'teaching' a different kind of pedagogical practice than the handing-down of received knowledge. What transpires is something much closer to the kind of mentorship in which the existence and dynamics of the mentoring relationship is itself doing genuinely pedagogical, rather than merely professional or social, work.

Lessons from Other Fine Arts Pedagogies

It might be illuminating to transpose these considerations into a brief discussion of one of creative writing's sibling fine arts. While completing my MFA at the Iowa Writers' Workshop, I got to know art practice MFA students who complained about the social and material privileges that they felt the painting students enjoyed. Just as with creative writing, there's a tale to tell about why painting has the pride of place that it does that pertains to the history of art pedagogy, as well as a conceptual hierarchy of the senses that privileges dating back at least to the Renaissance (Pallasmaa 2012: 18). I want to set aside this contingent history for a moment to think about painting as a craft which, though not necessarily containing its own *telos*, has become figured in the popular imagination as if it had one: as if the practices of European painting were just *painting* itself. The fact that we recognise the teaching of European painting as a cultural lineage of knowledge and skill transmission, one that proceeds along certain lines, already marks it off from creative writing. To learn to paint, one begins by learning to draw, to mix colours, and so on. Even if one ends up a Pollock or shooting at paint-filled assemblages in the style of Niki de Saint Phalle, these interventions are most legible in light of the broader tradition they contravene. If there were ever a time when the American poetry scene resembled something with such a clear map – and the map of painting, though massively oversimplified in my sketch here, is hardly easy to read – it isn't the present.

This account of painting pedagogy is far too quick and short, and neglects complexities of contemporary painting that may align it with the situation in creative writing. But even if the field of academic painting changes so much as to jettison drawing and colour-theory classes, we still have a sense of what technical or materials-related competence in that field could amount to (Meisel 2013: 26). In fact, art historian and critic James Elkins has suggested that, given that methods of teaching art, as opposed to artistic technique, are 'irrational and largely unknown' – though art teachers 'continue to behave as if they were doing something more than providing "atmosphere," "dialogue," or "passion"' – studio art departments must claim to offer their students more tangible alternatives (Elkins 2001: 92, 110). It's less clear what could play this role in creative writing pedagogy. One might point to poetic forms, as well as less strictly defined 'forms' of the story and essay. In the University of Iowa's English Department, where I taught Foundations of Creative Writing for the first year of my MFA and three advanced seminars as a Provost's Visiting Writer the year after graduation, this seemed to be the approach in the core Foundations of Creative Writing syllabus that I was invited to adjust. Students were asked to write within formal constraints, and to become acquainted with basic tools of poetic construction, like meter and rhyme. To paraphrase Thomas Lux, one might think that poems are akin to works of engineering, both in how they're made and how one is taught to make them (Lux 2011). (About the 'traditionalists' who thought that poetic forms 'exist to be solved for their own sake, as if the poet is an engineer', Richard Hugo declared: 'That's just foolish' [Hugo 1979: 33].)

But even if this pedagogical starting point weren't ideologically and aesthetically loaded – perhaps all painting pedagogy is, too – there are clear senses in which the materials of creative writing, namely language, differ from paint, palette and canvas. Since poems (treated here as metonyms for works of creative writing) can happen in speech, on paper, on a screen, or elsewhere, neither ink nor paper nor the human voice are, by themselves, the poet's materials; nor can poetry be isolated by appeal to the physical book, just as painting can't be isolated as artistic activity on a two-dimensional surface. Here another truism, that a writer's material is language itself, also turns out to be revealing. For language is, depending on who you ask, either the matter or the instrument of conscious thought, or both. To be a student in a creative writing classroom is to be asked to make art with the very materials of thought and self-constitution – to use language without the guardrails of scholarly or even social convention. It stands to reason that the work of teaching students how to use these materials, and their legitimate uses of them, will be as various as the forms of thinking and self-fashioning one encounters in the world. Creative writing's materials are the very materials of thought – not, as with scholarship, a subset of those materials. Attempts to transform academic creative writing into a 'respectable' discipline by certain kinds of standardisation risk contravening the maximal intellectual and aesthetic freedom to which it must remain committed if it seeks to make the fullest use of its materials.

I speak mostly of poetry here not only because the writing and study of it form the bulk of my own literary expertise, but because to invoke poetry is in many ways to invoke the problem of teaching creative writing *par excellence*, dealing as it does with the literary form arguably encountered least often in our shared cultural life. I suspect that what makes poetry more intrinsically anticanonical, more resistant to taming and taxonimisation, that explains the difficulties in teaching it as a craft, is precisely its focus on the materiality of language itself: what Kenneth Koch describes as a raising of sound to the importance of sense (Koch 1998). Teachers of poetry have the difficult task of productively alienating their students from a medium they're already intimately familiar with, and of doing so in a way that allows that alienation, and subsequent refamiliarisation, to recur. It's notable that the authors of a recent creative writing case study (Gulla and Sherman 2019) describe how useful they found taking their students to a gallery to describe visual art before moving back into the classroom to discuss poetry – as if the students had to experience the acquisition of another kind of fine-arts literacy to appreciate that, in entering the creative writing classroom, a new relation to language was called for.

Conclusion: Practice Beyond Pedagogy

In academic creative writing, as in other disciplines, the weight of received ideas is heavy, especially when their contingency isn't readily apparent. Consider the model of the creative writing workshop exported from Iowa, the first writing program of its kind, to the programs around the world that followed it. A distinctive approach in which the writer is silent and their submission discussed as if they were absent, what Joseph Moxley (2010: 230) calls the 'standard approach of the writing workshop' has been carried into the twenty-first century as if literary-critical history concluded with the New Criticism. Iowa's dominance as a cultural institution has had the effect of obscuring alternative pedagogical models, including American choreographer Liz Lerman's rich Critical Response Process framework (Lerman and Borstel 2003). The sense that serious workshops just *are* based on the Iowa model persists, in my experience – in part, I suspect, because there has been little professional conversation about alternatives, though that is changing. The Iowa model of the workshop hits all the right institutional notes if one thinks of creative writing as an academic discipline in precisely the ways I've been arguing we shouldn't. It outlines a 'test', a social and emotional one, that must be 'passed'; it separates the writer from the work in a manner familiar to academics, though not obviously appropriate to the work of creative writers; it suggests a routine to be followed in the creative writing classroom, as a painting class might gather students around an easel for a lesson in technique. By the time I'd arrived at Iowa, I had already completed a handful of workshops, most of which had employed the Iowa model. I missed the first workshop meeting of my MFA due to travel, and when I returned, I was told by my professor that the class had been offered a choice: Iowa model, or open salon. My classmates, I was shocked to learn, chose the former. Maybe it was what they'd come there for, after all.

If, as I've suggested, creative writing is neither a genuinely consensus-based discipline like other academic disciplines, nor substantially pedagogically akin to the other fine arts due to the nature of its materials, where does that leave the creative writing classroom in relation to this plurality of practices to which I've been referring? Pessimistically but not unreasonably, one might worry that my view leads to an image of the discipline (which, despite myself, I continue to refer to in the singular) as fundamentally solipsistic or balkanised, composed of isolated priests and priestesses uttering shibboleths to novitiates. But it need not. It might just as well lead to a conception of academic creative writing as a kind of productive anti-discipline – one unified in its disunity, so to speak, whose practitioners remain sceptical about the academy's relation to the art even as they put its resources to use. It might conceive of itself as deploying a pedagogy of structured mentorship, as discussed earlier. But these reconfigurations will require deliberateness, the questioning of creative writing's tendency towards 'wilful isolationism' (Wandor 2008: 159), and a willingness to acknowledge that the seemingly most neutral of the discipline's terms were never neutral. And it takes, too, resistance to the machinery of the corporatised university, hungry for students themselves hungry for clear-cut, itemised paths to sets of marketable skills. It requires conversations that may seem against our immediate self-interest as creative writers who want jobs teaching creative writing—who want, in material terms, to pay the rent by paying attention to poems and stories, and who can do this well enough without straining what may be an already marginal standing vis-à-vis university administration.

In time, though, if we don't work out answers to these questions, they'll be answered for us by those with little stake in whether the academic discipline of creative writing retains connections to the fertile underground of uninstitutionalised and uninstitutionalisable writing practices. If we want our students to be able to 'dwell in Possibility' (Dickinson 2016: 233) for the sake of their artistic development, the loss of connections to these diverse and divergent practices should concern us. This is so, I think, even if these practices lie beyond the reach of what academic creative writing pedagogy can invoke or model, and even if we can devise *ad hoc* ways to restore them ourselves in our seminars, lectures, and workshops. It would be antithetical to the spirit of my argument to suggest that attending to the tension between academic standardisation and the apparent unruliness ('apparent' because the unruliness in question may be another form of order) of non-academic creative practice should have a single practical or pedagogical upshot. There seem to me many ways one could consciously gesture towards the limitations of the forms of academic creative writing pedagogy while continuing to work within those forms: everything from explicit discussion of alternative pedagogical choices one could've made, to allowing students, whenever feasible, to choose from options. On the other hand, it's more straightforward, if gloomier, for me to imagine what the failure to preserve these connections might look like. For that possibility has already been actualised in certain institutions and cultural circles: in these arenas, success is tacitly defined in terms of one's ability to create a product that sells, whether on the academic market or in the public square.

This kind of flattening also occurs without the academy's help. And I don't want to downplay the efforts of teachers of creative writing to construct bulwarks against its bureaucratisation. But as a writer ensconced for the time being in the academy, as a past and current teacher of writing, I find myself alarmed at how readily I can be led (and so lead my students) to conflate the protocols, rhythms, expectations, patterns and forms of academic existence with those of the creative life – or lives. The alternatives to these familiar structures may be too numerous to list for ourselves or for our students, just as some may be unteachable, or even unintelligible. But to continually carve out space in our classrooms as we can, and with whatever language we can find, for the as-yet-unexplored, the as-yet-unknown – or even the explored and known but simply, again, unassimilable to academic contexts – is to remind our students that other worlds exist beyond the institutional one we share. These are worlds that we, and they, might even live in.

References

Ackerman, O. E. (2013), 'Wandering Lines: Robert Grenier's Drawing Poems', *Journal of Modern Literature*, 36(4): 133–153.

Antin, D. (2014), 'Afterword: An Interview with David Antin, Spring 2013', in S. Fredman (ed.) *How Long Is the Present: Selected Talk Poems of David Antin*. Albuquerque, NM:

University of New Mexico Press (Recencies Series: Research and Recovery in Twentieth-Century American Poetics), 373–381.

Auden, W. H. (1979). 'Writing', in *The Poet's Work: 29 Poets on the Origins and Practice of Their Art*. Chicago, IL and London: University of Chicago Press, 240–253.

Bennett, E. (2015), *Workshops of Empire: Stegner, Engle, and American Creative Writing during the Cold War*. Iowa City, IA: University of Iowa Press (The New American Canon: The Iowa Series in Contemporary Literature and Culture).

Dickinson, E. (2016), *Emily Dickinson's Poems As She Preserved Them*. Edited by C. Miller. Cambridge, MA and London: The Belknap Press of Harvard University Press.

Elkins, J. (2001), *Why Art Cannot Be Taught: A Handbook for Art Students*. Chicago, IL: University of Illinois Press.

Fontenelle, B. le B. de (1990), *Conversations on the Plurality of Worlds*. Translated by H.A. Hargraves. Berkeley, CA: University of California Press.

Galin, J., Haviland, C.P., and Johnson, J.P. (eds) (2003), 'Introduction', in *Teaching/Writing in the Late Age of Print*. Cresskill, NJ: Hampton Press, Inc., xix–xxxv.

Gioia, D. (2012), *Pity the Beautiful*. Minneapolis, MN: Graywolf Press.

Gulla, A. N. and Sherman, M. H. (2019), 'Difficult, Beautiful Things: Young Immigrant Writers Find Voice and Empowerment through Art and Poetry', in A. Cloud and S. L. Faulkner (eds) *Poetic Inquiry as Social Justice and Political Response*. Wilmington, DE: Vernon Press (Series in Literary Studies), 35–43.

Hickman, M. (2017), *Rayfish*. Richmond, CA: Omnidawn Publishing.

Hugo, R. (1979), *The Triggering Town: Lectures and Essays on Poetry and Writing*. New York and London: W. W. Norton & Company, Inc.

Koch, K. (1998), *Making Your Own Days: The Pleasures of Reading and Writing Poetry*. New York: Simon and Schuster, Inc.

Lerman, L. and Borstel, J. (2003), *Liz Lerman's Critical Response Process: A Method for Getting Useful Feedback on Anything You Make, from Dance to Desert*. Takoma Park, MD: Dance Exchange, Inc.

Lewis, D. (1986), *On the Plurality of Worlds*. Oxford: Blackwell.

Lux, T. (2011), 'The Poem is a Bridge: Poetry@Tech', in K. Coles (ed.) *Blueprints: Bringing Poetry into Communities*. Salt Lake City, UT and Chicago, IL: University of Utah Press and the Harriet Monroe Poetry Institute, Poetry Foundation, 114–125.

Meisel, L. K. (2013), 'How to Make Art', in *Photorealism in the Digital Age*. New York: Abrams, 26–31.

Middleton, P. and Marsh, N. (eds) (2010), 'Introduction: Pedagogy and Poetics', in *Teaching Modernist Poetry*. Hampshire, UK and New York: Palgrave Macmillan (Teaching the New English), 1–9.

Moxley, J. (2010), 'Afterword: Disciplinarity and the Future of Creative Writing Studies', in D. Donnelly (ed.) *Does the Writing Workshop Still Work?* Bristol, UK; Buffalo, NY; and Toronto, Canada: Multilingual Matters (New Writing Viewpoints, 5), 230–238.

O'Connor, F. (1961), 'Symposium on the Teaching of Creative Writing', *Four Quarters*, January, 10–22.

Pallasmaa, J. (2012), *The Eyes of the Skin: Architecture and the Senses*. West Sussex, UK: John Wiley & Sons.

Patchen, K. (1957), *Hurrah for Anything: Poems & Drawings*. Highlands, NC: Jonathan Williams.

Sikelianos, E. (2010), 'Sidelong and Uncodifiable', in J. M. Wilkinson (ed.) *Poets on Teaching: A Sourcebook*. Iowa City, IA: University of Iowa Press, 11–14.

Thorne, S. (2012), 'Call Yourself a Critic?', *Frieze*, 1 February. Available at: https://www.frieze.com/article/call-yourself-critic (accessed 15 October 2022).

Vaidyanathan, G. (2017), 'Could a Bacterium Successfully Shepherd a Message Through the Apocalypse?', *Proceedings of the National Academy of Sciences*, 114(9): 2094–2095. Available at: https://doi.org/10.1073/pnas.1700249114.

Wandor, M. (2008), *The Author is Not Dead, Merely Somewhere Else: Creative Writing Reconceived*. Hampshire, UK and New York: Palgrave Macmillan.

Wheen, F. (1999), *Karl Marx: A Life*. New York and London: W. W. Norton & Company, Inc.

White, S. (2022), *or, on being the other woman*. Durham, NC: Duke University Press.

Winters, Y. (1957), *The Function of Criticism: Problems and Exercises*. Denver, CO: Swallow Press.

3

Travel Guide to the Unconscious Practices of Creative Writers

Jason Wirtz
Hunter College, City University of New York (CUNY)

First, there is the meandering landscape of terminology. Not particularly glamorous in its vistas but necessary ground to cover in order to take in our major points of interest. Below are a few terms to consider, each of which we will encounter along the way, grouped under the two poles of conscious and unconscious.

Conscious	Unconscious
Explicit Rational Intellect Concrete Control Understanding Knowing Template Awareness Organised Explainable Effortful	Subconscious Implicit Nonconscious Preconscious Inspiration Felt Emotion Intuition Automatic Accident Surprise Receptive Effortless

Within the field of creative writing 'conscious' references cognition of which we are aware and can explain while 'unconscious' references cognition that we cannot fully explain, thus remaining mysterious to the writer. While stabilising definitions of conscious and unconscious can be helpful, it falls well short of what may be the principal goal of creative writing: to bridge the unconscious and conscious via writing. Here we have our first artefact for viewing from Ray Bradbury: 'Emotion, emotion wins the day. Intellect can help correct. But emotion, first, surprises creativity out in the open where it can be pinned down!' (1975: 19). What Bradbury champions here is pinning the unconscious down with words.

A critical clarification is that, for the creative writer, writing down what had been unconscious does not equate to complete understanding. In fact, a common theme within interviews with writers is the ideal of not understanding the totality of their writing – to record, yes – but not to achieve total understanding.

Poet William Olsen explains: 'If the end of the poem I write exceeds my understanding I know maybe it's worth staying with. Ultimately the end product has to outstrip an individual understanding, an individual consciousness' (2008).

Now that we have briefly surveyed the landscape surrounding several terms associated with the conscious and unconscious in creative writing practice we are ready to take in our four major points of interest – four ways that creative writers utilise writing to encounter the unconscious: *Automaticity*, *The Muse*, *Writing Leading the Writer*, and *Writing as an Independent Mode of Thought*. We will visit each in turn.

Automaticity

This may already be a recognisable sight to many as automaticity is a type of port city with many disciplines taking advantage of its location. Automaticity is the practice of learning a craft to the point that it becomes automatic. In this manner automaticity is a movement from conscious practice to unconscious, sublimated performance. Muscle-memory is a common exemplar of automaticity but this same phenomenon is at work within cognitive activities such as creative writing. Gene Yang, author of *American Born Chinese* (the first graphic novel to be a finalist for the National Book Award), encapsulates this phenomenon of automaticity well as he says, 'I think you have to learn it and then forget it, and then it sinks in. It goes from your brain to your gut' (2011). The notion of 'it sinks in' and moving from 'brain to your gut' is the successful transference of conscious practice to unconscious retrieval and performance. William Olsen also speaks about automaticity in terms of the writer's development of craft over time:

> I've read and written a lot. Poetry is an act of making as well as an act of seeing. In other words, it requires craft and one has to learn one's craft. You don't want to sit on a two-legged chair. I gave myself to learning that craft and now I can rely more on intuition.
>
> 2008

The way to develop automaticity is through practice and experience. Diane Seuss, winner of the 2022 Pulitzer Prize in poetry, articulates, 'I've been writing long enough, everything is internal and instinctive' (2008). To internalise and write with instinct requires a great deal of practice, of personal history with writing. Another Pulitzer Prize-winning poet, Yusef Komunyakaa, speaks to this process of sublimating craft using jazz musicians as his example: 'I think improvisation can occur when one has practised so long it seems effortless, but we know that isn't always the case. There's often a kind of tender agony expressed' (2008).

Our final stop along this point of interest is a local restaurant for a sit-down dinner. After we are all seated (which takes some time as there are over 20 of us), we each take turns telling our water, JC, just what we want and how we want it. JC begins to draw attention from some in our group because he doesn't write down any of our orders, instead he informs us that he is committing them to memory. We are astonished when he is able to verbally confirm our orders, even all the different types of salad dressings requested. This is no ordinary waiter as JC is clearly an expert with a developed memory in this particularly domain. JC, in fact, illustrates an important insight for automaticity – the ability of experts within a given domain to develop what is called long-term working memory (LT-WM).

JC, in fact, has been studied rather extensively (Ericsson and Kintsch 1995) to illustrate the use of LT-WM alongside other skilled performers within task domains such as chess, piano, sport, and medicine. LT-WM is an observable phenomenon wherein 'individuals can acquire memory skills to accommodate expanded demands for working memory in a specific task domain' (232). In other words, experts within a given task domain such as creative writing have observable differences from novices in terms of working memory ability.

What does LT-WM look like within the domain of creative writing? Here is an example from creative non-fiction writer Adam Higginbotham:

> I used to look forward to writing a story because once I'd done all that stuff I was talking about where you accrue all the information and you've got all the material, then you just live with it for weeks and you slowly arrive at some sort of synthesis of all of the information in your head so you can take it all on board and you can hold a lot of it in your mind simultaneously and then bits of it will drop out, you know, so you can see where the interesting parts are, you can see where the touchstones in the story are and a narrative will form itself. It's always been a very mysterious process to me how this stuff percolates through and becomes writable.
>
> 2013

This 'mysterious process' does in fact have a name – long-term working memory – and this phenomenon has been identified across several cognitive task domains. This phenomenon has been identified within eye tracking data as well where expert creative writers consistently demonstrate an ability to review large swaths of text produced so far to pick out important details that inform the writing to come. Expert writers are able to do this rapidly and without conscious awareness – two earmarks of automaticity. When I asked one creative writer about this process of quickly scanning several pages of text he articulated this response: 'I think what's happening is a quick check to make sure there's continuity. That the text flows. At least in broad terms. That there's rhythmic linkage. I'm orienting myself.' He concludes, 'Yes, I do think a type of long-term working memory is involved' (Rizzo 2022).

Experienced creative writers differ from beginning writers in ways that provide insight into the nature of creative writing practice. The ability to utilise LT-WM within the writing process as a result of prolonged experience with writing is one such insight. A host of automatised skills – what we collectively reference as 'craft' within the field of creative writing – further differentiates the novice from expert.

The Muse

The Muse is a classic, antiquated vista – Homer opens the *Iliad* and *Odyssey* with invocation to the Muse – but one with current applications and examples. Like the Roman Colosseum or Middle-Earth, even if you've never visited in person you carry a sense of what the Muse looks like in mind. The writer, in the case of the Muse, is positioned as an instrument to record events and dialogue seemingly taking place outside the writer's control, outside the writer's consciousness.

While in my own MFA program we had a visiting author, Charles Baxter, discuss his most recent novel. He described to us an experience of driving along a highway when he began hearing the characters from his novel-in-progress talking in his head. He quickly pulled over to the side of the road in order to write down what they were saying. At the time I thought this anecdote quite unusual, believing it to be idiosyncratic to this author, until I began interviewing writers only to come to find that they too share similar experiences. Robert Stickgold, a Harvard neuroscientist and sci-fi author, describes such an experience:

> I would literally just image the conversations and type them out. And in those cases I don't know what the different people are going to say in that conversation ahead of time and I don't feel like I often make a conscious decision that this is what the person should say.

Stickgold concludes, 'I think there's a lot of associative processing and language construction that, as an author, I will allow to happen outside of my control and awareness' (2013).

The experience of the Muse is to position oneself while writing as a conduit. Gene Yang says, 'You have to lose a little bit of control over the creative process in order for your project to have a life. If your project has a life of its own you're going to, it'll almost feel like it's making its own decisions at some point' (2011). This notion that the writing is 'making its own decisions' is a common theme to the Muse experience. The writing begins to take on its own persona, its own identity. Playwright Richard Maxwell expounds: 'No matter how much control you think you have over something, you can never steer it, and I wouldn't want to because then you kind of kill it. So the thing is, it's like a beast' (2013). There is an example of the Muse strategy on display within this collection from Shady Cosgrove: 'I used this strategy with writing the first draft of my latest novel-in-progress *The Housework of Desire*. When I sat down to write, I imagined the novel taking place on-stage and my only job was to scribe events' (2023).

Our next stop at this point of interest is to visit sixteen-year-old Bruce McAllister in San Diego in 1963. Weary of being tasked with finding symbols in the books assigned to him by his English teacher, he set out to find if writers consciously placed them in their writing in the first place. He sent out a survey to 150 well-known writers of the time asking if they consciously planted symbols in their work (Butler 2011). Remarkably, 75 writers responded including Jack Kerouac, Ayn Rand, Ralph Ellison, Ray Bradbury, John Updike, Saul Bellow, and Norman Mailer. The responses are fascinating still points of view into the writers and the time period with the prevailing sentiment being that writers do not consciously plant symbols in their writing. Jack Kerouac simply responds 'No', while some other writers go into greater depth in their response. Norman Mailer writes: 'Generally, the best symbols in a novel are those you become aware of only after you finish the work'. Ralph Ellison writes back: '... I think symbolism arises initially out of the subconscious', adding, 'Symbols which are imposed upon fiction from the outside tend to leave the reader dissatisfied by making him aware that something extraneous has been added'. Isaac Asimov engenders the general response, writing back about the integration of symbols: 'Consciously? Heavens, no! Unconsciously? How can one avoid it?' From the vantage of the Muse, it is indeed rather absurd to think of authors purposefully planting symbols in their work for readers to find like buried treasure. Writers continually place themselves to discover *as* they write rather than before they write.

Our last stop is Harvard University in 1957. The English department is considering Vladimir Nabokov as professor of Russian literature. Having recently published *Lolita*, Nabokov is well known among both English and Russian speakers. While several Harvard professors favour the appointment, a professor of Slavic Languages and Literatures – Roman Jakobsen – declares a counterargument: 'Gentlemen, even if one allows that he is an important writer, are we next to invite an elephant to be Professor of Zoology?' (Baena 2012). Nobokov was denied the appointment.

While Jakobsen's comment is unfortunately dismissive of creative writing craft, it conveniently points out an important difference between creative writing craft knowledge and critical reading knowledge. Often conflated, the knowledge of how to write creatively is fundamentally different from the knowledge of reading and talking about writing. Stuart Dybek articulates the difference:

> One of the things I've noticed in my creative writing classes is that people come in there as very good readers and they want to talk about a piece of writing as readers and what I keep trying to get them to do is talk about it as a piece of writing, how it was made rather than what it means.
>
> 2008

The concept of the Muse wherein the creative writer is using elements of craft and language as conduit to transfer unconscious knowledge into language is one such example wherein the differences between creative writing and critical reading knowledge are on full display for our viewing.

Writing Leading the Writer

Our penultimate point of interest – Writing Leading the Writer – at first glance looks to be a twin to the Muse. The difference here is that while the Muse positions the writer as a conduit for writing, Writing Leading the Writer positions the writer as taking full advantage of the unique affordances of written language to reach new destinations, insights and discoveries. The writer uses writing – specifically, what has been written by the writer – as a path to follow into unforeseen landscapes. Writing becomes a means of discovery, surprise, and accident. Stuart Dybek shares:

> Rather than looking to dominate this piece with a previous agenda what I'm looking to do is have this relationship with stuff that's already written that I'm going to surrender to, or that is going to prompt from me something I wouldn't ordinarily have written.... What you are trying to do frequently is place yourself in a situation where you don't know where you are going.... You want accidents to happen. You can't create the accident, but you're hoping to create the condition that might create the accident.
>
> 2008

As Dybek states, developing 'this relationship with this stuff that's already written' is a fine encapsulation of the strategy behind writing leading the writer. Other creative writers make similar points with their insights such as 'figuring out how to get out of the way' (Olsen 2008) and 'attending to the wisdom of the poem' (Seuss 2008). Joan Didion offers strong support of this strategy in her interview within 'The Art of Fiction': 'What's so hard about that first sentence is that you're stuck with it. Everything else is going to flow out of that sentence. And by the time you've laid down the first *two* sentences, your options are all gone' (1978).

Perhaps the finest illustration of this point of interest – Writing Leading the Writer – is an essay by Robert Frost titled 'The Figure a Poem Makes' (1939). The title itself illustrates the point and there are several lines that further clarify the approach. Frost argues that writing 'assumes direction with the first line laid down' and memorably articulates the value of attending to the writing with this description: 'Like a piece of ice on a hot stove the poem must ride on its own melting'.

Our final vista along this point of interest is to preview data from a recent eye tracking study with experienced creative writers. Eye tracking is a technology that allows us to see where a writer is looking in real time while writing. A significant finding is that creative writers take full advantage of one major affordance of writing: time. Unlike speaking, for example, writing allows the writer to travel back and forth in time, free from the constraints of chronology. The gaze points of experienced creative writers consistently illustrate writers positioning themselves to be responsive to their own writing. The points of fixation are recursive in nature with writers continuously looking back at the text produced so far in order to inform the text at the horizon. When the eye tracking data is shown to these experienced creative writers along with the accompanying question, 'What surprised you about viewing your writing via the eye tracker?' their responses proved insightful. Here is an example from creative writer and professor emeritus David Connor:

> How recursive my process was, (re)checking sentences before and after the one I was focusing on. So, not only does a 'targeted' sentence for revision require attention to see if it ends up right, it struck me that I appear to look at the sentence before and after – like top and bottom slices of a sandwich – to make sure what comes before and after also read correctly/smooth enough to my liking.
>
> 2021

Other experienced creative writers relate similar insights after viewing their writing process with the eye tracker. For example: 'I keep looking back at the previous few lines as I type, and it seems that I look at the chunk of writing (paragraphs, mainly) as a sort of whole. There's recourse to what I've already written as I think about what I'm about to add' (Barutcu 2021).

Experienced creative writers, as we have viewed, use what they have written as a guide toward what will be written. Part of what separates experienced creative writers from beginning writers is this practice of recursivity – of looking back at one's writing to find the way forward. Historical accounts of writing, interviews with accomplished writers and contemporary research methods such as eye tracking bring into focus for our viewing this principal practice of the writing leading the writer.

Writing as an Independent Mode of Thought

Does it seem plausible that writing can exist without the ability to talk about what we've written? Or without being able to read what we wrote?

Consider the following case of Neil, an adolescent boy who tragically suffers a brain tumour at the age of 13 (Vargha-Khadem, Isaacs, and Mishkin 1994). After the brain tumour Neil suffers from three conditions: anterograde amnesia (an inability to form new memories), visual agnosia (difficulty recognizing visually presented objects) and alexia (a loss of reading ability). Surprisingly, Neil receives passing grades in all of his school courses. How is this possible? Researchers come to find that his school had been providing him with recorded lectures along with questions posed by his teachers that Neil responded to in writing. Remarkably, while Neil is unable to verbally answer questions posed to him, he is able to respond in writing. As an example, when Neil is questioned about a book from his English course he is unable to recite even the title. When asked to write about this book, however, he immediately writes several lines, handing the paper over asking, 'What have I written?' Although Neil cannot communicate his responses through speaking he is able to write out responses even though he himself cannot read what he has written.

Similar to Neil, PW, a 51 year-old stroke victim, is able to provide written responses to questions that he is unable to answer with speech. Researchers share an illustrative example of PW's condition:

Examiner   Can you write the name?

PW   (writes) P-E-A-R

Examiner   Can you say it?

> PW   Fruit ... damn that's wrong. Piece of fruit that I love ... uh, uh, uh ... damn it ... Examiner: Can you come up with the name?
>
> PW   I can sit here and spell it for you all day long.
>
> Rapp, Benzing and Caramazza 1997: 72

There are several of these case studies (Caramazza and Hillis 1991; Rapp, Fischer-Baum, and Miozzo 2015; Rupareliya, Naqvi, and Hejazi 2017) within the literature on those with acquired communicative disorders (generally known as aphasia) wherein research subjects are able to access writing independent of conscious verbalization. What does this mean and what are the implications for writing? First and foremost, cases such as these push against the idea that writing developed entirely from spoken language. Instead it becomes clear that writing and speaking are in fact separate ways of knowing and interacting with the world. Within our brains writing and speaking can indeed be accessed independent of one another (Rapp et al. 1997). 'The findings reveal a brain that can neurally instantiate novel cognitive functions, such as written language, with considerable independence from the evolutionarily older functions and substrates from which they are likely to have originated' (Rapp et al. 2015: 893).

Researchers on writing have long pursued the possibility of writing as an independent mode of thought, separate from such closely related faculties as speaking, listening and reading. Janet Emig published 'Writing as a Mode of Learning' in 1977, delineating the ways that writing is 'a unique languaging process' (122). More recently David Galbraith (1998) makes a case for 'Writing as a Knowledge-Constituting Process' articulating a distinction between explicit and implicit processes. Whereas explicit, conscious processes are characterised by problem-solving and purposeful rhetorical planning (140), implicit, nonconscious processes are characterised by constitutive discoveries and insights surfaced exclusively through writing (156).

Peter Elbow argues that free-writing – the practice of writing without an agenda, without pre-thought – 'is the heart of one kind of invention; it's the kind of invention that in a rationalist society is most neglected.' Elbow continues to describe personally how writing is a unique mode of thought:

> I can't say it until I start writing. It's the act of keys on the keyboard or handwriting that lets the words come, and that probably comes from a life of writing. I've found that I can't get a thought straight in my head. And then once I start putting fingers down and moving my fingers fast, all of a sudden the sentence comes out.
>
> 2016

Interviews conducted with experienced creative writers offer further collaboration to the independence of writing thesis by surfacing the unknowns associated with writing, places where the writing process becomes unexplainable from the vantage of verbal reflection. Pulitzer Prize-recipient Donald Murray writes:

> We have to appreciate the fact that writers much of the time don't know what they are going to write or even possibly what they have written. Writers use language as a tool of exploration to see beyond what they know. Most texts and most of our research literature have not accepted this concept or dealt with its implications.
>
> 1978: 76–77

Tom Sleigh who writes poetry, essays and plays speaks to the primary reason he writes: 'The pleasure, not knowing what's going to happen. If it were like laying brick, I wouldn't go to it' (2010). Yusef Komunyaka echoes this sentiment:

> If the poem is a template of what we already know, it doesn't surprise us. I think that's why artists do what they do – they want to be surprised, they want to be able to laugh. I love when there's a moment when I'm laughing and I think, 'Oh gosh, where did that come from?' because it surprised me. 'Gosh, I really didn't intend to say that that particular way but it surprised me'.
>
> 2008

Several creative writers have posited the general thesis that 'I write to find out what I'm thinking' – a position upending the common assumption of thinking as a precursor to writing. In response to the question 'Why do you write?' Brenda Green responds: 'To find out what I really know. I wind up always journaling and writing to figure out what I really, really think. It forces me to slow down and to reflect and to really go deep down and to try and understand what it is that I've gained' (2013). The fact that several cases of aphasia and testimonials from experienced creative writers share the underlying premise that writing can serve as a means to understand one's own thinking provides a view of writing as a unique, independent mode of thought.

Departing Thoughts

Each of our points of interest – *Automaticity, The Muse, Writing Leading the Writer* and *Writing as an Independent Mode of Thought* – uniquely orbit the shared thesis that creative writing is frequently a practice of surfacing unconscious cognition via writing. This is to view creative writing as a unique mode of thinking and performing with inherent hierarchies of knowledge that differ from other forms of communication, especially those that rely most exclusively on explicit, conscious cognition. Mostly absent from writing research and pedagogy, this vantage of creative writing practice and developed craft knowledge is in further need of exploration.

References

Baena, V. (2012), 'Past Tense: Nabokov and Jakobson', *The Harvard Crimson*, 4 October.
Barutce, B. (2021), Personal interview. 24 November.
Bradbury, R. (1975), 'How Not to Burn a Book; or, 1984 Will Not Arrive', *Soundings* 7(1): 19.
Butler, S.F. (2011), 'Document: The Symbolism Survey', *The Paris Review Blog*, 5 December.
Caramazza, A. and Hillis, A. (1991), 'Lexical Organization of Nouns and Verbs in the Brain', *Nature*, 349: 788–790.
Connor, D. (2021), Personal interview. 20 September.
Cosgrove, S. (2023), 'Drafting, Revision, and an Author's Duty of Care' in M. Moore and S. Meekings (eds) *The Scholarship of Creative Writing and Practice*. London: Bloomsbury, 103–116.
Didion, J. (1978), 'Joan Didion, The Art of Fiction No. 71', *The Paris Review*, interviewed by Linda Kuehl, 74, Fall-Winter.
Dybek, S. (2008), Personal interview. 28 April.
Emig, J. (1977), 'Writing as a Mode of Learning', *College Composition and Communication,* 28(2): 122–128.
Elbow, P. (2016), Personal interview. 19 February.
Ericsson, K. A. and Kintsch, W. (1995), 'Long Term Working Memory', *Psychological Review*, 102(2): 211–245.
Frost, R. (1939), 'The Figure a Poem Makes', *The Collected Prose of Robert Frost*. New York: Holt, Rinehart, and Winston, 131–133.
Galbraith, D. (1998), 'Writing as a Knowledge-Constituting Process', in M. Torrance and D. Galbraith (eds) *Knowing What to Write*. Amsterdam, NL: Amsterdam University Press, 139–160.
Green, B. (2013), Personal interview conducted by Blanche Mackay-Williams. 13 June.
Higginbotham, A. (2013), Personal interview. 5 February.
Komunyakaa, Y. (2008), Personal interview. 22 October.
Maxwell, R. (2013), Personal interview conducted by David Allen. 21 March.
Murray, D. (1978), 'Internal Revision: A Process of Discovery'. In C. R. Cooper and L. Odell (eds) *Research on Composing: Points of Departure*. Urbana, IL: NCTE.

Olsen, W. (2008), Personal interview. 11 April.
Rapp, B., Benzing, L. and Caramazza, A. (1997), 'The Autonomy of Lexical Orthography', *Cognitive Neuropsychology*, 14(1): 71–104.
Rapp, B., Fischer-Baum, S. and Miozzo, M. (2015), 'Modality and Morphology: What We Write May Not Be What We Say', *Psychological Science*, 26(6): 892–902.
Rizzo, M. (2022), Personal interview. 16 May.
Rupareliya, C., Naqvi S., and Hejazi, S. (2017), 'Alexia Without Agraphia: A Rare Entity', *Cureus,* 9(6): 1–4.
Seuss, D. (2008), Personal interview. 8 July.
Sleigh, T. (2010), Personal interview. 21 July.
Stickgold, R. (2013), Personal interview. 7 August.
Vargha-Khadem, F., Isaacs, E. and Mishkin, M. (1994), 'Agnosia, Alexia and a Remarkable Form of Amnesia in an Adolescent Boy', *Brain*, 117: 683–703.
Yang, G. (2011), Personal interview. 9 February.

Faculty Creative Writing as Nationally/ Notionally Funded University Research

Darryl Whetter
Université Sainte-Anne, Canada

Universal Professor-Writer Questions in This Canadian Particular

What happens, as has been the case for myself and other Canadian artist-profs, when professor-writers pause their writing of fiction, poetry, creative nonfiction, stage and screenplays to write lengthy and onerous national grant applications that might, as has twice happened to me, win a professor's university (not that professor directly), roughly $50,000 to support the research, publication and promotion of creative writing that earned just $1000 in sales (SSHRC n.d.b)? Why are only a few of Canada's eligible writer-profs – who, unlike painting profs, use writing as their primary medium – either not applying or not winning these empowering and substantial federal 'Research-Creation' (R-C) grants from the Social Sciences and Humanities Research Council of Canada (SSHRC), a funding organization inaccessible to Canadian writers who aren't profs?

Switching from the writing-professor's career to the writing, for those of us who do the parallel writing of a complex federal grant application for creative writing[1] alongside that writing, what are the aesthetic, not just professional, advantages and disadvantages of writing a novel or poetry collection (et cetera) supported by an elusive federal grant? One each of my three novels and three collections of poetry enjoyed nearly $50,000 in state support when, like many Canadian writers, I earned less than $1,000 in royalties on those books.

My first novel, *The Push & the Pull*, was, like many first novels, a fictionalised version of my youngish life. My application for SSHRC support for pre-published drafts of that first novel invoked universal issues like caregiving but not flag-snapping-in-the-wind national issues. By my second novel, the onerous SSHRC application, rejected one year but funded the next, found me in a new compositional mode of actually pre-plotting a novel (or at least the counterfeit plot summary, in a novel with counterfeiting, for the grant application), a dualistic composition my SSHRC-funded first collection of poetry would rightly quote fossil lovers to recognize as 'Parts and Counterparts'. Concerning both aesthetics and career advancement, has the presence of these substantial, tenure-locking, personally and professionally enabling grants prompted any evolutionary mutations in CanLit akin to the 'award-bait' novel? Is a novel proposed for SSHRC funding more likely to receive funding if it concerns episodes of capital-H Canadian History (from the Vimy Ridge battles of the Great War to the *Front de libération du Québec* terrorist bombings of the late 1960s and 1970, et cetera) or contemporary social issues (e.g., Canada being an early global leader in legalizing same-sex marriage, recreational marijuana, and euthanasia)?

With my second novel, only in trying to find social issues to invoke in my SSHRC application did I think to turn my observations about Windsor, Ontario's high concentration of nude dancers and escorts into a bit of plot for a law student character: law student Kate Chan founds Safe Sisters, a legal-aid outreach network of female law students and sex trade workers (Whetter 2013b: 13–15ff.). Only in writing the justify-yourself grant application did I (i) finally read the research of Jacqueline Lewis (Sex Trade Advocacy and Research n.d.), a former campus colleague studying Canadian and Windsorian sex work then, percolation and pressure doing their work, (ii) transform that information into plot.

When the professors who teach your postgraduate writing then the deans and vice-presidents who evaluate your professorial career encourage you to apply for federal CW research grants, should you? In sum: if you're seeking tenure, hard yes! Post-tenure: only if you're feeling *very* lucky and/or need to splice a genome or travel extensively.

New Grant Footprints in the Canadian Snow

In a new research category for their career-cementing national faculty research grants and postgraduate scholarships SSHRC dubbed 'Research-Creation' (SSHRC 2021b), in 2003 SSHRC began allowing postgraduate students, tenured, or tenure-track artist-professors in Music, Theatre, Fine Arts, Creative Writing and the *very* few in Dance at Canadian universities to apply for multi-year funding, often in excess of $40,000 CAD for faculty, in federal research grants that empower both research and professorial careers (Social 2007).

To look at another, less hopeful column in the Canadian writer's ledger, according to The Writers' Union of Canada, (i) a Canadian writer's 'median net income [was] ... less than $4,000' in 2018, the last year for which they reported annual income (2018: 3) and (ii) 'writers are making 78 per cent less [in 2018] than they were making in 1998' (2018: 5). To earn $17,500 from a SSHRC national scholarship in the second year of a two-year CW master's degree while working on a book of poems that may well earn just $300 as an advance on royalties in the CanLit market risks being an early lifetime income peak for Canadian writers (Natural Sciences and Engineering Research Council of Canada 2022).

Any Canadian faculty researcher – including me twice but excluding me several times – who wins a SSHRC grant, including a Canadian writer-prof who wins a 'Research-Creation' grant, enjoys several career boosts inside the profession in addition to the actual research boon of money for travel or hiring out specialised services. From 2008–2011, at the University of Calgary (one of the two Anglophone Canadian schools offering a CW PhD), tenure-track CW prof Dr Christian Bök was granted $101,000 (SSHRC n.d.c) to alter bacteria so it would write 'poetry' (Vaidyanathan 2017). Other specialised services are more affordable than genetic manipulation. For a memoir I'm writing, I have submitted three slightly revised annual applications for a SSHRC R-C grant to (a) fund brain scans and a genome mapping which could (b) be discussed with me by a co-applicant neurosurgeon regarding a neurological disease that may run in my family. As (c) I could not and (d) should not pester such a neurosurgeon within Canada's beleaguered public medical system, this collaborative federal research grant would also allow me to obtain brain MRI scans our state medical system does not need to purchase and a genome mapping it almost certainly would never purchase for a seemingly healthy citizen.

For the individual prof, the professional benefits of a Canadian writer-prof winning a SSHRC R-C grant include, beyond funds for travel or expensive technical services, the general fact of grant success tending to beget grant success; institutionally, she also helps her host university hit competitive public benchmarks. In a media iteration of what many regard as Canada's weakness for monopolies or oligarchies in various industries (Daro 2018; Carney 2019), *MacLean's* magazine is not wrong to bill itself as 'Canada's magazine' (Macleansmag n.d.). For the past thirty years (Cision 2010), *MacLean's* annual ranking of Canada's universities has been central to their media centrality. The *MacLean's* ranking explicitly counts SSHRC dollars towards their '20 per cent' 'faculty' 'score' of any one university (Dyer 2021). Their published 'Methodology' for 2022 states: 'In addition, the magazine measures the success of faculty in securing research grants from SSHRC, NSERC and CIHR. *Maclean's* takes into account both the number and the dollar value received in the previous year, and divides the totals by each institution's full-time faculty count' (Dyer 2021; cf. Research Infosource 2022a; 2022b).

With SSHRC research grants so empowering to both research and careers, why do so few Canadian writer-profs win them? I count just 44 faculty CW R-C grants in nearly 20 years (although, notably, the programme had some pilot phases for its first ten years, with R-C grants not always available). More significant, while two early programme years, 2003 and 2006, had peaks of eight faculty CW R-C grants, from 2010 on only one or two have been awarded each year.[2] Only three writer-profs, Ted Bishop, now emeritus at the University of Alberta, Adam Dickinson, of Brock University, and myself have won more than one SSHRC R-C grant for CW. With career-making and book-empowering grants available to Canadian writer-profs, why are so few awarded?

Far more Canadian postgraduate CW students have their creative research federally funded compared to CW profs. From 2004 until 2021, the most recent year for which SSHRC makes grant data available with its *Awards Search Engine*, I count 198 master's CW R-C scholarships, 35 doctoral and just 44 faculty CW R-C grants.[3]

Traplines

Regardless of whether SSHRC, with its annually varied jurors, does or even can prefer big-issue Canadian novels, do professor applicants pre-assume that more personal stories are less likely to be supported than proposed novels ticking high-profile national and/or social boxes? To repeat: my first novel, with its Faulknerian 'human heart in conflict with itself', was not funded, but my prescient second novel, railing against Canada's federal marijuana prohibition just five years before it would be repealed, was funded. Regardless of whether or not these examples are Canadian, does the availability of career-enhancing grant support for the writer-professor reveal programmatic biases for the programmatic, rewarding writing and/or professorial skills more bureaucratic than artistic, promoting art/writing that defends well rather than reads well? In one of David Mamet's advice essays for actors and playwrights, with the notable title 'A Generation That Would Like To Stay in School', he contends, 'The classroom will teach you how to obey, and obedience in the theatre will get you nowhere' (1999: 18). In Canadian universities, my CW experience and this new research contend, SSHRC grants will 'get' writer-profs hired and promoted but will have little impact on whether or not the supported novel (etc.) is likely to be published or well-received. Having served on these highly subjective SSHRC juries for artist-profs three times, I have no hope they would have awarded a proposal from former Canadian CW prof Michael Ondaatje for what would become his *The English Patient*, winner not just of the Man Booker Prize but of the Golden Man Booker, 'the best winner of the Booker prize of the last 50 years, in a public vote' (Flood 2018). Like many, that good novel wouldn't look good in a summary, let alone a 'theorised' proposal.

The have/have-not equity remuneration scandal in university teaching, one very much both Canadian and global in CW pedagogy, is, regrettably, also exposed by SSHRC R-C funding. In *MFA vs. NYC*, Keith Gessen is right, however nationally myopic, to say, 'Practically no writer exists now who does not intersect at some point with the university system—this is unquestionably the chief sociological fact of modern American literature' (2014: 176). SSHRC faculty R-C grants are reserved for full-time, tenure or tenure-track CW profs, thus further exacerbating the equity divide between those with permanent or at least multi-year contracts versus those impoverished adjunct instructors who are hired year-in-year-out to teach CW courses in the same department but lack what SSHRC's 'Eligibility' page loosely if not collusively defines as sufficient 'affiliation' with a university (SSHRC 2021a). In my email interviews with various Canadian CW profs, Winnipeg writer Dr Jonathan Ball notes (2022), 'I am not allowed to apply for research funding, because the U does not consider me a real prof. SSHRC does not see me as a real prof'. Exemplifying the exploitation and precarity of the adjunct instructor, Ball's unpredictable and variable teaching income would consist of a meagre per-course rate times some uncertain number of courses per year at, he tells me, 'two universities, in four departments, since graduating, steadily over the course of the last 13 years' (2022). This summer, another Canadian writer and regular adjunct CW course instructor welcomed to teach but still shunned by SSHRC, Toronto poet Margaret Christakos, posted:

> 30 years ago in August 1992 I got my first Creative Writing teaching contract, at Ontario College of Art. At the time the pay was $6,089 for each course. This week there's a posting for a CW sessional position at OCAD [the same school, rebranded] this fall which is—I kid you not—paying $6,507.
>
> 2022

The exploitation and precarity of sessional CW course instructors like Ball and Christakos does not spare them being found guilty-by-association by the fellow writers who review their books or serve on non-SSHRC arts grant juries such as those at the Canada Council for the Arts. *Quill & Quire*, the Canadian equivalent of *Publisher's Weekly* (though one apparently not so keen on fact-checking), reviewed Ball's latest poetry collection, *The National Gallery*, claiming, 'Ball – who belongs to a coterie of other supposedly outsider Canadian poets who are almost uniformly tenured or tenure-track university professors, white and male' (Eckerlin 2019). In addition to the fact that Ball is not a tenured or tenure-track prof, the review's hostility towards writer-profs is central to its concluding line: 'if Ball is the Poet Laureate of Hell, it is perhaps fitting that it is a Hell writ large in and sanctioned by the halls of Canadian academe' (Eckerlin 2019). Despite teaching for thirteen years and having earned a SSHRC R-C doctoral fellowship, the prolific Ball is not 'sanctioned' enough by 'Canadian academe' to apply for SSHRC R-C faculty grants.

SSHRC faculty R-C grants, then, have certainly not been a boon to arts funding in general in Canada or any kind of redress for academic precarity and inequity. In the email interviews I did for this chapter, several tenured or tenure-track Canadian writer-profs spoke of feeling trapped between rocks and hard places when it comes to funding their research, lamenting that the SSHRC application process is too onerous, stealing precious writing time that could otherwise produce fiction or poems, not grants to support them, but also feeling too salary-privileged to apply to the Canada Council for the Arts and its provincial equivalents. Those Canadian writer-profs who do not feel, as one correspondent who asked to remain anonymous put it, 'too guilty' (a frequent interview reply) to apply to the Canada Council for the Arts worry that applications from professors for the CCA's federal two-year writing grants – capped at a *very rare* $50,000 for two years (Canada Council for the Arts n.d.), a low figure for SSHRC R-C grants – will be rejected by the fellow writer-jurors who feel professors are too privileged to apply to the CCA and provincial equivalents, including as the rare few who can apply to SSHRC.

The opportunity costs in lost labour, if not creative concentration, incurred by CW profs applying for SSHRC R-C grants are significant. Here are the obligatory section titles and word counts of my latest 2021 (unsuccessful) SSHRC R-C grant application, from a proposal in which a neurosurgeon would consult on my seeking brain and genome scans as part of writing a memoir.

As the references are actually a bibliography of works consulted, not just those cited, and as not all applicants will have to try to have a former formal grievance campus foe excluded as an assessor, a lighter word count here is 15,000 words to apply to win – in a meagre annual offering I did not know until I wrote

Table 4.1 Required categories and sample word counts for a 2021 SSHRC faculty R-C grant application

Section	Word Count
*Request for Multi/Interdisciplinary Evaluation	456
Summary	554
Detailed Description	4130
Knowledge Mobilization Plan	670
Expected Outcomes Summary	489
Team/Students/Output	2199
Budget Justification	872
*Exclusion of Potential Assessors	171
Relevant Research Contributions Over the Last Six Years (2015–2021)	1772
Description of R-C Support Material	201
Writing Sample R-C Support Material	3555
References	3695
Total	**18764**

this chapter – just one to two annual faculty R-C CW grants since 2013. Given how few of the Canadian CW profs I consulted endure these 15,000 slings and arrows applying for SSHRC R-C CW grants, and the (very) fewer still who receive them, most Canadian writer-profs presumably eye that labour buy-in and recognise that they could complete a few short stories or personal essays with that same amount of work. Recalling Mamet: who would rather write grant-speak than, say, fiction? My only sibling, the mediaevalist K. S. Whetter, is also a Canadian prof in an English department, a (prolific) literary scholar (Acadia University 2022). As he says,

> With the time and work I put into a SSHRC application, which lives or dies on the reports of two judges and probably won't get funded, I could research, write, and publish two articles – articles I am confident I will be able to publish. Why would I go through the wasted hope and wasted labour of trying to get a grant to enable publication when I can just do the same amount of work and know that I will publish something at the end?
>
> Whetter 2022

SSHRC jurors are not, I must reiterate, judging only R-C applications. Each of the three SSHRC juries I served on had us (i) evaluating scholarly projects in the same ranked competition as R-C projects with (ii) a majority of scholars who are not artists on the jury. At times, that lack of relevant experience leaves jurors, I contend with what I contend are not sour grapes, unqualified to properly judge R-C projects. For example, I have twice now received negative comments from jurors who regard my plan to hire a CW student researcher (strategically, a proposed expenditure which is all but obligatory) as not an effective learning strategy: I have applied to have a student assistant, who would be a CW major or post-graduate student to, in part, copy-edit different drafts of my manuscript (while also managing research to share on social media). If I were a student again, I could imagine few learning tasks more illuminating than watching my published writer of a supervisor revise her work, to see (and hear) how she contracts and expands a story in progress. Unimpressive, apparently, to the Victorian and Milton scholars who might be serving on a SSHRC jury doing out Canadian tax dollars earmarked for Canadian faculty research in the Humanities.

Fossilisation

I received SSHRC R-C grants for two of my seven books of creative writing: one novel and one collection of poems. My SSHRC rejections for a different novel and a proposed memoir are also illuminating. What became my 2013 marijuana-smuggling novel *Keeping Things Whole* (funded from 2011 to 2014 by SSHRC at $55,000 under the [better!] working title *Rowing to Cuba*) did, as my application claimed it would, touch on fascinating national issues and history involving smuggling, sex work, the liminality of border cities like its setting of Windsor, Ontario/Detroit, Michigan, et cetera. Still, that novel does not strike me as nationally and internationally relevant as my 2020 climate-crisis novel *Our Sands*, which was rejected by SSHRC in 2015 (with, as is the norm with my SSHRC rejections, one assessor giving a *Fund-this-now!* score and the second a *Down with CW!* score). Each novel is, I hope, prescient. My marijuana smuggling novel of 2013 questions Canada then spending hundreds of millions per year policing a drug seen, smelled, or heard about by every Canadian who has attended secondary school. By 2018, Canada surprised itself and the world by legalizing recreational, not just medicinal, cannabis (Parliament of Canada n.d.). In a notable pairing, my novel *Keeping Things Whole* includes the designer's pot leaf on the title page and the SSHRC logo and name in the non-diegetic frontispiece info. Yes, a novel set in Canada's marijuana smuggling industry captures plenty of historical and contemporary Canadian issues, including

American influence both negative (with our initial cannabis prohibition following theirs) and positive (with Canada moving from importing its marijuana to growing it (well!) following the exodus of American men and women into Canada, with more of the latter both coming and staying, during America's Vietnam War) (Hagan 2001: 122–124). All fascinating, I trust, but not as relevant, surely, as my rejected SSHRC 2015 proposal to write a novel set in Canada's Alberta tar sands, which *The Guardian* rightly calls 'one of the single biggest source sites of the carbon pollution that is choking the planet' (Goldenberg 2015). Noam Chomsky and Laray Polk rightly describe Canada's tar-sand oil as 'the dirtiest oil on the planet' (2013: 160). My rejected 2015 SSHRC grant proposal for a tar-sands novel cited various sources, including whistle-blowing physician Dr John O'Connor and (Indigenous) Anishinaabe author Winona LaDuke, to contend that Canada's notoriously toxic tar-sands industry, the run-off of which affects predominantly Indigenous communities, was proof that Canada's Indigenous genocide was not 'just' the 'cultural genocide' lamented by so many (Bolen 2012; Mako 2012: 191; Woolford and Benvenuto 2012: 374) but actual genocide. By 2021, international media began carrying stories about the mass graves of children found on Canada's former [Indigenous] residential schools (Austen 2021).

In my analysis and experience, SSHRC's R-C CW grants, selected as they are by just two jurors, who need not even be Canadian (SSHRC 2018), give no appropriate favouritism to how pronouncedly 'Canadian' or not the proposed project is. Poet/memoirist Emilia Nielsen's 2020 grant, which SSHRC's public *Awards Search Engine* and grant result tables they emailed me cross-reference to indicate was the only CW R-C awarded in 2020, seems (admirably) far more universal than Canadian (SSHRC n.d.d).

(Grant) 'Parts and Counterparts'

For my first SSHRC CW R-C faculty grant, in 2008, I was awarded just shy of $40,000 CAD for a poetry project then called *Match Destination Formatting* which was published, in 2012, as the poetry collection *Origins* (Whetter 2012); my publishing contract for the book was just $300 from a publisher who, like all Canadian literary publishers, would not exist without federal and provincial grants from other, non-SSHRC government agencies.[4] The $40,000 R-C grant was substantial for its proposed period of just twelve months compared, to my 2011–2014 SSHRC R-C grant of nearly $55,000 over three years.

Travel costs are eligible with Travel costs are eligible with a SSHRC grant, and much of both my proposed, grant-seeking expenditures and my actual grant spending (a wiggle room which Singapore, the other country where I have been a CW prof, would not abide) for the 2008 poetry project were devoted to numerous trips which contributed both directly and indirectly to several of the published poems. The one-sentence summary I eventually developed for *Origins* was 'A collection of poetry devoted to energy, evolution, and extinction as they have been, can be, and/or should be observed in the globally-unique fossil record found around Joggins, Nova Scotia'. In a book which contrasts the chance recordings of fossils with art as purposeful fossilisation, I made (undeniably fun) research trips to fossil museums and field sites in Canada: the Redpath in Montreal, the Royal Ontario Museum in Toronto, the Royal Tyrell Museum in Drumheller and the Burgess Shale Geoscience Foundation in Yoho National Park, British Columbia. Darwin's *On the Origin of Species* is overtly indebted to Canada's Joggins fossils, where he writes of 'Messrs. Lyell and Dawson found carboniferous beds 1400 feet thick in Nova Scotia, with ancient root-bearing strata', so of course I needed to visit Down House, the Darwin museum in England (Darwin 1859: 296).

With a poetry book divided into halves named after a fossil's 'Part' and 'Counterpart', which Harvard palaeontologist Stephen Jay Gould describes as 'two for the price of one—the fossil itself (called the part) and the impression of the organism forced into layers above (called the counterpart)—thumb and thumbprint, if you will' (1990: 93), surely a flight down to Mark Rothko's counterpart (the Rothko Chapel gallery in Houston, Texas) and part (its fourteen site-specific paintings) was required. Grant project and grant application, if you will.

Looking again at the thirty-nine poems published in *Origins*, I count nine that could not have been written without those research trips but sixteen that didn't need me to move beyond a bookstore or library. As the author of four books of fiction and three poetry collections, I am reasonably confident in my ability to imagine and/or extrapolate a scene from research while also simultaneously confessing that two of the book's landscape poems, 'Signed Inheritance: A Drumheller Glosa', and the ekphrastic 'The Rothko Chapel', that valentine to a suicidal painter, could not have been written without my travelling to those destinations. Each of those two poems has been reprinted elsewhere *after* the publication of the book, and in Canada most anthologies and journals prefer first publication (Whetter 2013a; 2019). In a national investment SSHRC could neither have anticipated nor shunned, what would turn out to be my only solo spot in my numerous panel appearances over four years at the *very robust*

Singapore Writers Festival was a full-hour reading and lecture from *Origins* (National Arts Council n.d.). That same Canadian federal government annually (and appropriately) spent new money, rather than capitalising on the old it had already invested in *Origins*, flying Canadian writers to Singapore for what some regard to be one of the most vibrant literary festivals in the world (Treagus n.d.).

Having already published two books of fiction, when I wrote my SSHRC R-C application for these fossil poems, a combination of confidence, industry savvy and late-early career cynicism found me thinking of the project more like producing a film than writing a book: I would write it if the money came together (i.e., if I won a grant). Also, gambling that national success is easier after international success, my SSHRC application regularly mentioned that I was applying for federal funds to, in part, deepen then share knowledge I had first gained while working as the editor of the provincially and nationally funded, but internationally sanctioned, UNESCO nomination dossier for what would become one of my province's major UNESCO World Heritage sites, the Joggins Fossil Cliffs (Boon and Calder 2007: 128). I would go on to publish six more books, but never again with such a combination of grant shrewdness and artistic pragmaticism. Fifteen years later, I still love a book I wouldn't have written without a SSHRC R-C grant.

Conclusion: (Un)'Inherited Design'

Between the evolutionary theory I read about while editing the Joggins Fossil Cliffs UNESCO nomination dossier then read in earnest for (i) a SSHRC R-C grant application and, even better, (ii) the poetry collection it enabled, I still think at least monthly of how evolution involves a series of gates opening and closing (for gene, species, biome, etc.). Stephen Jay Gould also revived attention to Dollo's law, a late nineteenth-century evolutionary breakthrough that recognises that once evolutionary success has been achieved, reversion to less biologically viable forms becomes impossible (Gould 1970). Gould would later summarise Dollo's law as 'History is irrevocable. Once you adopt the ordinary body plan of a reptile, hundreds of options are forever closed, and future possibilities must unfold within the limits of inherited design' (1994). As a CanLit writer, scholar and professor, and having applied repeatedly to SSHRC's R-C programme since their pilot-project year of 2003, and with my books funded and not only by that programme, but also by the Canada Council for the Arts and, provincially, Arts Nova Scotia, I cannot say that SSHRC's Research-

Creation programme is a substantial evolutionary success for Canadian writer-profs or even Canadian writers or for the ecosystem of CanLit. While SSHRC's R-C grants for master's and doctoral CW students are significant, with now just one or two faculty book-writing R-C grants awarded each year and many Canadian CW profs either shunning the work to apply or not being selected for funding while possibly also being rejected for writing grants from the Canada Council for the Arts, SSHRC's R-C faculty CW grants remain a chance mutation for the individual writer-prof organism in Canada, but not the species of Canadian writer-profs nor the landscape of CanLit.

Notes

1. As David Foster Wallace recognises, the words Creative Writing 'are capitalized because they understand themselves as capitalized. Trust me on this' (2014: 73). This chapter uses 'Creative Writing' to refer to the subject of academic study, where students can take courses or degrees at all levels of tertiary study. Lowercase 'creative writing' is used to denote the actual act of writing fiction, poetry, drama and/or creative nonfiction, the wordsmithing than can happen inside or outside a university. In this chapter, a Canadian professor of Creative Writing may apply to SSHRC to fund a creative writing project which will enrich her teaching of Creative Writing.
2. Although counting grants with SSHRC's public *Awards Search Engine* seems straightforward, especially with 'Creative Writing' listed in a 'Discipline' picklist, this iteration of their search engine does not easily find old projects with, I believe, the R-C category predating use of 'Creative Writing' as a discipline searchable in that field. My 2008 poetry project *Match Destination Formatting* is not easy to find as an R-C grant (but it was) (SSHRC, n.d.a).
3. Shifting names and categories within SSHRC make some data challenging to track. For example, the 'code' indicating a doctoral fellowship has changed, according to a posted SSHRC document, including both 752, for 'Doctoral Fellowships' then 767 for a presumably rebranded 'Canada Graduate Scholarship – Doctoral' (SSHRC n.d.e). The slightly different 'List of Sub-Disciplines and Codes' lists Creative Writing as '50818' (SSHRCl n.d.f). Email correspondence from SSHRC confirms that while faculty have won CW R-C 'Connection' grants (to present more polished research), my count here fixates on their book-writing 'Insight' and 'Insight Development' grants.
4. In terms too simple for one direct citation, there is no such thing as a professionally published literary book in Canada that has not been supported by government grants. For extensive details, see *Ultra Libris: Policy, Technology, and the Creative Economy of Book Publishing in Canada* by Rowland Lorimer, the founding director

of the Master of Publishing programme and the Canadian Centre for Studies in Publishing at Simon Fraser University. If you read Canadian fiction, poetry, CNF or drama, the book in your hand floats on several levels of government subsidy. Note as well that while both are federal government agencies, SSHRC and the Canada Council for the Arts are no more organizationally linked than, say, Health Canada and the Ministry of National Defence.

References

Acadia University, English. (2022) *Dr. Kevin Whetter*, Acadia University, Available online: https://english.acadiau.ca/dr-kevin-whetter.html (accessed 9 August 2022).

Austen, I. (2021), '"Horrible History": Mass Grave of Indigenous Children Reported in Canada', *The New York Times*, Available online: https://www.nytimes.com/2021/05/28/world/canada/kamloops-mass-grave-residential-schools.html (accessed 25 July 2022).

Ball, J. G. (2022), Email to Darryl Whetter, 16 July.

Boon, J. and J. Calder, (2007) *Nomination of the Joggins Fossil Cliffs for Inscription on the World Heritage List*. Joggins: Joggins Fossil Institute.

Bolen, M. (2012), 'UN Urged To Declare Canada's Treatment of Aboriginals "Genocide"', *The Huffington Post Canada*, Available online: https://www.huf- fingtonpost.ca/2013/10/18/genocide-first-nations-aboriginals-canada-un_ n_4123112.html (accessed 25 July 2022).

Canada Council for the Arts (n.d.), *Research and Creation*, Ottawa: Canada Council for the Arts, Available online: https://canadacouncil.ca/funding/grants/explore-and-create/research-and-creation (accessed 16 August 2022).

Carney, B. (2019), 'Monopoly-Friendly Canada "Does Not Treat Competition Policy Seriously"', *The Tyee*, 19 March. Available online: https://thetyee.ca/News/2019/03/19/Monopoly-Friendly-Canada-Competition-Policy/ (accessed 24 July 2022).

Chomsky, N. and Polk, L. (2013), *Nuclear War and Environmental Catastrophe*, New York: Seven Stories Press.

Christakos, M. (2022), *Margaret Christakos* [Facebook] 11 July. Available online: https://www.facebook.com/margaret.christakos.5 (accessed 9 August 2022).

Cision (2010), 'Maclean's Unveils Its 20th Anniversary University Rankings'. Toronto: Cision Canada. Available online: https://www.newswire.ca/news-releases/macleans-unveils-its-20th-anniversary-university-rankings-546250902.html (accessed 24 July 2022).

Daro, I. (2018), 'Canada Has an Oligopoly Problem—and We Need To Fix It', *THIS Magazine*, Available online: https://this.org/2018/11/30/canada-has-an-oligopoly-problem-and-we-need-to-fix-it/ (accessed 24 July 2022).

Darwin, C. (1859), *On the Origin of Species by Means of Natural Selection, or, the Preservation of Favoured Races in the Struggle for Life*. London: John Murray.

Dyer, M. (2021), 'Maclean's University Rankings 2022: Our Methodology', *Macleans.ca*, Available online: https://www.macleans.ca/education/macleans-university-rankings-2022-our-methodology/ (accessed 24 July 2022).

Eckerlin, J. (2019), 'The National Gallery by Jonathan Ball', *Quill & Quire*, November. Available online: https://quillandquire.com/review/the-national-gallery/ (accessed 30 July 2022).

Flood, A. (2018), 'The English Patient Wins Public Poll of Best Man Booker in 50 Years', *The Guardian*, 8 July. Available online: https://www.theguardian.com/books/2018/jul/08/the-english-patient-wins-public-poll-of-best-man-booker-in-50-years (accessed 31 August 2022).

Gessen, K. (2014), 'Money (2006)', in C. Harbach (ed.) *MFA vs. NYC: The Two Cultures of American Fiction*, New York: n+1, 175–185.

Goldenberg, S. (2015), 'The Tar Sands Sell-Out', *The Guardian*, Available online: https://www.theguardian.com/environment/ng-interactive/2015/may/28/carbon-bomb-canada-tar-sands-fort-mckay-town-sold-itself (accessed 24 July 2022).

Gould, S. J. (1970), 'Dollo on Dollo's Law: Irreversibility and the Status of Evolutionary Laws'. *Journal of the History of Biology*. 3(2): 189–212, doi:10.1007/bf00137351, Available online: https://link.springer.com/article/10.1007/BF00137351 (accessed 10 August 2022).

Gould, S. J. (1990), *Wonderful Life: The Burgess Shale and the Nature Of History*, New York: Norton.

Gould, S. J. (1994), *Eight Little Piggies: Reflections in Natural History*. New York: Norton. Available online: https://www.google.ca/books/edition/Eight_Little_Piggies_Reflections_in_Natu/RiDNndpF-YIC?hl=en&gbpv=1&dq=+limits+of+inherited+design+intitle:Eight+intitle:little+intitle:piggies+inauthor:Stephen+inauthor:Jay+inauthor:Gould&pg=PT118&printsec=frontcover (accessed 10 August 2022).

Hagan, J. (2001), *Northern Passage: American Vietnam War Resisters in Canada*. Cambridge, MA: Harvard University Press.

Lorimer, R. (2012), *Ultra Libris: Policy, Technology, and the Creative Economy of Book Publishing in Canada.* Toronto: ECW Press.

Macleansmag (2022), *Maclean's Magazine* [Instagram landing page]. Available online: https://www.instagram.com/macleansmag/?hl=en (accessed 24 July 2022).

Mako, S. (2012), 'Cultural Genocide and Key International Instruments: Framing the Indigenous Experience', *International Journal on Minority and Group Rights*. 19(2): 175–194.

Mamet, D. (1999), *True and False: Heresy and Common Sense for the Actor*. New York: Vintage.

National Arts Council (n.d.), *Annex B – Singapore Writers Festival 2017 Festival Tracks*. Singapore: National Arts Council. Available online: https://www.google.com/url?sa=t&rct=j&q=&esrc=s&source=web&cd=&cad=rja&uact=8&ved=2ahUKEwiP7an-ycH

5AhVvGVkFHTiEAN8QFnoECAIQAQ&url=https%3A%2F%2Fwww.nac.gov. sg%2Fdocs%2Fdefault-source%2Fnac-news-files%2Fsingapore-writers-festival-2017-celebrates-20th-edition_annex-b.pdf%3Fsfvrsn%3D1099e86d_0&usg=AOvVa w3wEe2sSH6uySwfR-7asmXR (accessed 9 August 2022).

Natural Sciences and Engineering Research Council of Canada (2022), *Canada Graduate Scholarships – Master's Program*, Ottawa: Natural Sciences and Engineering Research Council of Canada, Available online: https://www.nserc-crsng.gc.ca/Students-Etudiants/PG-CS/CGSM-BESCM_eng.asp (accessed 8 August 2022).

Parliament of Canada. (n.d.), *C-45: An Act Respecting Cannabis and To Amend the Controlled Drugs and Substances Act, the Criminal Code and Other Acts*, Ottawa: LEGISinfo, Available online: https://www.parl.ca/LegisInfo/en/bill/42-1/C-45 (accessed 24 July 2022).

Research Infosource (2022a), *About*, Toronto: Research Infosource Inc, Available online: https://researchinfosource.com/about (accessed 24 July 2022).

Research Infosource (2022b), *Canada's Top 50 Research Universities 2021*, Toronto: Research Infosource Inc, Available online: https://researchinfosource.com/top-50-research-universities/2021/list (accessed 24 July 2022).

'Search Results' (n.d.), *Awards Search Engine*, Social Sciences and Humanities Research Council of Canada, Available online: http://www.outil.ost.uqam.ca/CRSH/Resultat.aspx (accessed 11 July 2022).

Sex Trade Advocacy and Research/*Défense du travail du sexe et projet de recherche* (n.d.), 'STAR Team'. Available online: http://web2.uwindsor.ca/courses/sociology/maticka/star/launch_star_team.html (accessed 10 August 2022).

Social Sciences and Humanities Research Council of Canada (n.d.a), *Awards Search Engine*, Ottawa: SSHRC. Available online: http://www.outil.ost.uqam.ca/CRSH/RechProj.aspx?vLangue=Anglais (accessed 30 July 2022).

Social Sciences and Humanities Research Council of Canada (n.d.b), *Rowing to Cuba: A Novel*, Awards Search Engine, SSHRC. Available online: http://www.outil.ost.uqam.ca/CRSH/Detail.aspx?Cle=80213&Langue=2 (accessed 17 July 2022).

Social Sciences and Humanities Research Council of Canada (n.d.c), *The Xenotext Experiment*, Awards Search Engine, SSHRC. Available online: http://www.outil.ost.uqam.ca/CRSH/Detail.aspx?Cle=80213&Langue=2 (accessed 30 July 2022).

Social Sciences and Humanities Research Council of Canada (n.d.d), *Life Writing and Life-altering Disease: Engendering Counternarratives of Chronic Illness*, Awards Search Engine, SSHRC. Available online: http://www.outil.ost.uqam.ca/CRSH/Detail.aspx?Cle=197137&Langue=2 (accessed 9 August 2022).

Social Sciences and Humanities Research Council of Canada (n.d.e), *List of Sub-Disciplines and Codes*. Ottawa: Social Sciences and Humanities Research Council of Canada. Available online: http://www.outil.ost.uqam.ca/CRSH/Liste_Info.aspx?Info=5&Langue=2. (accessed 15 August 2022).

Social Sciences and Humanities Research Council of Canada (n.d.f), *List of Funding Opportunities and Codes*. Ottawa: Social Sciences and Humanities Research Council of Canada. Available online: http://www.outil.ost.uqam.ca/CRSH/Liste_Info.aspx?Info=2&Langue=2 (accessed 15 August 2022).

Social Sciences and Humanities Research Council of Canada (2007), *Formative Evaluation of SSHRC's Research/Creation in Fine Arts Program*. Ottawa: SSHRC. Available at: https://publications.gc.ca/site/eng/9.834253/publication.html (accessed 13 July 2022).

Social Sciences and Humanities Research Council of Canada (2018), *Application for a Grant: Insight Grants Instructions (Web)*, Ottawa: Social Sciences and Humanities Research Council of Canada, Available online: https://webapps.nserc.ca/SSHRC/Instructions-Help/ig_instr_e.htm (accessed 9 August 2022).

Social Sciences and Humanities Research Council of Canada (2021a), *Insight Development Grants*, Ottawa: Social Sciences and Humanities Research Council of Canada, Available online: https://www.sshrc-crsh.gc.ca/funding-financement/programs-programmes/insight_development_grants-subventions_de_developpement_savoir-eng.aspx#4 (accessed 31 July 2021).

Social Sciences and Humanities Research Council of Canada (2021b), *Definition of Terms*, Ottawa: Social Sciences and Humanities Research Council of Canada, Available online: https://www.sshrc-crsh.gc.ca/funding-financement/programs-programmes/definitions-eng.aspx?pedisable=false#a22 (accessed 16 August 2022).

Treagus, P. (n.d.), 'The World's Best Literature Festivals', *The Reading Lists*, Available online: https://www.thereadinglists.com/the-worlds-best-literature-festivals/ (accessed 10 August 2022).

Vaidyanathan, G. (2017), 'Could a Bacterium Successfully Shepherd a Message through the Apocalypse?' *Proceedings of the National Academy of Sciences*, 114(9): 2094–2095. Available online: https://doi.org/10.1073/pnas.1700249114 (accessed 30 July 2022).

Wallace, D. F. (2014), 'The Fictional Future', in C. Harbach (ed.) *MFA vs. NYC: The Two Cultures of American Fiction*, New York: n+1, 73–80.

Whetter, D. (2012), *Origins: Poems.* Kingsville, Ontario, Canada: Palimpsest.

Whetter, D. (2013a), 'Signed Inheritance', in J. Ferguson (ed.) *A Crystal Through Which Love Passes: Glosas for P.K. Page*, Ottawa: Buschek Books, 70–73.

Whetter, D. (2013b), *Keeping Things Whole: A Novel.* Halifax, Nova Scotia: Nimbus.

Whetter, D. (2019), 'The Rothko Chapel', *The Ekphrastic Review*. Available online: https://www.ekphrastic.net/ekphrastic/the-rothko-chapel-by-darryl-whetter (accessed 23 July 2022).

Whetter, K. S. (2022), Email to Darryl Whetter, 8 August.

Woolford, A. and Benvenuto, J. (2012), 'Canada and Colonial Genocide', *Journal of Genocide Research*, 17(4): 373–390.

Writers' Union of Canada, The (2018), *Diminishing Returns: Creative Culture at Risk*. Toronto: The Writers' Union of Canada.

5

Write a Novel in Twelve ~~Easy~~ Steps

Lania Knight
Open University, UK

This chapter considers the writing of my second novel *Remnant* (2018) and explains the process through the structure of the Alcoholics Anonymous twelve-step addiction recovery model (2001: 59–60). The genesis of the novel was a fairly long period of intense personal difficulty, and the twelve-step model resonates because my life at the time felt unmanageable. The novel deals with a dystopian society in the American Midwest 100-plus years in the future, and certain elements of the story had their roots in my studies in Plant Science and Environmental Conservation, as well as in my experiences driving a long commute through Central Illinois soon after my son suffered a health crisis.

The idea for utilising the Twelve Steps as a frame for creative process comes from one of the generative exercises I use with creative writing students, 'How to ____ in Five Easy Steps'. First, they write out the steps of a process they are familiar with or expert at. They borrow my title, inserting their own process, such as: 'How to Leave Your House in Five Easy Steps'. The results are often surprising because of the paradox implied in the title of each piece. Why would you need to explain how to walk to the corner shop? Next, the students shuffle the practical, concrete instructions with emotional, perhaps abstract reminders, which can add a dimension of tension: *Open the front door and step outside, but only after you've looked left and right for your mother's most recent boyfriend.* Last, labelling it 'easy' is a way of using a common marketing strategy and turning it on its head – the student writer soon realises there is nothing 'easy' about their task.

Alcoholics Anonymous is a twelve-step mutual aid addiction recovery program that originated with Bill Wilson and Bob Smith in Akron, Ohio in 1935 (Cheever 2005: 160). I am familiar with AA because my best friend from primary school has been in AA for decades. When I went home for my ten-year high-school reunion, I met with him and his wife. They were going through a very difficult time awaiting trial for their teenaged daughter. He and his wife were attending AA and Narcotics Anonymous meetings two and three times a week. It was what had helped them get sober, and it held them together as a family during this dark period.

Years later, I experienced a dark period of my own with my teenaged son. The summer I received my PhD, he experienced a health crisis. His dad drove two hours from Kansas City when I told him something was terribly wrong. Dr A. examined John, and while we waited in the corridor, John's dad leaned on the counter near the nurse's station, his face gone red. I had only ever seen him cry once or twice in the twenty-four years I'd known him. John was in hospital for more than two weeks. When he was released, those first hours were a haze of him trying to say goodbye to our house. The moving truck was parked out on the street filled with boxes and furniture. I had accepted my first professional job as a new PhD back in February and was due to start in August. We were set to move nearly three hundred miles away. While John was in hospital, I had alternated between numbness, despair and indecision. I was supposed to be making ready to move, but I kept wandering from room to room, not able to sort anything. My sister-in-law drove over from Kansas City and packed my kitchen into boxes because I couldn't do it myself. I could not organise the plates and cups and jars of jam. I could not organise anything. None of us – his dad, his stepfather, nor me – knew if John could handle the move east to a new house, a new town, a new state, so we persuaded him to fold himself into his father's pickup truck, which was parked behind the moving truck, and he went west to live with his dad.

What options are available to us in responding to and living with trauma? Writers and academics Arthur Bochner and Nicholas Riggs suggest that 'We depend on stories almost as much as we depend on the air to breathe. Air keeps us alive; stories give meaning to our lives. They become our equipment for living' (2014: 196). When our lives derail, as writers we have the option of creating something – a story, a poem – to restore meaning in our lives and make sense of what might feel senseless. Dancer, poet, and academic Celeste Snowber, in her essay on detours, asks, 'How can we lean into the uninvited guests of our lives?' (2004: 152) There are many ways to cope – or not cope – with uninvited guests.

On my first day of work in August, I was shown the tiny, windowless room that would be my office. There was enough space for a small desk and a single chair where students could perch during my office hours. I was under tremendous pressure to make the most of it: there were few jobs available, and I was lucky to be employed at all. I was a published fiction writer, but I'd also studied and written creative nonfiction and I'd taken playwriting classes and written several plays. A 10-minute play was read at a regional festival, and a full-length play was produced locally. I was able to teach in more than one genre, which is a large part of why I got the job. A woman I'd been hired with was given the fiction classes I'd thought I'd be teaching. She and another new colleague installed themselves in their new offices, more than triple the size of mine and filled with sunlight. My office though was a step up from the basement I'd shared with multiple PhD students at my alma mater, so I arranged my books on the track shelving over my new desk and promised myself I'd bring posters to decorate the walls. I cobbled together a playwriting syllabus for my one creative writing class and, for my other three classes, recycled the syllabus for Freshman Composition that I'd taught when I first started as a PhD student. I was lucky to have a job. I was the only member of my PhD cohort to get a tenure-track job straight after graduating, and I was only teaching four classes. I had friends teaching five and six classes across multiple community colleges and universities. Each morning before my commute, I'd gather my things and strap on my seatbelt and vow that I could do it for one more day. I sometimes made the hour-long drive with new colleagues but eventually chose to drive by myself. The confines of a car felt too intense to share with anyone else – I needed that time alone to pull myself together and find a way to face my students.

The idea for my second novel *Remnant* came during one of those commutes through Central Illinois. Regimented rows of corn interspersed with swathes of yellowing soybean fields spanned the horizon in every direction. It should have been a pleasant drive through the countryside, but Central Illinois is more open-air factory than landscape. When French explorers Louis Joliet and Jacques Marquette arrived in 1673, this land formed one continuous prairie. Now, less than 0.01 per cent of the 21 million acres of Illinois prairie Joliet and Marquette would have encountered remain (Forest Service n.d.), along with the many animal species like bison and prairie dog and grassland birds that once called the flat expanse home.

One morning during that drive, I was listening to the audio version of Michael Pollan's book *Botany of Desire* (2002b). I was thinking about genetic mutation, plants, and Pollan's argument that the language of domestication seduces us into thinking we have tamed the plant kingdom. A friend recommended Pollan's book, and it helped ease the strain of the commute, keeping my mind busy. My son was hospitalised four more times during those first two years of my new job. He came to live with us for brief periods. We attended family counselling – he, my husband, my daughter and I – trying to understand how to support him during this difficult time. I needed something to keep my mind occupied during my commute, so I started listening to audiobooks. One morning, while Pollan was explaining the history of apples, an eighteen-wheeler full of livestock overtook me on the interstate. At that moment, a question rose in my mind: *what if that truck were full of humans?* I can identify this as the initiation of what writer Shaun McNiff describes as accepting 'what we do not know and can never know [...]' and which 'helps us to be more completely open to the forces that are alive and moving through present experience unseen, perhaps innately searching for new ways of being organised and presented in awareness' (2018: 30).

Step One of recovery is to admit that you are powerless over your addiction. In my case, Step One was an opportunity to admit that there were forces in my life – my job, my son's health – that I had little or no control over, and that because of, or alongside these, my life felt unmanageable. My son had recently turned eighteen, a legal adult if not an adult in terms of his ability to function independently. This meant his father, his stepfather, and I had at best a tenuous connection to his health care given the laws at the time. My worry over whether he would be okay was itself a kind of trauma. In her book *The Science of Stuck*, therapist Britt Frank explains what trauma is and why it can be so damaging. She quotes Peter Levine, an expert in trauma recovery, in describing trauma as anything that is 'too much, too fast, or too soon' (Frank 2022: 56). It was my first year as an academic, something I'd been studying and preparing myself to do for the previous ten years, and I was in the midst of trauma. Each phone call from an unknown number, each text message or phone call from my son or my ex-husband or the hospital sent my heart racing. I was taking pills to fall asleep every night because I couldn't stop thinking. I rotated through paracetamol and ibuprofen and caffeine to keep my head from aching and to stay focused on designing the courses I was teaching as well as reading and marking student work. Changing jobs or quitting wasn't an option. We'd just relocated nearly three hundred miles, bought a new house, my husband didn't have a job yet, and of course as a new hire at a time when the economy was in a tailspin, I couldn't make demands of my new department. *You want me to work in a broom closet? Sure, I'll work in a broom closet. You want me to teach X? Yes, of course I'll teach X.* I had no way out, so I had to find a way to keep going.

Step Two of recovery is to believe that a power greater than yourself can restore you to sanity. Stories have a kind of magic, a power that I see as greater than myself. Because of stories, I was able to survive my childhood mostly intact. Stories convinced me to leave home, to marry, to move across the country, and later, to move across the world. I believe in stories, and at some point while listening to *Botany of Desire* I realised it was a story that was going to anchor me.

Not a story in the therapeutic sense – nothing like *here's how to make sense of your life and what's happening now*. Rather, a story I could lose myself in, a story I could fall into, a story so strange and complicated, so far removed from my day-to-day life that I could only go there if I set down the trappings of my real life and entered a space entirely separate.

One of my favourite quotes to give new writers is from Flannery O'Connor: 'Anybody who has survived his childhood has enough information about life to last him the rest of his days' (1969: 84). As a child, one of my tools for survival was to cultivate my inner, imaginative life. Another tool was to get lost in the woods. In Illinois, I couldn't lose myself in the woods and I couldn't escape the rage and helplessness I was feeling, but, on that hour-long commute to and from work, I could listen to books and begin to imagine characters living a life very different to mine. Michael Pollan described in *Botany of Desire* the rainforests that were cleared for soya plantations in South America as an example of how plants have domesticated us to do their work for them. An image developed in my mind of a future where we as humans have a very different kind of relationship to plants. I started imagining a reciprocal relationship, one based on sensitivity and communication between plants and humans. It was likely influenced by something I'd read years before about indigenous shamans sleeping near a particular plant, dreaming dreams the plant had given them to understand the relationship between plants and humans. I had the initial ingredients for creating the world of a novel that was very different from my own lived experience.

Around this time, I had a dream of a river flowing beneath the floorboards of a friend's apartment. In the dream, I was straddling two pieces of furniture, astonished at the water flowing just below my feet. This is how finding my second novel felt. I was opening to McNiff's idea of 'forces that are alive and moving through present experience unseen'. Here was my life, this mess and tangle worrying about a son who was unwell while working at my first professional job, and then beneath it all is a story about a clone living fifty miles west near an ancient Native American burial ground, 100-plus years in the future. The powerful forces of my own time – environmental catastrophes, the rising Republican nominee who would become President Number Forty-Five, multinational corporations profiting from plant genetics – these found their way to the future world of my book. These present-day 'forces that are alive' were 'innately searching for new ways of being organised and presented in awareness' and made their way into my book.

Step Three is to make a decision to turn your will and your life over to a higher power as you understand it. I chose at some point to turn my life over to this new book idea as I understood it. The question of fiction is *What if?* and when that livestock truck overtook me on Interstate 35, I had the beginnings of something. As I listened to Pollan, an additional new idea (for me) was emerging. From *Botany of Desire*:

> In the wild, a plant and its pests are continually coevolving, in a dance of resistance and conquest that can have no ultimate victor. But coevolution ceases in an orchard of grafted trees, since they are genetically identical from generation to generation. The problem is very simply that the apple trees no longer reproduce sexually, as they do when they're grown from seed, and sex is nature's way of making fresh genetic combinations.
>
> 2002a: 52

A new way of thinking about sexual reproduction was surfacing. And it was connected to an opposing idea, something about King Minos. King Minos was like that grafted tree, cloning versions of himself to rule in perpetuity instead of letting a new generation with its fresh – and perhaps revolutionary – ideas take over. On that commute, I was making the decision each day to turn over my will to this new book, to the strange story that was emerging 100-plus years in the future.

Writers and academics Webb, Atkinson, and Williams posit that,

> More than a bridge, creative writing can be conceived as a series of bridges and pathways, across and between personal experience and social history. [...] We write [...] as members of a nation and a global community dealing with trauma and turning to science for answers to the crises heralded by fire, floods, and the pandemic, and to creative work for consolation and the capacity to endure.
>
> 2021: 11

As I listened to Pollan during my commute, the crossing pathways of my own trauma and that of the agricultural landscape of Central Illinois began to merge and coalesce into a story that turned my gaze toward science and history to find 'the capacity to endure'. The external landscape changed over time – a harvest soon after I arrived left the brown soil dotted with corn stalks. I finished Pollan's audiobook and moved on to reading Ursula LeGuin's *The Word for World Is Forest* (2010) and Margaret Atwood's *Oryx and Crake* (2004). I reread Wendell Berry's essays in *The Gift of Good Land* (1981), Alan Weisman's *The World Without Us* (2007) and Kazuo Ishiguro's novel *Never Let Me Go* (2005). Snow fell and lasted throughout winter, often blowing horizontal over the miles of open agricultural fields and shifting across the interstate days and weeks after the last snowstorm. A world was forming in my head during that first year, a world that felt to me as unkind as the landscape I found myself driving through week upon week.

Michael Pollan's book has a long section on apples, including a bit about Johnny Appleseed. Apples got me thinking, connecting the landscape of the past and the present to something of the future. Before listening to his book during those car journeys, I'd never realised that apple orchards grown by early settlers were intended for making apple cider – 'hard' apple cider. With the 'apple-a-day' campaign in the US in the early twentieth century, I, like most Americans, associated apples with health. However, during the early days of colonisation, apples were a means for producing one's own alcoholic beverages and for taming a bit of wilderness. It is disturbing when you realise a baseline understanding, a concept not even worth questioning or investigating, turns out to be false. Something about the whitewashed message that 'apples are for health', when they were utilised for something entirely different by my predecessors, rankled me.

Step Four is to make a searching and fearless inventory of yourself. On my daily drive, that hour alone of transitioning from home to work opened any of a range of feelings from escape to descent, from rage to relief. My 'searching and fearless inventory of myself' often included regret and fear that I had brought about some irreparable damage to myself and my family. I felt guilty for moving away when my son was struggling with his health. Those times when he came to live with us in Illinois, it felt like we were waiting for the next terrible thing to happen. In the evenings, I would check on him when I got home, and then I'd sit in the corner of the kitchen on a stool, watching my husband prepare dinner. His days were challenging – he was looking for a job and struggling with having moved away from family and lifelong friends. I wanted to describe my days to him, my despair, but there was no room for my complaints. By the end of my second year, I found I could no longer read anything academic or analytical or dark unless it was necessary for teaching. That summer, I went to hear a Young Adult author speak at the local library. Afterwards, I read nothing but YA for months. YA's promise of a somewhat predictable hero's journey told in first person was all I could handle in a story. I needed the gentle nudges that help the reader understand why our protagonist would do this or that.

Step Five is to admit to a higher power, to yourself, and to another human being the exact nature of your unmanageable life. One evening, one of my former PhD supervisors visited campus to give a reading from her new book. She and I had stayed in touch, and she'd said yes when I asked if she'd give a reading at my new university. Later that evening, after a few hours of dinner and drinks with my colleagues, I dropped her off at her hotel. She paused before she got out of the car. There's something better out there for you, she said. She'd listened to my new colleagues, who spent most of the evening praising one of the women who'd been hired alongside me. It was humiliating. I was grateful, though, to have a witness. In her 2004 article 'The Tale of Two Bethanies', Creative Writing teacher Vicki Lindner writes of the power of witness in supporting a victim of trauma to heal. Because of the trauma of what was happening with my son, what I was experiencing at work also felt like trauma. If my PhD supervisor hadn't been at that dinner, I might have been overwhelmed by my new colleagues' poor manners. Instead, I realised what they'd said was petty and unkind, and with her encouragement, I tried to hold on for that 'something better'.

One weekend, when my son was staying at his dad's house, my husband and I went out for dinner at our favourite barbeque restaurant. I was in a particularly low place. He'd gotten a job teaching ESL in our town, and his commute was short enough that he could walk to work or take the bus. His colleagues were positive and supportive, and his students were grateful for instruction in English. We were seated at a table near the bar. I sipped my beer and complained about my day. It was probably one of many such conversations. He said something like, you went to school for this for years, you need to stay with it for at least half as long as you've studied. I felt trapped. Hopeless. I raised a silly bet: let's see what the waiter says. If he says I can work in another field, I will. If he says you need to stay put, I will. It turned out that though he was young, he'd made a complete life change and gotten out of a job he hated, even though it meant he didn't have much money while he was training in a new profession. He was fine waiting tables in the meantime, loved the banter and the crazy questions from customers like me.

Of course I wasn't going to change my life just because some waiter said yeah, that's the thing to do. A few years previous, I'd helped my husband make a major career change, had sat with him for hours listening to how much he hated his job, how trapped he felt. I'd encouraged him to get trained in a new field, and he did, which changed his professional life. But now, when I needed him, when I felt like I couldn't carry on, I was on my own. It reminded me of what my grandmother told my mother when she married my father: 'you've made your bed hard, and now you've got to lie in it'. I had made the decision to accept this job, to move my family, and now I had to deal with the consequences. I had to lie in the hard bed I'd made and hold on for something better.

Step Six is to be entirely ready to have your 'higher power', aka my book-in-progress, remove all the defects of your challenging life. I had made the choices that got me to this moment, but somehow, according to the Twelve Steps, I wouldn't be able to get myself out of this mess. I accepted it, though. I saw that, for now, there was little to nothing I could do to remove the defects of my challenging life. I had to carry on. And at some point, I let the book-in-progress carry the weight for me. I began shaping my characters, giving them aspects of myself or of people in my life, and I began moving them around on the board – bashing them or strengthening them to suit my needs. Soon, I was plumbing depths of violence on the page I'd never let myself explore. In the past, I'd always struggled with making my characters suffer. Not anymore. On reflection, years later and living an ocean away, I see how the violences of my childhood, my schooling, my relationships, and my country were making their way through me and into my fictional world. The trauma in my own life, and the larger violence of my country and culture, were beginning to press through into the edges of my awareness and make themselves known as character and plot and dialogue.

Step Seven is to humbly ask your book-in-progress to remove your difficulties. This step requires dialogue, which I'd already begun because my characters were talking with me and with each other. There was a little girl, a clone being prepared for an ultimate harvest: she had been cultivated as a sacrifice to increase the longevity of the original human from whom she'd been cloned. Rereading Ishiguro's *Never Let Me Go* had lodged a dark, dreamlike sense in me of what impending violence of this sort can look like in a novel. Neal Shusterman's *Unwind* (2007) takes on a similar trope of human sacrifice for the sake of others, body-part-by-body-part, but I found it during my 'I can't read anything too dark' phase, and I didn't read it until much later, when *Remnant* was nearly finished. In *Remnant*, there was also a scientist character, a clone who detested what he'd become within the artificial environment of the compound where he was cultivated and had lived his entire life. There was a migrant worker character, a clone whose work crew were also clones of himself. These workers were losing access to a drug that for years had kept them subdued, and hence, they were losing control of themselves and sinking into unthinkable violence. All these characters were moving into a circle that was spinning tighter and tighter. In their article 'First, Do No Harm', Creative Writing teachers Sarah DeBacher and Deborah Harris-Moore write about their experiences teaching Creative Writing in the midst or the aftermath of traumatic events, including Hurricane Katrina and various school shootings. 'Even though our instinct is [...] to rise above a horrible event, the immediate push to intellectualise or reflect on an event may be emotionally damaging and even paralysing' (2016: para 17). At the time, I could not write about what was happening to my son. Each time he was admitted to hospital, he came out a different person. I was trying to find ways to cope and adjust, and I developed a saying for myself: 'Love always gets another chance'. I was experiencing what Pauline Boss (2016: 270) calls 'psychological ambiguous loss', the psychological loss of a family member where they are physically present but psychologically missing. The family member is 'there, but not there'. My son looked like my son, but he no longer seemed to me like my son. That time is a blur, and when I think of it, I cannot separate the despair over him from the frustration of everything else.

When I moved to Illinois, I left behind a landscape that I loved, the Ozarks. In Columbia, Missouri, I lived at the northern edge of the Ozark Plateau, but every summer, I drove south to visit the Ozark Mountains with my family and a group of friends, camping and kayaking the rivers, losing myself and entering 'river time'. Because of my choice to accept a job in Illinois though, I couldn't easily get back to the Ozarks. My characters could, so I pushed them and pulled them across the landscape. The Ozarks in the world of my novel were decimated by decades of forest fires, and my characters find themselves not in the mountainous terrain of my memory, but rather a landscape scorched by the elemental equivalent of the rage and helplessness I felt in my own life. In *Remnant*, the clone characters who are a legacy from the current time-period would be lost without the one 'natural born' character. She has a sensitivity to plants and is able to help the others forage for food while they travel from Illinois west to the Ozarks. The mindset that has led to ecological destruction in my novel, which includes plant monocultures and eventually the cultivation of human worker clone monocultures, destroying prairies for corn and soybean rotations, selling off national parks to the highest bidder, harvesting body parts of clones to keep the old non-clone generation alive – all these things are the old way. This natural-born character, a half-formed mutant who is sensitive to plants, makes right the balance between humans and the natural world. Through her, it becomes clear in my book that humans are in fact domesticated by plants as Michael Pollan argues in *Botany of Desire*. Rather than fight that, the way forward in *Remnant* is to submit, to enter a new kind of relationship of reciprocity and humility. Which echoes the humility of the dialogue one is asked to enter at this seventh step in the recovery process. I asked my book-in-progress to remove my difficulties, and what it did was allow a part of me escape and hope when the rest of me had to stay put.

Step Eight is to make a list of all harmed and become willing to make amends. Wendell Berry, in his book *The Gift of Good Land* (1981), opens with an essay about visiting traditional indigenous farmers in Peru. I read this essay in university when I was studying Plant Science and Environmental Conservation.

What struck me, when I re-read it, was that I'd absorbed many of Berry's observations and, over time, come to think of them as my own. One of the most insightful ideas I'd absorbed was that of tending to just enough land that you can look after yourself. The miles and miles of land taken over by agribusiness in the flat portions of the Midwest are a stark contrast to the oak-hickory forests of the Ozarks. It's a rugged terrain, but in my novel, it is one of the few accessible places to live where there is water flowing close to the surface. This kind of landscape of necessity requires small-scale food production. Taken even further, it lends itself to hunting and gathering, which my characters begin doing to survive. It's the big picture – thinking of the Anthropocene and how much damage/change has been caused by humans and what we'll be known for long after we're gone – it's this I'm trying to say something about in my novel. By embodying a sensitivity to plants and giving it power through the mutant, the one character who can rebalance humanity's relationship with plants, I'm trying to make amends for the harm we have caused as humans.

Step Nine is to make amends wherever possible, except when to do so would injure. In the bigger picture of the novel, most of humanity and much of the planet has been harmed. In the smaller picture of my own life, it's me who's been harmed. There's a photograph of me from the summer after I left home. I went back briefly to visit my mother, and in the photo, I'm sitting on a towel on a beach in Galveston, Texas. Part of what this book is about is making amends to that seventeen-year-old girl. Letting her finally have her say about what it felt like to be her. If the question of fiction is *What if?*, the question of poetry is *What is it like?* Early in the book, I wrote a scene describing how the main character Esme is being prepared for a partial harvest, her body lashed to a tripod while her scalp is shorn in a brutal ritual that's repeated every year. The menace and control in this scene are an intensified, visual description of what I felt like as a teenager. Esme is living an altered version of my life – one where the violence is amplified to the point that others can recognise it, and where her increased agency allows her to respond to her jailers with something more than silence.

Step Ten is to continue to take personal inventory and when you're wrong, admit it. I was fortunate with my editor at Burlesque Press in that he did some developmental editing with me on parts of the book he thought might be difficult for the reader to navigate. Writing this book was a very 'interior' kind of process for me, so his insight into the reader's experience was invaluable. In one editorial comment, he wrote 'This is too confusing for page two. The reader needs to understand the first order reality here before entering an imaginary one'. Esme, like me, survived by creating an imaginary world to retreat to, but it took some time to find the right balance between the 'first order reality' I needed to establish for the reader and the imaginary world she lived in much of the time. Of course, when you think your work is done, it's difficult to hear that it needs more, but I listened, and the book is better for it.

Step Eleven is, through prayer and meditation, to seek conscious contact with a higher power, in my case the book-in-progress. I prayed/asked only for knowledge of my book's will and the power to carry that out. In a kind of answer, I was awarded a four-week residency at Vermont Studio Centre, where I spent each day in a studio overlooking the Gihon River. In a way, for the first time since the onset of my son's health crisis and the start of my new job, I felt seen, even if it was only the walls of my studio and my fellow writers and artists in residence. My husband, dealing with his own work issues by now and grieving the death of his mother, had grown tired of hearing me complain about my job and the perceived or real slights and injuries of working in a toxic environment. He'd asked me to stop talking about work with him. He alternated between confusion and frustration over my son, so I tried not to bring it up with him. I needed someone to witness my pain, though, and ultimately it was my novel-in-progress, pinned to the walls of my studio in Vermont, that held that space for me; and the other writers and artists in residence. The story of *Remnant* is a journey told from alternating characters' points of view. It helped me to read my characters' voices and trace their steps on my studio walls alongside maps of the Ozarks National Scenic Riverways. In that studio in Vermont, I learned something new about what chapters can and can't do, and how to structure a complex novel.

Later, when I returned home to Illinois, I visited Cahokia Mounds National Park. While reading the museum displays, I realised the journey my characters were making was a micro-retracing of a large-scale cycle of exponential growth, decline, and dispersal that had taken place on this same land more than 1,000 years before. Here too I found Timothy Pauketat's book *Cahokia: Ancient America's Great City on the Mississippi* (2010) and read of the rise and fall of the indigenous people who lived near Cahokia Mounds, a cycle induced by reliance on maize, which I found eerily like the present-day reliance on corn. I also visited East Saint Louis to observe the criss-crossing maze of highways and railroad bridges my characters would be traveling, with an eye to trying to imagine the state of roads and trestles one hundred years in the future. The more I gave my time to the book-in-progress, the less it mattered how difficult my life had become.

Step Twelve is, having had an awakening as the result of these steps, to carry this message to others and to practice these principles in all my affairs. My life situation – the ailing son, the difficult job – sorted itself with time. There was nothing I could have done to hurry them along. Instead, I built a world in my mind, and I was lucky enough to get it down on paper, to find a publisher who loved it, an editor who believed in it, and readers who 'can both delight in and be terrified by' it (Vowler 2018: front cover). I found a way to endure – one scene, one character, one chapter at a time.

References

Alcoholics Anonymous (2001), *Alcoholics Anonymous: The Story of How Many Thousands of Men and Women Have Recovered from Alcoholism*, New York: Alcoholics Anonymous World Services.
Atwood, M. (2004), *Oryx and Crake*, New York: Anchor.
Berry, W. (1981), 'An Agricultural Journey in Peru', *The Gift of Good Land: Further Essays, Cultural and Agricultural*, San Francisco: North Point Press, 3–46.
Bochner, A. and Riggs, N. (2014), 'Practicing Narrative Inquiry', in P. Leavy (ed.) *The Oxford Handbook of Qualitative Research*, Oxford: Oxford University Press, 194–222.
Boss, P. (2016), 'The Context and Process of Theory Development: The Story of Ambiguous Loss', *J Fam Theory Rev*, 8: 269–286.
Cheever, S. (2005), *My Name is Bill*, New York: Washington Square Press.
DeBacher, S. and Harris-Moore, D. (Summer 2016), 'First, Do No Harm', *Composition Forum* 34, no pages. Available online: https://compositionforum.com/issue/34/first-do-no-harm.php (accessed 7 October 2022).
Forest Service (n.d.), 'Science in Action: Midewin National Tallgrass Prairie', United States Department of Agriculture. Available online: https://www.fs.usda.gov/main/midewin/learning/nature-science (accessed 6 October 2022).
Frank, B. (2022), *The Science of Stuck*, London: Headline Home.
Ishiguro, K. (2005), *Never Let Me Go*, New York: Vintage.
Knight, L. (2018), *Remnant*, Tennessee: Burlesque Press.
Le Guin, U. (2010), *The Word for World is Forest*, New York: Tor Books.
Lindner, V. (2004), 'The Tale of Two Bethanies: Trauma in the Creative Writing Class', *New Writing*, 1(1): 6–14.
McNiff, S. (2018), 'Philosophical and Practical Foundations of Artistic Inquiry', in P. Leavy (ed.) *Handbook of Arts-Based Research*, New York: Guilford Press, 22–35.
O'Connor, F. (1969), *Mystery and Manners: Occasional Prose*, London: Farrar Straus & Giroux.
Pauketat, T. (2010), *Cahokia: Ancient America's Great City on the Mississippi*. New York: Penguin Library of American Indian History.
Pollan, M. (2002a), *Botany of Desire: A Plant's Eye-View of the World*, New York: Random House.

Pollan, M. (2002b), *Botany of Desire: A Plant's Eye-View of the World*, Audible Audiobook – Unabridged. New York: Random House Audio.

Shusterman, N. (2007), *Unwind*, New York: Simon and Schuster Books for Young Readers.

Snowber, C. (2004), 'Leaning Absolutes: Honouring the Detours in Our Lives'. In D. Denton and W. Ashton (eds) *Spirituality, Action And Pedagogy: Teaching from the Heart*, New York: Peter Lang, 124–135.

Vowler, T. (2018), Blurb for *Remnant*, Tennessee: Burlesque Press.

Webb, J., Atkinson, M., and Williams, J. (2021), 'Literary bridges: Creative Writing, Trauma and Testimony', *TEXT: Journal of writing and writing courses*, 25(2): 1–18.

Weisman, A. (2007), *The World Without Us*, New York: Thomas Dunne Books

6

The Writer as Citizen

Creative Writing, Social Action, and Political Responsibility

Jen Webb
University of Canberra

In her introduction to *Negotiating with the Dead*, Margaret Atwood identifies 'three questions most often posed to writers, both by readers and by themselves: *Who are you writing for? Why do you do it? Where does it come from?*' (Atwood 2002: xix; emphasis in original). This chapter operates on similar terrain, but is more interested in the first two questions in her list, which have been part of the conversation about writing and writers across history. What is being interrogated in these two questions is not the mechanics of writing – the third in Atwood's list, and the one that emerges in such venues as writers festivals where authors are also interrogated about the technicalities of their practice. While this may be of some interest, for writers and scholars of writing practice, the *why write* question provides springboards into understanding better what motivates writers to write, and what writers identify as the value, for themselves and others, of their practice and its products.

Of these, the two that are frequently discussed by creative writers based in universities is how to address the balance, or lack thereof, in our approved reasons for writing. Within the academy, it often seems that writing for its own sake is less valued than writing designed to generate or transmit knowledge. This is an aspect of the craft/research dichotomy that Tim Mayers (2009) sets out, when he observes that academic creative writing is divided into either a knowledge or a craft focus. For him, the addition of the word 'studies' to 'creative writing' heralds a departure from writing itself and for itself, as well as a movement away from training students to become good writers, to training them in the techniques of scholarship and research (2009: 218).

He contextualises this, noting that his observations and concerns were located in tertiary education institutions in the USA. Where I live and work, in Australia, writers based in the academy have found approaches that ensure creative practice, pedagogy, craft training, and research can cohabit comfortably. In this model, the practice and craft of creative writing comprises part of a research methodology, the writer's attention flowing to and fro between the craft and knowledge orientations, and each acknowledging and drawing on the affordances provided by both modes of practice (Webb 2015). The products that emerge from such a project are likely to incorporate (at least) two discrete outputs: a literary work, and an essay that explores and explicates the issues pursued during the project. Each has its own identity, and each typically seeks a different audience: general readers for the first; scholarly readers for the second. This model allows writers in the academy to deploy combinations of craft, creative play, teaching, thinking, experiment, making and research: a multifocal practice that is increasingly adopted not only by university-based writers but also by university-trained writers who make their careers outside the academy.

Australian novelist Kate Grenville, for example, completed a doctorate in writing, in the course of which she produced a novel, *The Secret River* (2005), that relied for its content on the techniques of history research. She pursued this knowledge activity not to produce a history – or even an historical novel – of nineteenth-century Australia but, she says, to craft 'a work of fiction. Like much fiction, it had its beginnings in the world, but those beginnings have been adapted and altered to various degrees for the sake of the fiction'. This, she continues, is 'what fiction writers do: take the world and modify it' (Grenville 2007a: 66–67). Her 'modification' of the world generated a great deal of public discussion about settler history, and an empathic sense of what that period of history might have felt like for those living it, whether settlers or Indigenous Australians. It is closely researched; it is not history, but precisely a work of *literature*, whose excellence has been recognised by Australian and international literary awards. She explains her answers to the questions *why write*, and *for whom* in a number of interviews and essays. With respect to the why question:

> I realised that I knew much more about the frontier and its violence than I'd ever let myself know that I knew. I may not have known the details, but I'd always known the broad outline of the story.
>
> It also dawned on me how the language was an accomplice in this knowing-and-not-knowing. There was a linguistic sleight of hand going on – the land wasn't really 'taken up', it was just 'taken'. The word 'dispersed' that I came across

so often in the sources – as in 'we dispersed them in the usual manner' – this bland little word often meant shoot.

Grenville 2007b

Which is why the product of her work was fiction, and not history; her focus was not merely on researching and telling stories of settler Australia, but also on interrogating language itself, particularly its relationship on the one hand to material/experiential reality, and on the other to the shoring up of a particular moral and national framework.

With respect to the 'for whom' question: it is first for herself, to clarify her own understanding of history, and then for other settler Australians. She writes:'I'd expected resistance to this book, even anger. What I've found is a huge hunger to know – the same hunger that drove the writing [...] What should we feel about the stolen gift that our forebears have made to us?' (ibid).

The prizes and awards; the translation of the novel into a stage play and a TV miniseries; the many keynote addresses and interviews she has been recruited to offer – this suggests that her initial interest in telling a story about her own ancestor has been transmuted into a work of literary quality that also offers (white) Australian readers the opportunity to reflect on this 'stolen gift', the uncomfortable fact that we are living in an historical crime, and to consider how to live, as an ethical person – a good citizen – in the twenty-first century. Grenville points out that fiction is a safe place to perform this work, because it 'offers a compensatory pleasure that offsets the discomfort – the satisfactions of narrative and the sensual pleasures of language' (ibid). In short, it does double duty – as fiction; and as a comparatively safe place to encounter a more explicit sense of the lived world, and of how individuals might respond to their being in that world.

There are many examples of creative writers producing work that does double duty – generating literary work that also conveys new knowledge or pedagogical material; or producing discrete bodies of work in each mode. T. S. Eliot does the latter, with his poems and critical essays operating in different spaces, and arguably for different audiences and different purposes. As a body of work, though, this straddles the craft/knowledge divide, since both his poems (craft) and his critical essays (knowledge) remain important, both for readers in general, and for teachers and researchers in both creative writing and literary studies courses. Kevin Dettmar (2019) suggests that this continued interest in Eliot's writings is in no small part because of the 'brio' of his writing style. That is to say, his capacity in both *poiesis* (the art of making) and *technê* (the craft of shaping), along with his capacity to think, analyse and add to knowledge, keep his work current, and of value to literature and to learning.

Perhaps it is the maker aspect, the art and craft of writing, that renders the knowledge aspect more accessible and more palatable. Jay McInerney (2005: 4) seems to be saying this, in his essay about the value of storytelling. He opens by noting that his own essay is non-fiction and as such: 'is unlikely to be as vivid, or textured, or as faithful to the author's deepest convictions and emotions as his own fiction, as linguistically adventurous or as revealing about the way it feels to live now as the latest novels by Salman Rushdie or Zadie Smith'.

Perhaps; essayists might take issue with this; but at the heart of McInerney's *Guardian* essay is a cry for readers and writers to take seriously the affordances of the craft of fiction, not merely for the pleasure of the text, but also for particular types of knowing: the sort of modification of the world, and empathic engagement, that Grenville essays. As he writes: 'It is to the novel, ultimately, that we turn to confirm our own senses and emotions, to create narratives that reveal to us how we feel now and how we live now, to reveal emotional truths' (2005: 4). This is craft – the quality of writing that can capture a reader; but it is also knowledge, because without technical skill, the capacity to bring something into being in a way that has impact, and the background knowledge to produce a grounded representation, it is unlikely that the work would achieve the results McInerney identifies.

Beyond Binary Thinking

This view of practice, and its claims for the legitimacy of creative writing to deliver knowledge and political responsibility would probably offend Plato, because it appears to ignore the concerns about the 'ancient quarrel' raised in several of the writings that appear under his name (see, e.g., *The Republic*, 607b). In broad terms, Plato characterises this quarrel as being between poetry (or creative writing more generally) and philosophy (or knowledge more generally). The former, for Plato, is predicated on intuition, emotion, and mimesis, and is therefore intellectually and morally unreliable; the latter, being built on a solid foundation of reason and evidence, offers value to the Republic and its citizens.

But imagination vs evidence, or appeal to emotion vs appeal to intellect, or any of the other possible divides between the two modes of writing are really only the product of a particular set of values, and frameworks for knowledge that are themselves built on an arbitrary binary logic. The problem with such logic is that, as Jacques Derrida argued, there is no clean or clear divide between the elements in a binary structure. The energy in an either/or structure is not located in the difference, but in the relationship: on what Derrida describes as *différance*, or a way of thinking same and difference simultaneously (1982: 19). There is always a shared quality between two elements that are apparently set in opposition to each other: which suggests that the apparent divides in the domain of creative writing are not necessarily matters of radical or oppositional dissociation; rather, each perspective or practice relies on and draws their meaning from the other (Webb 2008: 59). Plato's own writing – or Plato-channelling-Socrates – seems to confirm this: in the *Phaedrus*, he quotes Socrates to the effect that though the unreliability of 'poets' is because they are afflicted with a species of 'madness' – being possessed by the Muses – their passion and their craft skill not only generate the pleasure of the text, but also have a knowledge-function because such writing 'adorns ten thousand works of the ancients and so *educates posterity*' (*Phaedrus* 244E–245A; emphasis added).

At the heart of the craft/knowledge, intuition/research divide is the point, or the value, of writing. To what should writing aspire – what are its ends? And what is the responsibility that rests on writers? This has engendered metres of publications on the topic as much by writers with a small or local reputation as from the globally known. I want to focus on three key issues that emerge from this discourse, by considering the words and works of three very influential twentieth-century writers. First, Oscar Wilde, who writes in his preface to *The Portrait of Dorian Gray*, 'There is no such thing as a moral or an immoral book. Books are well written or badly written. That is all' (1908: 5); which implies that the purpose of writing is to add to the stock of quality literature. Milan Kundera, by contrast, raises a very different issue in his assertion that 'A novel that does not discover a hitherto unknown segment of existence is immoral. Knowledge is the novel's only morality' (1988: 6). Theodor Adorno looks to ethics rather than art for art's sake, or new understandings. For him, it is neither craft nor knowledge that proves the measure of a 'good book' but, instead, an ethical encounter with history. This is articulated in the widely (and often mis-)cited statement that 'To write poetry after Auschwitz is barbaric' (Adorno 1981: 34). Which is to say: the 'why write' is to engage actively, responsibly, with the failures and catastrophes of society.

While each author seems to hold a very firm position in their essay-statements, an examination of their literary works suggests a different imperative, or motivation. The quality, clarity, and imaginative properties of Wilde's oeuvre demonstrate his deep concern with 'well written' books but, as so many of his publications reveal – *The Happy Prince and other Tales* (1888), for example, or

The Ballad of Reading Gaol (1897) – he was also deeply concerned with social problems and the ethics of human interaction. For Kundera, the care taken in his writing evidences a strong focus on craft that he does not mention in his insistence on knowledge-as-morality. Moreover, a few pages after that statement he writes, 'The novel's raison d'etre is to keep "the world of life" under a permanent light and to protect us from '"the forgetting of being"' (1988: 17). This is not the same as the knowledge claim he makes earlier, but closer to ethics, manifest in the almost palpable rage at political brutality found in, for example, *The Book of Laughter and Forgetting* (1980) and *The Unbearable Lightness of Being* (1984). Rounding out this trinity of authorised commentators, Adorno's apparent blanket ban on the writing of poetry after Auschwitz is not in fact an insistence on morality-as-censorship; rather, it is a call for writers to be attentive about the matters they are exploring and the possible effects of their writing. He calls on writers neither to 'surrender to cynicism' nor to write 'helpless poems to the victims of our time' (1977: 188, 189); not to use our powerful aesthetic tools in production of a work that might make 'an unthinkable fate appear to have had some meaning', because this would allow for the possibility that 'something of its horror is removed' (1997: 189). Which suggests that for Adorno, poetry (literature more generally) matters in ethical terms precisely because of its capacity to illuminate the world, modify understandings, highlight or hide matters that deserve attention.

In fact, all three of these writers, who initially appear to identify just one motivation and justification for writing, in fact show that they value a wider arc of practice; as do most writers, it seems. In one context, *poiesis* is more important; in another it is *technê* that matters; and in a third the focus is on social responsibility, or passion, or economics, or politics or (et cetera). Margaret Atwood notes that the product of trawling publications and conversations with writers about their motivations for writing was a torrent of answers that fill two pages (xix–xxi) of *Negotiating with the Dead*. They include all the motivating factors one might imagine: aesthetic sensibility, social activism, record-keeping, chaos-defeating, income-earning, instructional, perceptual, celebration, sorrow, et al. In his influential essay 'Why I Write', George Orwell boils Atwood's pages down to just 'four great motives for writing'; which, he continues, 'exist in different degrees in every writer' (1946). They are 'Sheer egoism' (which he acknowledges, but does not approve); 'Aesthetic enthusiasm' (which he acknowledges as inevitable); 'Historical impulse' (which he notes, without evaluating); and 'Political purpose' (which he uses in the expanded sense: the desire to change the world; to change people's minds).

Joan Didion offers a similar, though differently nuanced, account in her own 'Why I Write' essay. She first explains that she discovered 'I was no legitimate resident in any world of ideas. I knew I couldn't think', and that it took her some time 'to discover what I was. Which was a writer'. What she does as a writer – and what, she suggests, other writers do too – is engage in 'the act of imposing oneself upon other people, of saying *listen to me, see it my way, change your mind*' (1994: 224; emphasis in original). She calls this a 'hostile' attitude, but we could equally describe it as 'persuasion', as a mode of political communication. Philosopher Martha Nussbaum makes the point that, because 'Literature is in league with the emotions' (1995: 53), a literary work 'is a morally controversial form, expressing in its very shape and style, in its modes of interaction with readers, a normative sense of life'. As such, 'it has the potential to make a distinctive contribution to our public life' (1995: 2). This echoes Orwell's comment, in his list of the motives for writing, about political purpose: 'no book is genuinely free from political bias', he writes; 'the opinion that art should have nothing to do with politics is itself a political attitude' (Didion 1994). From Didion's and Orwell's experience, it seems, all writers necessarily engage in political actions, deliberately or not, because they are showing readers another way to see, another mind to think.

This is only effective, though, if readers choose to read; because though writing is typically a solitary activity, it results in a communal event: which is the reading and the discourse that follows. Once a text enters society, armed with the capacity to capture a reader's attention (and/or heart), with the potential to move readers, or change, inform, inflect, offend, enlighten, or even bore them, the writer/text/reader have entered into communion and community, through the world conjured by, and the values incorporated within, the text.

Writing [as] Ethics

Worldmaking, and values, raise the question of the ethics of writing, a topic that is never far from the surface, especially for university-based writers and research students; but one that more often results in disagreement or discomfort rather than evidence-based arguments. There is no final, or rather, comprehensive answer to the question of what constitutes ethical writing (Rose 2011); not surprisingly, since there is no final or comprehensive answer to the question of what constitutes ethics more generally. Philosopher Martha Nussbaum's statement that 'there are certain norms that are so honoured and so central to people's discourse and daily lives that their precise contours are not studied with clarity' (2016: 58) suggests that ethical choices and the moral frameworks against which they are measured can be just a little too intimate for comfort.

Michel Foucault offers a way out of this problem when he writes, 'Ethics is the considered form that freedom takes when it is informed by reflection' (1977: 284). That is, as writers we are free to think and write the works we do; but if we are to address the question of ethics, we will have consciously reflected on the meanings we are making, on the world we are representing. It is the term 'reflective' that is central, here, because it is a reminder that writers are not just telling a story or conveying an image, but actually organising meaning, crafting what Michel de Certeau describes as 'an imposed system (... analogous to the constructed order of a city or of a supermarket)' (1984: 169). If we are to attract de Certeau's readers to wander through our 'city', our (ethical) writing, it cannot be work that preaches, or insists on moral purity; not only is that likely to be tendentious, didactic, quickly dated, it is also less welcoming to readers. We writers are not, after all (*pace* Shelley) legislators, whether acknowledged (2001: 717) or otherwise, and art is neither policy nor law.

Art/Life

It is, though, a human activity, and one that carries certain responsibilities of citizenship. This is another very indeterminate concept, and in the research on the topic I conducted in the post-September 11 years, it was a question that attracted some pretty varied responses. On the whole, those I interviewed agreed that they were distressed and angered by the disasters that fill the daily news, and the attacks on rights and freedoms that were so evident in their own nations and globally. But, they said, while it might be a *human* responsibility to engage politically, it is not their responsibility *as artists* to do so. This is an attitude I tend to share; but just as Kate Grenville came to realise that she did in fact know about the violence of Australian settlement, so too I slowly came to realise that my attitude was more likely to be a product of the unthinking in which I operate because of my social privilege – being educated, having spent my life in reasonably democratic nations, and above all, being white. Artists living in other contexts are often less sanguine about the artist/citizen divide: as the South African writer Zakes Mda says:

> I have dismally failed to respond to the strange aesthetic concepts so cherished in the western world that profess that artistic creation is an end in itself,

independent of politics and social requirements. I draw from the traditional African aesthetics where art could not be separated from life.

1984: 296

This resonates with Wittgenstein's insistence that 'Ethics and aesthetics are one and the same' (1974: 6.421). What this might mean in practice for each writer is likely to be the result of a process of consideration, reflection, and investigation in which they develop more refined understandings of the value of what they write and why they write, as well as how they personally evaluated the quality of their finished work – its fitness for purpose as a novel, or poem, or script, for example. The philosophical concept of axiology may be a useful foundation in this task of thinking how to produce writing that is both ethical, and aesthetically satisfying.

Conclusion: Writing/Righting the World

Axiology (from the Greek *axios* or worth; and *logos* or reason) is a comparatively new term, being only a little over a century old (Hart 1971: 29), but the concept has been a part of philosophy and society throughout recorded history. It is concerned with what we value, and how we attribute value; and while it is used to make sense within and evaluate various scholarly disciplines, there are, as Roger Sansi observes, 'deep, unavoidable connections between ethics and aesthetics' (2017: 374). These connections manifest in encounters with questions and decisions such as: why a writer might choose to write about one specific topic rather than another; why wrestle with the slippery confounding nature of language itself; and how to determine when the text is ready to enter the world.

Julian Meyrick, Robert Phiddian and Tully Barnett (2018) have conducted a major research project into the cultural sector, considering where value lies in this field. They dismissed the usual creative industries metrics approach, adopting instead an axiological approach that identified several elements associated with creative value. These include that a work should have purpose that makes contributions beyond the economic domain; it should accommodate meaning and the making of meanings; and it should be future-minded, capable of looking forward rather than similarly rehearsing the already known. They write, 'Value is constitutive. It not only *is* something, it *does* something, leaving us changed as well as rewarded. Paradoxically, this is most obvious in culture, where stories of personal transformation abound' (2018: xxvii; emphasis in original). And they provide a structure within which the value of creative production can be narrativized.

In considering these issues of ethics, aesthetics, values, and the motivation for writing, Claudia Rankine's ground-breaking work *Citizen: An American Lyric* (2014) kept impressing itself on me. It is, I'd say, a work that is sui generis because it evades categorisation. Poetry of course, with tastes of memoir, essay, commentary, and polemic, it has had an enormous impact on readers and critics alike. It begins with an epigraph from the French filmmaker Chris Marker's *Sans Soleil* (1982): 'If they don't see happiness in the picture, at least they'll see the black'. This quotation points, arguably, to the problem of providing an unproblematic representation. For Marker's film essay, the black is void, and it is the opposite of the 'happiness' that, the voiceover tells viewers, he tried to represent in the images of children that followed. We may not see, or perceive, happiness as he did; but we can't help but perceive what cannot be represented: the black leader that precedes the children, the happiness.

I would not presume to suggest why Rankine chose this as her epigraph; but the 'see the black' notion, scrolling as it does on to a scene of children in a lyrical setting and then forward to scenes of war machinery, can be read in terms of the *Phaedrus* concept of art-as-affect. In Marker's film essay, this sequence captures its audience, infusing them with emotion while simultaneously illuminating an aspect of contemporary history and alerting viewers to social and global crises. For me, Rankine's narrative structure does something similar in its opening sequences. First, in its use of the second person singular, it propels readers into the position of the narrator's gaze, the focalisation perspective. But almost immediately readers who, like me, are not African American are propelled (or, at least, I am) into the uncomfortable reality that the *you* who is narrating this first memory is not *me*, the reader. In fact, I am more closely identified with the girl whose name the narrator can't remember; the girl who cribbed the narrator's schoolwork and later patronised her in racist terms: 'she tells you you smell good and have features more like a white person' (2014).

The first two pages that set out this story entrance me with the lyrical technique deployed, the dream sense of an event recalled, the imagery that is woven through each word and line. And then, ka-pow, they confront me with the reality of a life I never had to lead, courtesy of the privilege I had of being born white and in a settler nation that, as in the US, refused to confront fully the crimes of its own history, the erasure of so many of its citizens. As the book unfurls, the Marker quote – *at least they'll see the black* – begins to take on other dimensions. The early sections confront erasure, how those living lives of privilege refuse to 'see the black', and the struggle people of colour must engage in to resist their erasure. As the text unfolds, shifting from voice and context and orientation, I find myself simultaneously captivated by its Wildean 'well written' qualities; chagrined by my failure and/or incapacity to understand in any material ways what it is to be an African American woman; but not simply scolded – rather offered a gift of illumination.

None of us can know, or experience, lives that are not our own; but we can be instructed in empathic understandings through literature that performs a way of seeing and being, a sense of community, in which it draws to readers' attention our common humanity, and our limited understanding. And it recalls de Certeau's argument that to write is 'to produce a more humane world' (1986: 199). A more humane world, dare I say, is one that includes work that is well written; that sheds new light on the world; that is oriented toward ethical values – in short, work that understands the generative potential of creative axiology.

References

Adorno, T. (1977), *Aesthetic Theory*, trans. R. Hullot-Kentor, London: Athlone Press.
Adorno, T. (1981), *Prisms,* trans. S. and S. Weber, Cambridge MA: MIT Press.
Adorno, T. (1997), *Aesthetics and Politics*, London: Verso.
Atwood, M. (2002), *Negotiating with the Dead: A Writer on Writing* [also published as *On Writers and Writing*], London: Virago.
Certeau, Michel de (1984), *Practice of Everyday Life,* trans. S. Rendall, Berkeley: University of California Press.
Certeau, Michel de (1986), *Heterologies: Discourse on the Other*, trans. B. Massumi, Minneapolis: University of Minnesota Press.
Derrida, J. (1982), *Margins of Philosophy,* trans. A. Bass, Brighton: Harvester Press.
Dettmar, K. (2019), 'A Hundred Years of T. S. Eliot's "Tradition and the Individual Talent"', *The New Yorker* (27 October), https://www.newyorker.com/books/page-turner/a-hundred-years-of-t-s-eliots-tradition-and-the-individual-talent (accessed 6 June 2021).
Didion, J. (1994 [1976]), 'Why I Write', in G. H. Muller with A. F. Crooks (eds) *Major Modern Essayists* (2nd ed.), Englewood Cliffs: Prentice Hall, 224–228.
Foucault, M. (1997), *The Essential Works of Michel Foucault, Vol. 1: Ethics: Subjectivity and Truth*, New York: The New Press.
Grenville, K. (2005), *The Secret River*, Melbourne: Text Publishing.
Grenville, K, (2007a), 'The History Question: Response', *Quarterly Essay*, 25: 66–72.

Grenville, K. (2007b), 'Unsettling the Settler: History, Culture, Race and the Australian Self', *Psychoanalysis Downunder* 7B (February), https://www.psychoanalysisdownunder.com.au/issue-7b (accessed 6 June 2021).

Hart, S. L. (1971), 'Axiology – Theory of Values', *Philosophy and Phenomenological Research*, 32(1): 29–41.

Kundera, M. (1988), *The Art of the Novel*, trans. L. Asher, London: Faber.

Marker, C. (1983), Sans Soleil [Sunless], Paris: Argos Films.

Mayers, T. (2009), 'One Simple Word: From Creative Writing to Creative Writing Studies;, *College English*, 71(3): 217–228.

McInerney, J. (2005), 'The Uses of Invention', *The Guardian* (17 September): 4

Mda, Z. (1984), 'Extracts', in M. J. Daymond, J. U. Jacobs and M. Lenta (eds) *Momentum: On Recent South African Writing*, Pietermaritzburg: University of Natal Publishing, 295–297.

Meyrick, J., R. Phiddian and T. Barnett (2018), *What Matters? Talking Value in Australian Culture*, Melbourne: Monash University Publishing.

Nussbaum, M. C. (1995), *Poetic Justice: The Literary Imagination and Public Life*, Boston: Beacon Press.

Nussbaum, M. C. (2016), *Anger and Forgiveness: Resentment, Generosity, Justice*, Oxford: Oxford University Press.

Orwell, G. (1946), 'Why I Write', *Gangrel*, 4 (Summer): 5–10.

Plato (1998 [c370BCE]), *Phaedrus,* trans. J. H. Nichols, Ithaca, NY: Cornell University Press.

Plato (2004 [c380-350BCE]), *Republic*, trans. B. Jowett, New York: Barnes and Noble.

Rankine, C. (2014), *Citizen: An American Lyric*, Minneapolis: Graywolf Press.

Rose, J. (2011), 'Theft is Theft: The Ethics of Telling Other People's Stories', *The Ethical Imaginations: Writing Worlds Papers*, AAWP, https://aawp.org.au/wp-content/uploads/2015/03/Rose_0.pdf (accessed 11 November 2013).

Sansi, R. (2017), 'Ethics and Aesthetics: Afterword', *World Art*, 7(2): 373–380.

Shelley, P. B. (2001 [1840]), 'A Defence of Poetry', in V. B. Leitch (ed.) *The Norton Anthology of Theory and Criticism*, New York: W.W. Norton, 699–717.

Webb, J. (2008), *Understanding Representation,* London: Sage.

Webb, J. (2015), *Researching Creative Writing,* Cambridge: Frontinus Press.

Wilde, O. (1908), 'Preface', *The Picture of Dorian Gray*, Leipzig: Bernhard Tauchnitz.

Wittgenstein, L. (1974), *Tractatus Logico-Philosophicus*, trans. D. F. Pears and B. F. Guinness, London: Routledge.

But What about the Imagination?

Representation, Other People's Stories, and Fiction Writing

Dr Tresa LeClerc
University of California, San Diego

Introduction

Throughout my years teaching creative writing and attending writers' talks, it has not been uncommon to hear questions relating to how authors write characters who are significantly different to themselves. Inevitably, the question of the imagination's role in writing these characters comes into play, particularly when those characters occupy a more marginal position in society than the author. This has been referred to as 'writing other people's stories' (Leane 2016; Wright 2016), or 'writing the Other'. Yet the imagination, and its ability to accurately represent groups of people, has been called into question. This is because stories of this kind, which portray a significant power difference between author and subject, may be misrepresentative of the group of people they seek to represent, and in the process, reinforce dominant and harmful stereotypes. This is especially the case when that misrepresentation involves a level of exploitation: for example, when the writer has made a large sum of money from the publication while authors from the group represented remain underpaid and under-published.

Cases such as these raise questions about author representation of marginalised communities and the 'imagination'. Claudia Rankine and Beth Loffreda (2015), Jeanine Leane (2016), and Alexis Wright (2016) have criticised the use of the imagination in this context, pointing out that it is part of the racial imaginary, in which marginalised authors, particularly Black and Indigenous characters, are constructed as inferior to white characters. Furthermore, the literary industry is dominated by white authors (Spread the Word 2015; Lee & Low Books 2020; So and Wezerek 2020) and this has led to a crisis of misrepresentation for culturally marginalised communities. However, we still have little information about how the writings of marginalised characters are produced by writers who are not themselves of that background, aside from brief descriptions in the prologues and epilogues of such books (LeClerc 2016).

One approach to broaching this topic has been to consider the discipline of ethnography and its methodologies, which focus on ethical research, as a guide to representing otherness. The line between fiction and nonfiction is one that has been hotly contested in the discipline, particularly when ethnographic method has been used to write fictional accounts. In 'That's Enough about Ethnography!' anthropologist Tim Ingold (2014: 385), sees ethnographic description as 'more an art than a science' and 'no less accurate or truthful for that', but he argues that novel ethnographic forms have led to a distortion and devaluing of the discipline. This raises the question, what are the limits of ethnography and the imagination when constructing a fictional novel?

To examine this, as part of my dissertation I wrote three drafts of a novel manuscript, using the ethnographic methods of fieldwork, interview, and feedback, to better analyse this process of writing, and reflected upon the politics of writing Otherness. This also meant that as part of my creative practice project, the findings were represented in fictional form. The manuscript contained four characters from refugee backgrounds, and the story was set across a day in Melbourne. One of the characters was of Chilean background. This character was closest to my own background: my father is from Chile (though not from a refugee background) and my mother is Irish-American. At the time of writing the manuscript I was living in Melbourne, though I grew up in Southern California. This chapter argues that, within the current context of racial under-representation in the literary industry, authors profiting off of a trend toward racial diversity while still occupying a privileged position has led to instances of backlash, particularly when that representation is seen to feed into false or stereotypical national narratives. Using ethnographic methods, and following the work of Loffreda and Rankine, Leane, and Wright, this chapter problematises the idea that the 'imagination' is an adequate way to represent a historically situated culture. While increased discussion with the community represented may help to mitigate these issues, stronger methods for writing don't help to resolve the issue of underrepresentation of Own Voices writers in the book industry.

Background

Many different labels have been applied to the use of fiction to present social research, such as experimental ethnography, ethnofiction, ethnographic fiction, the ethnographic novel, literary tales, new journalism, and parajournalism (Behar and Gordon 1995; Van Maanen 1998, cited in VanSlyke-Briggs 2009: 336). These works challenge the boundary between fiction and nonfiction. While there is an overlap between the ethical discussions around representation in ethnography and the growing criticism of representing others in literature, this area historically lacks theorisation (Laterza 2007: 125).

A look into how writers may construct narratives about characters from more marginalised backgrounds is necessary, in order to gain more insight into how representation can be created, including misrepresentation. Creative practice could be of use here, because it allows for precisely this kind of theorisation. In my doctoral work, I used an ethnographic methodology that would enable me to examine in detail the process through which characters were constructed. In *All the Time Lost*, ethnographic data was represented through the use of the field notes, interview transcripts, and participant feedback on the manuscript. These were used to mirror different methods authors may use to write characters of other backgrounds. Among those mentioned by authors are 'empathy', the 'imagination', and 'sensitivity'.

'Imagining' the lives of others or 'putting oneself in another's shoes' implies some measure of fictionalisation, as it is a project of thinking through the positionality of another person. As fieldnotes do not involve formal conversation with the subject, the writing of a character through these also uses a measure of imagination and empathy. As I have previously written on the topics of empathy (see LeClerc 2018) and sensitivity (see LeClerc 2020), this chapter reflects specifically on the use of ethnographic field notes and the imagination to write fiction. The fictionalisation of that data, and the blending of it with literary elements, allowed me to examine how these forms complement each other, and at times overlap. However, I also note that too much faith in the imagination's ability to accurately represent another's experience is problematic. The imagination is supplemented with information that constructs the other through various sources, such as the mediascape (Appadurai 2015). This, along with the possibility of over-empathy, may impact representation and reproduce tropes and stereotypes.

Ethnography's Use in Fiction

Before discussing *All the Time Lost*'s use of ethnographic methods to write fiction, it is useful to consider fiction's relationship to ethnography. Fiction's use within ethnography has been contemplated at length within the field of anthropology (see Clifford and Marcus 1986; Atkinson and Hammersley 1994; Narayan 1999; Augé 2013). The literary turn, the point where ethnography began to examine its own writing processes and systems (and politics) of representation, led to the notion that the findings of research could be conveyed through other means, such as visual, sensory, or literary forms (Rapport 2012). This meant a heightened awareness of the similarities between literary and ethnographic forms. Harrison (1996: 90; cited in VanSlyke-Briggs 2009: 335) draws attention to American canonical writer Zora Neale Hurston's early training as an ethnographer and her representation of participant-observer ethnography in *Mules and Men*. Unfortunately, at the time of its writing in the 1930s, literary representations of ethnographic research were not considered academic, and thus failed to be recognised by the academy (Harrison 1996: 90, cited in VanSlyke-Briggs 2009: 335). While innovative forms of ethnography (see Pink 2015) are becoming more common, more theorisation has the potential to contribute to the literary debate around fictional character representation.

Literature has sought to translate the human experience through fiction. During the literary turn, anthropologists began to use literature as a source for exploring culture (Rapport 2012). Marilyn Cohen's *Novel Approaches to Anthropology: Contributions to Literary Anthropology* (2013) is a collection of studies using ethnographic methods to interpret literary fiction. As opposed to a field site, anthropologists looked to the fictional novel to tell them about a particular culture at a certain point in time. As traditional anthropology is impossible in this context, Cohen states that literary anthropologists 'read the scene' observing and interpreting the described environment and artefacts in order to provide the 'essential empathy anthropologists bring to their fieldwork and interpretations of cultures' (Cohen 2013: 3). In this sense, fiction can be considered a form of ethnography (Laterza 2007: 124). Therefore, this can be thought of in two ways: the use of literature to produce an ethnographic study, and the use of the ethnographic novel to convey ethnographic findings, which take on a literary form (Laterza 2007: 125).

As a literary form, the question of whether the ethnographic novel should be considered literature, anthropology or a cross-disciplinary work remains. Ethnofiction, for example, blurs the line between ethnography and literature, yet is still largely situated in the discipline of anthropology. Behar and Gordon (1995, cited in VanSlyke-Briggs 2009: 336) see ethnofiction as 'creative anthropological representations of meaning'. Ethnofiction is 'creative ethnography' that actively seeks to elicit readers' personal connection to the work (VanSlyke-Briggs 2009). Aside from the use of fiction, what differentiates this from the ethnographic novel that presents ethnographic findings, is perhaps that the author will not directly state what he/she intends to communicate (VanMaanen 1988, cited in VanSlyke-Briggs 2009: 336). Yet, both fiction and ethnography seek to understand human life, and both have their foundation in writing (Fassin 2014: 41). Clifford (in Clifford and Marcus 1986: 6) saw ethnographic writings as fictions in the sense that they were 'made' and 'fashioned', but maintained the importance of ethnography not being 'made up', but 'real'. Fiction and ethnography can be seen as complementary forms, striving to reach the same goal: to understand and translate culture.

In the last ten years, we have seen more experimentation with this form. Marc Augé describes his ethnofictional novel *No Fixed Abode* as 'neither an academic study nor a novel', but a 'narrative that evokes a social fact through the subjectivity of a particular individual that is 'imagined'' (Augé 2013: vii). To VanSlyke-Briggs (2009: 341), what differentiates ethnofiction from the novel is the emphasis on the reader's witnessing of a place and time rather than their identification with the protagonist. He sees ethnofiction as a blending of the field notes, interviews, and collected data told through a fictional method. While insignificant details may be fictionalised, significant events should be created through observation and field notes. Thus, ethnofiction and the ethnographic novel are written after the collection of data.

However, I wanted to know what would happen if I started with fiction rather than observed data. As a result, my writing of *All the Time Lost* deviated from this form in that the characters were created before the inclusion of field notes. Therefore, the ethnographic data informed the novel rather than being the basis of the novel. Within this frame, I describe the manuscript as 'ethnographically informed', rather than an ethnographic novel. This allowed me to compare characters that were created through the author's imagination with the versions written after fieldwork.

Creative Practice Methodology

To examine how the manuscript was written, I used a practice-led methodology. Here I draw on Candy, Amitani, and Bilda's (2006) definition: the research was done through the process of writing the novel itself which leads to new understandings about practice. However, this research can also be considered practice-based in that the research is also demonstrated through the creative outcome (Candy et al. 2006), *All the Time Lost*. As a result, the investigation is undertaken partly through practice and partly through the outcomes of that practice (Candy et al. 2006).

Graham Harper (2013: 114) points out two main criticisms against creative writing as a discipline. The first is that creative writing research is not easily replicable as each writer's situation is different. Because it is not replicable, creative writing cannot be developmental, or build upon existing knowledge. Harper counters this, arguing that shared situational knowledge is the foundation of what society is built upon, and that the focus of creative writing is on methodology, rather than replicability. I would add that it may be likened to the social sciences, in that social sciences investigate, amongst other things, the ways in which people do things and the reasons why they do them. Creative writing practice can be seen to be an investigation into the ways writers write, an investigation into 'creativity'. As such, while the artefact may not be replicable, the process used to create the artefact may be. A writer in the future may use ethnographic methodologies to write a book that centres around otherness by following the process that I have described. By looking at the difficulties I have identified through my reflective practice, and suggestions for future practice, improvements may be made to this process and thus knowledge built upon it.

Furthermore, creative practice researchers tend to adapt methods and research strategies from qualitative traditions (Haseman and Mafe 2009: 212). Simon Holloway (2013) compares the creative writing PhD to a pocket watch. He posits that while more traditional PhDs may take apart the watch to examine how it may have been created, the creative practice PhD builds a watch, and through this process, examines the method of its construction. In doing so, practice is used as a means of making tacit knowledge available to research (Niedderer and Roworth-Stokes 2007). In order to interrogate the inner workings of the 'pocket watch', I modelled each phase of my project on collaborative ethnographic methods: fieldwork, interview, and feedback.

I began writing the first draft of *All the Time Lost* with the initial premise of four characters, who travelled at various times on public transport. I decided that they should be going to the city at some point, to follow the lines of the railways and tram tracks. During my time writing the draft, I attended a protest in the city, and this became the point where all the storylines intersected. The last part of the story was based on my experience attending a public university lecture. I thought this would make a good addition, since most of the city's tramlines end at the university. These aspects formed the 'core story'.

The first draft was written while I conducted fieldwork in the refugee community. It was written as fiction, based on my field notes. But I noticed that while I thought I was creating these storylines using my imagination, after re-reading my drafts, I noticed that my past experience working with people from migrant backgrounds inevitably played a role in how I imagined the characters. Furthermore, as one of the characters is from a Chilean background, some of this story was also drawn from my personal experiences. This raised the question – what do we as authors mean when we say 'imagination'?

The Imagination

According to Braddock (2012: 667), many early theorists framed the imagination as a kind of magical power or genius, the spontaneity of which enabled invention, originality, and creativity. Baldick (2015) points to Coleridge's *Biographia Literaria* (1817), which 'emphasised the imagination's vitally creative power of dissolving and uniting images into new forms, and of reconciling opposed qualities into a new unity'. This provides a clearer definition of how the imagination operates, using images already present in the mind of the author. Later, in the nineteenth and twentieth centuries, it was noted that the imagination relied on intuition and feeling; it began to be more strongly associated with the intellect and expression, a kind of conscious imitation of reality (Braddock 2012: 673). Blackburn (2016) observes it as, 'the ability to create and rehearse possible situations, to combine knowledge in unusual ways'. This focus on knowledge draws attention to what the author already knows or believes to be true.

Rankine and Loffreda (2015) describe the racial imaginary. They point to how race is constructed in the eyes of a white audience. Following from this, Jeanine Leane (2016) argues that 'literary representations are never just benign descriptions; they enter into and shape our national discourse'. Leane describes books in which Aboriginal people were written out of the picture, what she refers to as the 'literature of erasure'. She elaborates using *Coonardoo* by Katharine Susannah Prichard (1929) in which the colonial scheme was cast as a way to 'save them from themselves'. As Alexis Wright (2016), in her seminal essay 'What Happens When You Tell Somebody Else's Story?' asserts, 'Aboriginal people have not been in charge of the stories other people tell about us'. Wright discusses the national narrative in which stories are told on the behalf of First Nations people, supposedly 'for their own good', and the dangerous impacts of these narratives. Wright points out that the playing field has never been even and has always worked in favour of whiteness.

We might also look at Appadurai's (2015) mediascape, to see how the distance from the subject means that they are more likely to constructed in the imagination of the producer through the media's representation. Appadurai discusses the concept of the mediasphere. He identifies several scapes which shape our understandings of imagined worlds. With the landscape of the media, our images are constructed not only with fiction texts, such as films and TV, but also with nonfiction texts, like the news and documentary. If a person were to describe what someone in the mafia may look like, their description will depend upon whether they have encountered a person from the mafia in reality. If not, the image they see in their mind may be constructed through what they have seen in the news and in film. In other words, how writers construct fictional characters within the mediasphere depends on our proximity to those characters. A writer is more likely to rely on these past media representations if the writer has less experience with the people they seek to represent.

My reliance on the 'imagination' revealed that I had, in the early stages of writing, seen the imagination in much the same way as early theorists, as something almost magical and unrelated my previous ideas of people from refugee backgrounds. However, the imagination cannot be separated from the pre-existing ideas of the author. My experiences before my fieldwork played a role in the early draft's interpretation of characters and ultimately their representation.

The Imagination and Literary Representation

Backlash against more privileged authors who write marginalised characters can be observed online though opinion pieces in magazines and journals and on social media, in spaces like Twitter. Two notable cases are Jeanine Cummins's *American Dirt* (2020), a fictional novel about a treacherous migration journey from Mexico to the USA, and Kate Clanchy's *Some Kids I Taught* (1999), a memoir about life lessons Clanchy learned from the children of multiple diverse backgrounds whom she worked with as a teacher. Of *American Dirt*, Myiram Gurba's (2019) viral review in *Tropics of Meta* noted the stereotypes of the 'Latin lover, the suffering mother, and the stoic manchild' along with cliched tropes, like an assassination at a quinceañera. Rajesh's (2021) *Guardian* article reported

Clanchy was criticised for her descriptions of children's racial background, class and ability, using terms like 'chocolate coloured skin' and 'flirty hijab'. Both books where criticised for stereotypical and offensive descriptions of characters, and in each case, the larger discussion of discrimination of writers from marginalised backgrounds was brought to the forefront. The backlash stems from the recognition of these stereotypes as a way of perpetuating the racist system.

No Friend but the Mountains is an own voices nonfictional account of life in Manus Regional Processing Center, referred to in the book Manus Prison, written by Behrouz Boochani (2018). It provides some insight into how this racist system is perpetuated in refugee narratives. In it, Boochani describes Manus Island as a prison and the way the guards and bureaucratic systems work to establish and reinforce not just power but ideology. The Kyriarchal system, he writes, operates using intersecting social systems of dominance and oppression. Boochani identifies these structures, like racism, heteronormativity, coloniality, as multiple and interlocking. As Ghassan Hage (2014) writes, white Australian culture can stifle conversations about race. He describes condescending racism, which takes the form of a casual acceptance of racism and disavowal of the person calling out the racist act, with such dismissals as 'oversensitive' or 'too serious'. In doing so, relaxation of racialised forms of interaction can become routinised or normalised (Hage 2014: 234). In the same way, of the prison, Boochani writes that: 'Manus Prison as an ideology hinders or eliminates opportunities to know; to know in nuanced and multidimensional ways both about the violent atrocities and about the unique lived experiences of the prisoners' (2018). In effect, it becomes easier not to discuss racism because to do so involves social punishment. To avoid this, authors may reproduce the typical tropes about refugees. According to Boochani, 'it is possible and acceptable to be both pro-refugee and anti-refugee in different ways' (2018).

This resonates, as reported in my article 'The Controversy of Writing in the Voices of Others' (LeClerc 2018), the findings of the project showed that fieldwork without direct interviews tended to replicate a dominant narrative told about refugees, which played down racism and played up victimhood. It showed that the more direct engagement with the community represented through interviews and feedback, the more likely those narratives are to be countered. But I was careful to point out that the best way to counter harmful representation is for the industry to enable opportunities for marginalised groups to represent themselves.

Therefore, using the ethnographic method of fieldwork to write creative fiction did not solve the issue of representation because fictionalisation involves the imagination and the imagination is not a neutral space, nor is it free of the influence of dominant narratives and tropes. As Hammersley (1992: 3) notes, while ethnography could represent one reality rather than 'reality' itself, lending itself to the notion of being perceived as a rhetorical device, such as fiction, it does not represent a direct relationship between ethnography and practice fiction (see Krieger 1984 and van Mane 1998, cited in Hammersley 1992).

Conclusion

The finished version of *All the Time Lost* can be thought of as a palimpsest, a text in which elements of the original have been scraped off or replaced. Thus, this creative practice study was my attempt to make those layers visible, in order to 'track' the creation of the text and provide further insights into how works about the lives of others may be constructed. While the ethnographic method of fieldwork enabled a closer observation of the methods used by writers to produce fiction, it can still produce problematic representations that reinforce a hierarchical power structure. Misunderstandings about the power of the imagination are pervasive in the writing industry, which may overlook how stereotypes from the media or privileged cultural positioning may impact the lens through which they write. Recent cases of social media backlash show a growing movement against narratives that perpetuate a Kyriarchal system. A previous look into ethnographic interviewing and feedback to mitigate this impact reveals that it can help in terms of identifying racist tropes (LeClerc 2018), but I argue that it is not as effective as Own Voices writing in addressing issues of misrepresentation and underrepresentation. This examination has implications for the field of creative practice, in that it provides more detailed information on how refugee narratives are constructed, and how ethnographic methods can be applied to creative practice research. It calls for caution when representing marginalised communities in writing and more action to be taken by the publishing industry to enable writers from these backgrounds to publish stories that counter popular nationalist tropes and narratives.

References

Appadurai, A. (2015), 'Disjuncture and Difference in the Global Cultural Economy', in *Colonial Discourse and Post-colonial Theory*, Abingdon, UK: Routledge, 324–339.

Atkinson, M. and Hammersley, P. (1994), 'Ethnography and Participant Observation', in N. K. Denzin and Y. S. Lincoln (eds) *Handbook of Qualitative Research*, Thousand Oaks, CA: Sage, 248–260.

Augé, M. (2013), *No Fixed Abode*, London: Seagull Books.

Baldick, C. (2015), 'Imagination', in *The Oxford Dictionary of Literary Terms*, Oxford: Oxford University Press.

Blackburn, S. (2016), 'Imagination', in *The Oxford Dictionary of Philosophy*, Oxford: Oxford University Press.

Boochani, B. (2018), *No Friend but the Mountains: Writing from Manus Prison*. Sydney, NSW: Pan Macmillan Australia.

Braddock, J. (2012), 'Imagination', in R. Greene, S. Cushman, C. Cavanagh, J. Ramazani, and P. Rouzer (eds) *The Princeton Encyclopedia of Poetry and Poetics: Fourth Edition*. Ebook, Princeton, NJ: Princeton University Press.

Candy, L., Amitani, S., and Bilda, Z. (2006), 'Practice-Led Strategies for Interactive Art Research', *CoDesign*, 2(4): 209–223. Available online: https://www.tandfonline.com/doi/abs/10.1080/15710880601007994 (accessed 30 August 2022).

Clanchy, K. (1999). *Some Kids I Taught and What They Taught Me*. London: Picador.

Clifford, J. and Marcus, G. E. (1986), *Writing Culture: The Poetics and Politics of Ethnography: A School Of American Research Advanced Seminar*, Berkeley, CA: University of California Press.

Cohen, M. (2013), 'Introduction: Anthropological Aspects of The Novel', in M. Cohen (ed) *Novel Approaches to Anthropology Contributions to Literary Anthropology*, Lanham, MD: Lexington Books, 1–26.

Cummins, J. (2020). *American Dirt*. New York: Flatiron Books.

Fassin, D. (2014), 'True Life, Real Lives: Revisiting the Boundaries Between Ethnography And Fiction', *American Ethnologist*, 41(1): 40–55. Available online: https://anthrosource.onlinelibrary.wiley.com/doi/abs/10.1111/amet.12059 (accessed 30 August 2022).

Gurba, M. (2019), 'Pendeja, You Ain't Steinbeck: My Bronca with Fake-Ass Social Justice Literature', *Tropics of Meta*, Dec 12. Available online: https://tropicsofmeta.com/2019/12/12/pendeja-you-aint-steinbeck-my-bronca-with-fake-ass-social-justice-literature/ (accessed 30 August 2022).

Hage, G. (2014), 'Continuity and Change in Australian Racism', *Journal of Intercultural Studies*, 35(3): 232–237.

Hammersley, M. (1992), *What's Wrong with Ethnography?* London and New York: Routledge.

Harper, G. (2013), 'Creative Writing Research', in G. Harper and D. Donnely (eds) *Key Issues in Creative Writing*. Ebook: Bristol, Buffalo, Toronto: EBSCO Publishing.

Haseman, B. and Mafe, D. (2009), 'Acquiring Know-How: Research Training for Practice-Led Researchers', in R. T. Dean and H. Smith (eds) *Practice-Led Research, Research-Led Practice In The Creative Arts*, Edinburgh: Edinburgh University Press, 211–228.

Holloway, S. (2013), 'How to Make a Pocket Watch: The British Ph.D. in Creative Writing', in G. Harper (ed.) *A Companion to Creative Writing*. Ebook: Chichester: John Wiley & Sons, Ltd.

Ingold, T. (2014), 'That's Enough About Ethnography!' *HAU: Journal of Ethnographic Theory*, 4(1): 383–395.

Laterza, V. (2007), 'The Ethnographic Novel: Another Literary Skeleton in The Anthropological Closet?' *Suomen Antropologi: Journal of the Finnish Anthropological Society*, 32(2): 124. Available online : http://www.academia.edu/726440/The_ethnographic_novel_another_literary_skeleton_in_the_anthropological_closet (accessed 29 December 2017).

Leane, J. (2016), 'Other People's Stories', *Overland*, 225. Available online: https://overland.org.au/previous-issues/issue-225/feature-jeanine-leane/ (accessed 30 August 2022).

LeClerc, T. (2016), 'Fictionalising the Stories of Others: Reflections on Teaching Collaborative Life Writing and Fictionalisation in the Creative Writing Classroom', *Writing in Practice Journal of Creative Writing Research*. Available online: https://www.nawe.co.uk/DB/current-wip-edition-2/articles/fictionalizing-the-stories-of-others-reflections-on-teaching-collaborative-life-writing-and-fictionalization-in-the-creative-writing-classroom.html (accessed 30 August 2022).

LeClerc, T. (2018), 'The Controversy of Writing in the Voices of Others', *TEXT Journal* Special Issue: Identity Politics and Creative Writing, 53. Available online: http://www.textjournal.com.au/speciss/issue53/LeClerc.pdf (accessed 30 August 2022).

LeClerc, T. (2020), 'The Privilege of Common Sense: The Cultural Appropriation Debate in Creative Writing', *Overland*, 29 July. Available online: https://overland.org.au/2020/07/the-privilege-of-common-sense/ (accessed 30 August 2022).

Lee & Low Books (2020), 'Where is the Diversity in Publishing? The 2019 Diversity Baseline Survey Results', *The Open Book Blog*, January 28. Available online: https://blog.leeandlow.com/2020/01/28/2019diversitybaselinesurvey/ (accessed 30 August 2022).

Narayan, K. (1999), 'Ethnography and Fiction: Where is the Border?' *Anthropology and Humanism*, 4(2): 134–147.

Niedderer, K. and Roworth-Stokes, S. (2007), 'The Role and Use of Creative Practice in Research and its Contribution to Knowledge', *International Association of Societies of Design Research Conference*, 12–15 November. Available online: http://niedderer.org/IASDR07SRS.pdf (accessed 30 August 2022).

Pink, S. (2015), *Doing Sensory Ethnography* (2nd ed.), Los Angeles: Sage.

Rajesh, M. (2021), 'Pointing Out Racism in Books Is not an "Attack" – It's A Call for Industry Reform', *The Guardian*, 13 Aug. Available online: https://www.theguardian.com/books/2021/aug/13/pointing-out-racism-in-books-is-not-an-attack-kate-clanchy?CMP=Share_iOSApp_Other&fbclid=IwAR2XwtP2sg_5erku_wZPx25bQT5W6HtcjKvNNajmHvVLC73Q8aqgjrIn5io (accessed 30 August 2022).

Rankine, C. and Loffreda, B. (2015), 'On Whiteness and The Racial Imaginary', *Lit Hub*, April 9. Available online: https://lithub.com/on-whiteness-and-the-racial-imaginary/ (accessed 30 August 2022).

Rapport, N. (2012), 'Literary Anthropology', *Oxford Bibliographies*. Available online: http://www.oxfordbibliographies.com/view/document/obo-9780199766567/obo-9780199766567-0067.xml (accessed 30 August 2022).

So, R. J. and Wezerek, G. (2020), 'Just How White is the Book Industry?' *The New York Times*, Dec 11. Available online: https://www.nytimes.com/interactive/2020/12/11/opinion/culture/diversity-publishing-industry.html (accessed 30 August 2022).

Spread the Word (2015), *Writing the Future: Black and Asian Writers and Publishers in the UK Market Place*. Available online: https://www.spreadtheword.org.uk/wp-content/uploads/2016/11/Writing-the-Future-Black-and-Asian-Authors-and-Publishers-in-the-UK-Marketplace-May-2015.pdf (accessed 30 August 2022).

VanSlyke-Briggs, K. (2009), 'Consider Ethnofiction', *Ethnography and Education*, 4(3): 335–345.

Wright, A. (2016), 'What Happens When You Tell Somebody Else's Story?' *Meanjin*, 75(4): 58–76. Available online: https://meanjin.com.au/essays/what-happens-when-you-tell-somebody-elses-story/ (accessed 30 August 2022).

8

Drafting, Revision, and an Author's Duty of Care

My Novel 'Housework of Desire' and the Near-Destruction of a Thirty-Year Friendship

Shady Cosgrove
University of Wollongong NSW

In a speech at the Art Gallery of New South Wales, Australian writer Charlotte Wood spoke about the process of drafting her award-winning novel, *The Natural Way of Things*. She stated:

> To free myself from the sometimes-paralysing fear of uncertainty, I've learned a few mental tricks. One of these is to conceive of my story in progress as a kind of performance that I am only there to watch take place, rather than to control. And in my mind's eye, the unfolding performance of my novel has always taken place in the hushed dark of a richly textured circus tent.
>
> 2018

I used this strategy with writing the first draft of my latest novel-in-progress 'Housework of Desire' (working title), a book about friendship, couple-swapping, and desperation in the context of neoliberal America. When I sat down to write, I imagined the novel taking place on-stage and my only job was to scribe. The word count was staggering – over a two-week stay as a Bundanon Trust Artist-in-Residence, I produced 40,000 words. However, there was cost – when a dear friend read the draft, she was appalled by the likeness between herself and one of the characters. Do you really see me like that, Carolyn (not her real name) asked. I was flummoxed. It's true, I had been thinking of her when writing, but the character of Sabine was by far my favourite in the book. I loved her complexity, her ambition, and her ability to call people on their bullshit. If I'd written my friend into the book, I'd written the parts of myself I wanted to embrace and develop. As well, even though it had been unintentional, and my friend unidentifiable, confidential stories she had shared with me had clearly made it into the novel. When I gave her the draft, I had worried Carolyn might be affronted by the sexual content in the book (would she think I wanted to sleep with her husband, would she think I had been imagining her having sex?) but that did not faze her. As she wrote, after reading this essay, 'I remember you saying that I might feel a little weird about it . . . but honestly I thought it was cool imagining breaking down those boundaries and reading your sex scenes.' Carolyn's issue, instead, was the relationship between creative artefact and lived experience, and the feeling I'd violated the boundaries of our friendship by exploiting her difficult experiences, making me wonder: what right do we have to our lived experiences, and what is an author's ethical duty of care to their loved ones? What is the difference between creative engagement and exploitation? What processes or systems can be used to mitigate conflict, and is that even desirable? And how does the very creative process itself impact these questions?

This chapter will examine ideas of the unconscious, writing process and duties of care when the 'research' of our creative practice is lived experience. Using my experiences drafting 'Housework of Desire' as a case study, I will tease apart issues of inspiration, creativity, feedback and trust, arguing that authors have to navigate a duty of care when deciding what material to include (and how to represent it) in their fiction – but timing and redrafting can prove critical in allowing the freedom and unknowingness of the creative process.

Creative Process

The writer sits at their desk, gathers faith and faces the blank screen. What then, what strategies can assist us in navigating the liminal, in making the plunge from cursor to story? Writer Andre Dubus III refers to E. L. Doctorow, saying that writing a novel is like driving at night:

> 'You can only see as far as your headlights'--but you keep going until you get there. I've learned over the years to just report back anything that I see in front of the headlights: Are they yellow stripes or white? What's on the side of the road? Is there vegetation? What kind? What's the weather? What are the sounds? If I capture the experience all along the way, the structure starts to reveal itself. My guiding force and principle for shaping the story is to just follow the headlights. That's how the architecture is revealed.
>
> 2017: 63

This metaphor of following the headlights and reporting on the side of the road is not unlike entering the circus tent and bearing witness to action on a stage. Both involve accepting a passive activity as creator. Driving is arguably the more active metaphor – imaginary motion as a consequence of the writer – but both conceptions demand the writer as observer, and the object of observation is their own consciousness.

When I used Wood's circus tent method, I imagined an old-fashioned tent, with heavy curtains – warm inside, but empty. I'd walk halfway down, and sit on the aisle, always on the left-hand side, and wait for the red velvet curtain to rise. When the lights came up, my novel was depicted on stage and my job was to write as witness. While this description maybe seems more in-keeping with the experience of attending a play or live performance, there was a cinematic quality to the imagining as though I were in the presence of a circus-movie, with all of the perspective of a moving camera. Still, it was a conscious observing, as I was not making anything up, I was not *working*. This not-working was critical to the endeavour. As Dubus III states:

> There's a profound difference between making something up and imagining it. You're making something up when you think out a scene, when you're being logical about it. You think, 'I need this to happen so some other thing can happen.' There's an aspect of controlling the material that I don't think is artful. I think it leads to contrived work, frankly, no matter how beautifully written it might be.
>
> 2017: 62

Though I have published short fiction and two other book-length creative works, this was the first time I consciously used the circus tent method; it was useful as a first-draft writing strategy as it freed me from the pressure of the blank page. Frequently, as I sat down to write, I would re-read the previous paragraphs and wait to see what emerged onstage. The experience seemed more of a 'dropping-in' to story than a conscious creating of story, and in that sense reminiscent of meditation. This method certainly helped get words on the page, but they were still in need of substantial work and review. Large sections of the manuscript would need to be overhauled, if not deleted entirely upon revisiting later – not because of my friend's concerns but because had I not taken character deeply enough into account (I was still getting to know them) or I had undercut rising tension with unnecessary plot points. In future projects, I might devote more time to understanding character and motivation before commencing this process – though too much preparation risks impeding the desired free-flow.

At the 2008 Sydney Writers' Festival, writer Paul Auster said you can feel when a story goes off track, and writer Siri Hustvedt agreed, saying she experiences 'an internal sensation of rightness or wrongness' when drafting fiction. Arguably, this makes no sense – the story has never been written, why should it go any direction at all? And yet, I connect with Hustvedt's idea of 'internal rightness' and have felt it before as a physical sensation when writing, certainly in my longer works. With 'Housework of Desire', the experience of 'rightness' and 'wrongness' was not an analytical one – they were not thoughts, at first. They began as feelings that occurred in my brain and gut simultaneously, and demanded trust and openness. I was forced, on some level to relinquish conscious control, reminding me of Dubus III's comment that sometimes he needs to 'back the fuck off' when writing.

> I've learned over the years to free-fall into what's happening. What happens then is, you start writing something you don't even really want to write about. Things start to happen under your pencil that you don't want to happen, or don't understand. But that's when the work starts to have a beating heart.
>
> 2017: 62

Or writer Aimee Bender, who needs to 'get out of the way – when I let go a little bit, I surprise myself' (2017: 4). Or, in the classroom, writer Kathryn Harrison often repeats the phrase, 'Please stop thinking' because 'people really write better without thinking, by which I mean without self-consciousness' (2017: 111). For her, the writing process is akin to groping toward something, 'not even knowing what it is until I've arrived' (ibid).

The idea of the subconscious at work or the unconscious influence is a common theme in discussions about the writing process, and while I'm wary of the idea of writer-as-medium there is a consistency to these descriptions that bears considering. As novelist Kathryn Harrison states, 'writing is a process that demands cerebral effort, but it's also one informed by the unconscious. My work is directed by the needs of my unconscious' (2017: 110). Writer Don Delillo describes it as a 'zone' that he aspires towards – 'there's a higher place, a secret aspiration. You want to let go. You want to lose yourself in language, become a carrier or messenger. The best moments involve a loss of control. It's a kind of rapture…' (1993: 1). This idea of the 'zone' or 'getting out of the way' involves a relinquishing of control. If the writer gets out of their own way, they are making space for something not-fully-conscious to propel the story – and this can be uncomfortable. If we relax into the nether-reaches of our brains, it is unknown what will emerge – it may well be stories or details that don't 'belong' to us. It may be descriptions or scenes that have stayed in our brain because we worry about the people who have told them to us. It may be these details emerge and those close to us feel exposed at seeing their experiences on the page without consent even if we were compelled by a profound unconscious (sometimes dangerous) caring.

The Writer and Duties of Care

Much work has been undertaken on the ethics of reading and criticism (Eaglestone, 1997; Keen 2006; Hale 2020, 2009). Narratologist and philosopher Tom Cochrane argues that reading is important because it teaches us to discern narrative and consider fictional situations as possible realities, inciting the question: What might I do in a given situation? He states, 'The benefit of providing character models is drawn from a long tradition of regarding the fictional narrative as a sort of thought experiment' (2014: 307). And narratologist Faye Halpern reminds us that the reading experience is a complicated one, that eliciting the reader's sympathy effectively 'depends on the reader's engaging in ethically suspect kinds of role-taking and 'we should accept its ethical complexity: otherwise we will fail to account for its power' (2018: 126). Or, as ethicist Anne Surma surmises, 'the role of sympathy is ethically fraught and '[t]he privilege of writing... brings with it responsibilities and obligations to others whom writers address and in whose communities texts circulate' (2005: 1). But these thinkers ask us to consider the reading process generally; they do not assume a personal relationship between reader, writer, and text. Surma states: 'We look to see ourselves (our identities, interests, values) engaged within the texts written to us, to see ourselves addressed or acknowledged, so that a space for our potential response is opened up' (2005: 3). What if we actually do see ourselves and our private struggles represented in the text? And what is the writer's ethical obligation to loved ones when these similarities are pointed out?

Many have argued the life-appropriating artist-writer has little to answer for. As *New York Times* columnist Robert Kolker writes, 'artists, almost by definition, borrow from life. They transform real people and events into something invented, because what is the great subject of art—the only subject, really—if not life itself?' (2021: 1). Kolker was writing in the context of Dawn Dorland and Sonya Larson, two writers whose (arguable) friendship turned to lawyers and court cases, based on accusations Larson wrote about Dorland's experience of donating a kidney and plagiarised one of Dorland's Facebook posts for the short story 'The

Kindest'. The Dorland–Lawson saga is an example of the tensions that can erupt between the lived, the reported and the written.

The situation with 'Housework of Desire' was different. When my friend Carolyn voiced concerns, this was in the context of a longstanding, formative friendship of almost thirty years. We had seen each other through surgeries, deaths of parents, radical work changes, big financial decisions, and hard parenting calls. When I was overseas in college, she enrolled me in the subject that would inspire me to become a writer. Despite this considerable, intimate history, after she had read my draft, her therapist advised her never to talk to me again; and I struggled with how and whether to proceed with the project. On one hand, I was (obviously) attached to the novel. On the other, I was not interested in the role of a writer-vampire, feeding off of loved ones' experiences. I wanted to write about life in an effort to explore and understand, to connect with readers; I did not want to exploit lived experience. And yet, what exactly is exploitative writing and how does one avoid it? And if I had exploited her experience, what was the harm of this 'borrowing'? Writer Phillip Lopate states:

> Some writers get around the problem by showing their manuscripts to the people being written about and asking if they object to anything. I understand the scrupulosity of this position, but I could never do it myself. Having made the decision to go ahead and write about someone, and having done it to my satisfaction, I don't want to give that person such power over me! Once you invite people to make changes on your unpublished manuscript, they will. Besides, it's my moral dilemma, not theirs. Giving them the option to revise would be like shifting the ethical burden onto them.
>
> n.d.: 1

Lopate is writing about non-fiction here, not fiction, but the sentiment also applies. I do not believe showing a manuscript to people being written about necessarily shifts the ethical burden onto them – the writer is still responsible for the final text. Sharing it may inspire alterations, but the decision resides, ultimately, with the author. However, I do understand Lopate's objection to seeking approval from external sources for his writing – readers will inevitably operate from a position of bias and may not acknowledge or be aware of the subjectivity of their experience. When drafting the memoir *She Played Elvis* (2009), a project that directly referenced family members, I was wary of inviting readers to offer objections for these very reasons. With 'Housework of Desire', I did not share my manuscript with Carolyn for the purpose of getting her 'okay' regarding content. Carolyn read the draft to offer feedback, and, in so doing, felt her lived experience had been exposed without warning. As she said, 'Some combination of factors led me to identify too heavily with the character and from there I was off and running'. And yet, if roles had been reversed, I would have felt uncomfortable with this 'combination of factors' as well – too much detail (that was not necessary to the story) was identical to her lived experience.

Moreover, she was troubled by a couple of scenes and wanted to understand why I had included them when they did not seem to serve the structural arc. As these conversations took place, I did not feel she had 'power over me' or that she was making objections lightly. At that stage, I was not entirely sure of the answers to her questions – the project was still in its early drafting stages and the story hadn't yet 'settled'. I explained that I had experimented with the creative process, and she clarified key details that made her uncomfortable, as well as more general issues of character representation and plot development that seemed lacking or problematic to the larger arc of the story. As we spoke, it became evident the character of Sabine in my head was not on the page; and these were matters of aesthetics and craft: the character needed a deeper arc, with more vulnerability. Her motivations needed to be clearer. And, in a twist, I realised I needed to be more compassionate to the parts of Sabine that weren't working on the page because they were actually resonances of myself, not Carolyn. Our discussions provided a breakthrough that forged the novel, and those conversations, along with a period of intense daily meditation, coincided with feedback from my agent and informed a large-scale rewrite that focused on point-of-view. That is, what began as an exercise in duty of care transformed into an aesthetic exploration that profoundly impacted the book for the better (certainly in my opinion).

To be clear, at no stage was my friend recognisable, and two of the details she cited as making her uncomfortable had been drawn from entirely unrelated situations. While she inspired some aspects of the novel, she also read her experiences onto unrelated ones, highlighting that it may not be possible to write a story with which friends and loved ones *ever* feel comfortable. Wayne Booth references Roland Barthes when he says, '"What takes place" in a narrative is from the referential (reality) point of view literally *nothing*; "what happens" is language alone, the adventure of language, the unceasing celebration of its coming' (1988: 124). This raises the question: if *nothing* has taken place, what crime had I committed against my friend? And indeed, if this 'nothing' was inspired by completely unrelated events, what is my ethical duty of care? These questions pertain to more than this novel project. My short fiction and prose poetry tend to capture moments of change and points of crisis for characters, and sometimes are inspired directly from events in my life. If this is the case, I often change key details (gender, context, plot points) for privacy but again, I wonder: how is the author to proceed in good faith when the lived inspires the creative?

With 'Housework of Desire' I did not blankly change the novel according to Carolyn's concerns. Rather, I was compelled by Andrew Harrison's observation (quoted in Booth 1988: 1) that, 'A work of art is … a bridge, however tenuous between one mind and another'. I wanted loved ones to cross my novel-bridge, while also honouring the workmanship and skill that made it tenable as a bridge. I considered novelist Glenice Joy Whitting's words, 'My ethical responsibilities were to people, to the contract between writer and reader, to myself as a writer, and to the work' (2011: 1). I found this delineation useful – attention needed to be paid to my friend, the work, readers, and myself as writer. Keeping all of this in mind, I used the rewriting process to amend events and sharpen character arcs to make the novel stronger and take account of Carolyn's observations. Sometimes these changes were neutral. Other, more dramatic changes actually made the novel significantly better such as providing deeper motivations for character decisions and changing a climactic move (from San Francisco to New York) to the end of the novel. Sometimes I kept details that made Carolyn uncomfortable, explaining to her my purposes for doing so. Critically, these revisions did not take place within the imagined 'circus tent'. As per Dubus III:

> Now dreaming your way through a story is very useful at first – for the first draft, maybe the first two drafts. But once the revision process begins, you've got to change your approach … once you dream it through, try to look at the result the way a doctor looks at an X-ray. You've got to be terribly smart about it. In the secondary period, you get more rational and logical about what you've dreamed – while still cooperating with the deeper truths of what you've made.
>
> 2017: 64

There were places in the story where my subconscious had been lazy and used 'easy' details – drawing, I suspect, from my friend's experiences – instead of combing for more telling ones, specific to the story. The circus draft offered a strong outline, with clear emotional impulses, but the work of crafting was still required. Writer Claire Messud describes revision as 'a kind of creative destruction' where scenes are condensed to eliminate repetition. 'To have a more efficient and more intense fragment is going to be better. So you compress, the same way that to make something very tasty you might reduce the sauce' (2017: 243). I worked on this compression, frequently eliminating unnecessary details, sometimes ones that had elicited Carolyn's discomfort. Sometimes, too, I deleted material simply because I had faith I could do better. As Delillo says,

> If I discard a sentence I like, it's almost as satisfying as keeping a sentence I like … The instinct to discard is finally a kind of faith. It tells me there's a better way to do this page even though the evidence is not accessible at the present time.
>
> 1993: 1

Freedom, Unknowing, and Revision

T.S. Eliot states, 'Immature poets imitate; mature poets steal; bad poets deface what they take, and good poets make it into something better, or at least something different' (1920: 114). Eliot references literary plagiarism here, and yet this chapter asks a related question: can life itself be plagiarised? Do we have a right to the expressions of our experiences? The issue for Carolyn was not one of libel. She was not concerned about being recognised. My crime with Carolyn, I suspect, was bad writing. I'd defaced what I'd taken instead of making it something better. And revision proved the key to resolving this. The implication here is that aesthetics can provide the answer to authorial ethical quandaries: write your way through duty-of-care by writing better. While this may have proved the case with 'Housework of Desire', I am uncomfortable with the assertion more generally. After all, who can judge 'better writing'? And how can one account for the many and varied ways ethics and representation might conspire with writing and duties of care?

Ideas of plagiarism have dogged literary circles for decades. Journalist Ligaya Mishan reminds us,

> The root of 'plagiarism' lies in the Latin plagium, defined in Roman law as the crime of kidnapping, specifically enslaving free citizens or seizing and extorting labor from someone else's slaves … Only in the first century A.D. was the term deployed, by the poet Martial, to highlight a false claim of authorship. Later, it became a specific reference to the abduction of children, and is still cited as such in Scottish law, while another derivative, plagio, formerly a statute in Italian law, is loosely translated as brainwashing: the subjugation of another's mind, bending it to one's will.
>
> 2018

Contemporary understandings of plagiarism involve writerly theft and false claims of authorship, however the history of the word demonstrates the tension between the lived and the written. Enslaving, child abduction, brainwashing: these are all verbs connected with human and lived experiences. Carolyn was not worried about my words, she was worried that her experiences had been used and, I suspect, that they'd been written about in a way that did not engage deeply enough with the complexities of her lived experience. As writer Angela Flournoy says, 'It's when you've somehow failed to make fully nuanced and three-dimensional characters that people start to say, *What right do you have?*' (2017: 181). I believe our actions demonstrate our ethics and admit, when Carolyn raised concerns, I wondered what kind of person I was: would I prioritise art or friendship? Where were my loyalties? What kind of friend was I, really? I was relieved (and lucky, perhaps) to find solutions that honoured both Carolyn and the text, but it did imprint on me the importance of communication and open listening. If either Carolyn or I had become defensive I suspect our friendship would not have survived (and the book would be weaker).

The revising process was a conscious endeavour, and provided a context for considering duties of care: what to include, what adjustments to make. Ethicist Sara Button references George Saunders, in seeing 'revision as a key to writing more generous, more ethical fiction' (n.d.: 1). That is, I could use the circus tent method to produce a workable draft, but conscious revision proved critical to considering representation, giving me space to make decisions about what information, scenes and place names to include. As another author in this volume, Jen Webb, states, 'ethical writing is the writing we do when we have consciously reflected on the meanings we are making, or the world we are representing' (2010: 1). This conscious reflection is key to being deliberate with the meanings and representations we create.

Writer Norman Mailer relates the writing process to exploring '…you're getting into something where you don't know the end, where the end is not given' (2017). And Neil Gaiman concurs, expanding:

> For me, writing fiction should be, in some way, a voyage of discovery. You assume that the writing part of yourself is smarter and bigger than the human part of yourself. The writing part of yourself, actually, is competent to deal with everything and will find out what the things are, and for me, that's the difference between your first draft and your second draft. Your first draft you're figuring it out in a way. And the second draft you read the first draft, and you go, 'OK, actually, these are the things, this is what I'm saying, therefore anything that doesn't help I can lose and I can add stuff in the buttresses'.
>
> n.d.: 1

Gaiman allows for the experience of discovery in the first draft, and uses the second draft to discern the project's deeper meanings, and edit back or expand as needed. For me, this 'voyage of discovery' in the first draft proved critical. Facing the blank page was already difficult work, and I experienced more freedom in knowing it was not set: I could return to the work if larger concerns of craft or duty of care arose. Karl Ove Knausgård asserts that writing and literature is 'a space where I can be free in every sense, where I can say whatever, go wherever I want to. And for me, literature is almost the only place you could think that that is a possibility' (n.d.). Knausgård has been criticised for exposing the private lives of his family members (his paternal uncle tried to halt publication of the first volume of his autobiographical series *My Struggle*), and yet I appreciate this idea of boundless possibility. My argument here is that, as per Gaiman, writers should be allowed (and allow themselves) unconscious freedom with early drafts, and bring matters of craft and ethics to later ones.

In conclusion, every writer must make their own decisions regarding the priorities of the lived and the written. I posit the drafting, workshopping and redrafting process can be used to support both the creative process and a duty of care to those who may be affected. I suspect the circus-tent method inspired my writing to come from a deeper imaginative place than in previous projects, and this involved a certain 'unknowing' as the process unfolded. It was revising that then provided a site for engaging with craft and duties of care, and ultimately made the novel stronger, while keeping important friendships intact.

References

Barthes, R. (1984), *Image Music Text*, trans Stephen Heath, London: Fontana.
Bender, A. (2017), *Light the Dark*, New York: Penguin, 1–6.
Booth, W. (1988), *The Company We Keep*, Berkeley: University of California Press.
Button, S. (n.d.), 'Ethics in Fiction', Stanford McCoy Family Center for Ethics in Society. Available online: https://ethicsinsociety.stanford.edu/research-outreach/buzz-blog/ethics-fiction (accessed 4 January 2022).
Cochrane, T. (2014), 'Narrative and Character Formation', *The Journal of Aesthetics and Art Criticism*, 72(3): 303–315.
Cosgrove, S. (2009), *She Played Elvis*, Sydney: Allen and Unwin.
Delillo, D. (1993), The Art of Fiction No 135, *The Paris Review*. 128, Fall. Available online: https://www.theparisreview.org/interviews/1887/don-delillo-the-art-of-fiction-no-135-don-delillo (accessed 21 October 2020).

Dubus III, A. (2017), 'Do Not Think, Dream', *Light the Dark*, New York: Penguin, 61–68.

Eaglestone, R. (1997), *Ethical Criticism: Reading After Levinas*, Edinburgh: Edinburgh University Press.

Eliot, T. S. (1920), *The Sacred Wood*. London: Methuen & Co. Ltd..

Flournoy, A. (2017), 'A Place to Call My Own', *Light the Dark*. New York: Penguin, 179–184.

Gaiman, N. (n.d.), interviewed by Mia Funk for *The Literary Review*. Available online, https://www.theliteraryreview.org/book-review/neil-gaiman-the-creative-press/ (accessed 4 January 2022).

Hale, D. (2009), 'Aesthetics and the New Ethics: Theorizing the Novel in the Twenty-First Century', *PMLA*, 124(3): 896–905.

Hale, D. (2020), *The Novel and the New Ethics*. Stanford, CT: Stanford University Press.

Halpern, Faye. 2018. 'Closeness Through Unreliability: Sympathy, Empathy, and Ethics in Narrative Communication', *Narrative*, 26(2): 125–145.

Harrison, K. (2017), 'Please Stop Thinking', *Light the Dark*. New York: Penguin, 109–114.

Hustvedt, S. (2008), Sydney Writers' Festival, Sydney Theater. In conversation with Paul Auster.

Keen, S. (2006), 'A Theory of Narrative Empathy', *Narrative*, 14(3): 207–236.

Knausgård, K. O. (n.d.), *Conversations with Tyler*. Available online: https://conversationswithtyler.com/episodes/karl-ove-knausgard/ (accessed 4 January 2022).

Kolker, R. (2021), 'Who Is the Bad Art Friend?' *New York Times*, 5 Oct. Available online: https://www.nytimes.com/2021/10/05/magazine/dorland-v-larson.html?auth=login-google1tap&login=google1tap (accessed 19 July 19 2022).

Lopate, P. (n.d.), 'The Ethics of Writing About Other People', *Creative Non-Fiction*, 40, Winter. Available online: https://creativenonfiction.org/writing/the-ethics-of-writing-about-other-people/ (accessed 16 July 2022).

Mailer, N. (2007), The Art of Fiction No 193, *The Paris Review*. 181, Summer. Available online: https://www.theparisreview.org/interviews/5775/the-art-of-fiction-no-193-norman-mailer (accessed 21 June 2022).

Massud, C. (2017), 'Words on Paper Will Outlast Us', *Light the Dark*. New York: Penguin 239–246.

Mishan, L. (2018), 'In Literature, Who Decides When Homage Becomes Theft?' *The New York Times Style Magazine*. Available online: https://www.nytimes.com/2018/10/08/t-magazine/literature-homage-theft-appropriation.html (accessed 4 January 2022).

Surma. A. (2005), *Public and Professional Writing: Ethics, Imagination and Rhetoric*, London: Palgrave Macmillan.

Webb, J. (2016), 'Ethics and Writing', *The Conversation*. Published 4 August, Available online: https://theconversation.com/ethics-and-writing-63399 (accessed 4 January 2022).

Whitting, G. (2011), 'Omissions and Additions: Ethics and the Epistolary Writer', *Ethical Imaginations: Refereed Conference Papers of the 16th Annual AAWP Conference*. Available online: https://aawp.org.au/wp-content/uploads/2015/03/Whitting_0.pdf (accessed 4 January 2022).

Wood, C. (2018), The Lady and the Unicorn and *The Natural Way of Things*, speech. Art Gallery of NSW, 9 May. Available online: https://www.charlottewood.com.au/the-lady-and-the-unicorn.html (accessed 4 January 2022).

9

A New Vision of Beauty in Creative Writing Practice

Belinda Hopper
Macquarie University, Sydney

Aesthetics has been a contested idea in the realm of art and literature since the idealised beauty dilemma spawned the 'modernist paradox'. The attempt to defend beauty from 'pre-modernist kitsch' left it exposed to 'postmodernist desecration'; beauty was 'caught between two forms of sacrilege, the one dealing in sugary dreams, the other in savage fantasies' (Scruton 2011: 160). From the modernist 'cult of ugliness' (as coined by Ezra Pound in 1954's 'The Serious Artist'), postmodernism deconstructed the refined, elegant whole in favour of the raw and disjointed parts, exchanging a cohesive narrative for the fragmented. The aesthetic of beauty was sidelined to make way for the edgy, the gritty, the cool. Realism succumbed to hyper-realism and the quest for authenticity led to an apologetic of 'ugly'. With the death of the author, it fell to the reader to interpret the ambiguous, open-ended, or often meaningless denouement.

Enter Marilynne Robinson with her Pulitzer prize-winning novel, *Gilead* (2004), which has been reviewed as 'a beautiful work'(Wood 2004). *Gilead* tells the story of a dying Congregationalist minister, the Reverend John Ames, living in Iowa in 1956. Throughout the novel, Robinson salvages what aesthetics philosopher, Roger Scruton, sees as the traditional, sacred function of beauty: to transcend and redeem suffering. Mark S. M. Scott (2016: 17) observes, 'Beauty is not an elixir for life's sorrow'; it does not take Ames' suffering away, but it works as an emollient. Ames disciplines himself to notice small graces; a kind gesture, the beauty in nature; simple joys that ameliorate his suffering. Reflecting on the unexpected beauties of his final birthday helps Ames rise above his suffering to the point that he expresses his reluctance to leave this life. He writes, 'I hate to think what I would give for a thousand mornings like this. For two or three' (Robinson 2004: 184).

In my second interview with Robinson in 2018, we discussed the neglect of aesthetics in the arts and about writing from an apologetic of beauty. She said,

> I think, for whatever reason, beauty is something that people tend to put aside as if it meant something like ornamentation ... When in fact it is a sort of falling together of what is potential in experience and the perceiving mind, and something that is continuously new, as it is newly understood. And I don't think we pay enough attention to the answerability of the existing world, to consciousness.
>
> Hopper and Robinson 2018

In this chapter, I offer Robinson's definition of beauty and outline the reasons why she believes aesthetic categories are overlooked in literature. I discuss what Robinson sees as the shift in the demands on the reader when writers ignore aesthetic considerations in favour of received expectations of what should feature in a work of fiction. I explore Robinson's inspiration for writing her own fiction from an apologetic of beauty and discuss her theory of narrative and the literary devices she uses in pursuit of beauty. I then turn to Robinson's fiction and offer excerpts from the novels that form her Gilead Quartet, to demonstrate her aesthetics in practice. I outline the advice Robinson's writing teacher, John Hawkes, gave her and finish with the advice she gives her students in regard to bringing aesthetic considerations to bear on creative writing practice.

Robinson's Definition of Beauty

Robinson (2018a: 106, 112) describes beauty as an active principle; a mysterious, pervasive force in reality that we have no instruments to measure, except our minds and senses. She describes it as part of 'entelechy', possessing a sense of wholeness; 'that beauty manifests itself in one thing or another, even asserts itself when accident permits'. She says that beauty persists even through different eras where standards of beauty change or differ from one another, as if beauty is continually redefining itself and moving continuously in a 'collective conscience' (ibid: 112). In terms of creative writing practice, Robinson says, 'beauty disciplines. It recommends a best word in a best place and makes the difference palpable between aesthetic right and wrong' (ibid). Yet the word 'beauty' has always seemed unsatisfactory to Robinson. She feels there is an essential quality for which we have no word, and we are therefore driven back on beauty or elegance; words used by mathematicians and physicists to endorse theories that are likely to be true because of their 'efficiency and soundness of structure' (Robinson 2014: 125). Robinson's core definition of beauty is, 'that it is both rigorous and dynamic and that it somehow bears a deep relationship to truth' (ibid). She considers beauty to be a 'conversation between humankind and reality', to which we bring essential gifts, like 'reflection and creation' (Robinson 2018a: 217). As a result, Robinson's work has the aim of 'reauthorizing experience, felt reality, as one important testimony to the nature of reality itself' (ibid: 103). She insists upon the necessity of reauthorising experience because she understands the act of writing fiction to be the mind exploring itself and its 'impulse to create hypothetical cause and consequence' (Robinson 2014: 131).

The Resistance to Beauty

Robinson (2012: 144) proposes we 're-mystify' consciousness and experience, and points out the irony that on one hand, science constrains our capabilities by genetic determinism, and on the other, it frees us by claiming that the human brain is the most complex known object in the universe. Her pushback against determinism has bearing on creative writing practice because to have the sense of human presence about him or her, a character must seem free and constrained simultaneously, or else all credibility is lost (Robinson 2018a: 104). To imply humanity is wholly deterministic in nature is to fail to acknowledge 'the beauty and complexity of individual human experience' (Robinson 2014: 125). It also denies the moral choices we face in everyday life, which sustains narratives and brings drama and tension to the lives of fictional characters.

The resistance to the recognition, analysis, and celebration of beauty in departments of literature has been described by scholars as 'stultifying' (McNelly Kearns 2009: 66). Robinson (2018b) has also said she finds it strange that her graduate students have said to her they had never heard the word *beautiful* applied to a piece of prose until they came to the Iowa Writers' Workshop. She considers it bizarre that we do not apply aesthetic categories to a major art form, a reluctance she blames on the emergence of Theory. Robinson argues:

> Literature had been made a kind of data to illustrate, supposedly, some graceless theory that stood apart from it, and that would be shed in a year or two and replaced by something post- or neo- and in any case as gracelessly irrelevant to a work of language as whatever it displaced. I think this phenomenon is an effect of the utilitarian hostility to the humanities and to art.
>
> Sorensen 2018

Scruton (2009) agrees with Robinson that utilitarianism is to blame for the dismissal of beauty in the arts. Robinson (2012) laments that we now seem to feel beauty in literature is an 'affectation' of some sort. When she asked her students at the Workshop to write a beautiful paragraph, she found most of them didn't know what to do because the concept of beauty was unfamiliar to them. Contemporary creative writing advice is to 'kill your darlings'. Conversely, Robinson (2018b) says to keep the beautiful paragraph and throw out the rest; to start from a place of beauty, not discard it. She argues that he term 'beauty' is excluded from describing literature, because from the point of view of objectivity as presently understood, 'the accepted means of establishing what is real cannot acknowledge beauty' on the basis that it is considered a transcendental, along with goodness and truth, which positivism does not allow (Robinson 2018a: 37). Yet Robinson warns that if we strip anything of the 'beauty and dignity' proper to it, then we reduce it to nothing more than 'parody' (Robinson 2014: 130). If we dismiss individual experience, or testimony, we impoverish our understanding of ourselves and each other (Robinson 2010: 61–62). Robinson's aim in her fiction is to acknowledge the beauty and complexity of individual human experience (2014: 125). If we erase individuality and personal agency, then we have no way of differentiating one character over and against another or raising any questions of morality.

Robinson sees the flow-on effect of this 'abeyance of beauty' is that readers are asked now to react instead of to consider. Writers address the nervous system of their readers, through action and plot, instead of their minds, through a thoughtful consideration of ideas (ibid: 129). Robinson seeks to redress the reactionary by asking us to once again contemplate, along with her characters, what it is to live quiet, ordinary lives, revering our very existence as 'sacred'. She believes that fiction is akin to science, written in an implied subjunctive, with the character of hypothesis about it, which means that 'reality is greater than any present circumstance' (ibid). Also, because the beauty of language 'is rigorous and exploratory' and allows us to participate in a sense of coherency that in some way reflects experience itself (ibid).

Robinson's Aesthetic Inspiration

Robinson found a corrective to positivist determinism in John Calvin's theology of aesthetics, as his sacramental vision encompasses our experience and perception and puts the mind as the locus of revelation (Fate 2006). Robinson (2014: 129) concedes it is unfashionable, but necessary, to put active consciousness at the centre of a discussion of what we are as humans. In crafting her characters, Robinson's standard is 'strictly experiential' (2018a: 105). There is no higher priority in her fiction than to explore what it is to be human, in all our glory and frailties. These priorities play out in that fast-paced action and plot do not feature in her fiction, so much as the rich interior lives of her characters. She is concerned that when a writer feels that something 'has' to appear in their narrative, to satisfy some arbitrary notions of pace or drama, for instance, it is akin to censorship and robs the writer of their artistic freedom to write what they want to write about, which for Robinson (2012: 32) is the small drama of conversation.

Recapturing Beauty Through Metaphor

The ideal novel, for Robinson, galvanizes language – its sound, its ability to simulate experience, and its capacity to circle and collapse meaning through the extended metaphor (Schaub and Robinson 1994: 235). Robinson became interested in metaphoric language through the American Transcendentalists, which she studied at Brown University (Fay 2009: 443). She admires Emily Dickinson's skill in using metaphor as a 'sensorium' tool of language to aid and explore perception (Gardner 2006: 47–48). Robinson lauds metaphor, or analogy, as 'the essential form of thinking' (Schaub and Robinson 1994: 244) for its dexterity in making 'the familiar new', and 'the unfamiliar understandable' (Vogelzang 2018: 749). She deploys metaphor in Dickinson's sophisticated manner: to explore questions of metaphysics, with the assumption that there is more to reality than we perceive and that our individual experience is addressed to us. When Robinson implores writers to pay close attention to their experience, it's not to fulfil the creative writing program-era adage to, 'write what you know' or to write about personal experience (McGurl 2009: 81). Rather, for Robinson, perception is a language through which things are communicated to us, and metaphor is the means of trying to articulate our perception of reality or experience (Gardner, 2006: 48). Vogelzang (2018: 744–753) argues that Robinson's 'deeply moving attention to the quiet luminosity of life' gives her fiction the appearance of modernism, but where modernists typically portray a kind of 'tortured despair' at the inadequacies of the literary metaphor, Robinson takes the stance of 'sacred wonder'.

Beauty in Robinson's Fiction

Modernism led to a questioning of beauty for its subjectivity; for its visionary, or revelatory quality, which depends upon our powers of perception. John O'Connor (2011: 114) draws attention to the ambiguity of experiencing and understanding beauty as 'revelatory', suggesting there could be a 'revelatory tension' between our experience and our understanding of that experience. Robinson makes a strong correlation between beauty and experience, yet in *Gilead*, Ames also demonstrates this 'revelatory tension' in reflecting on the beauty of his wife's voice, and the laughter between two motor mechanics. He comments, 'I really can't tell what's beautiful anymore' (Robinson 2004: 5).

Theory of narrative is a fundamental act of consciousness, according to Robinson (2014: 138). She believes the working of the human mind is astonishing and beautiful, and that by focusing on the inner lives of her characters, she locates their beauty (Robinson 2018a: 113). In looking for the beauty in every character, there are no villains in Robinson's fiction, which is an anomaly in literature and counterintuitive to what is generally considered to be a narrative force. Consider Philosopher Simone Weil's assessment that:

> Imaginary evil is romantic and varied; real evil is gloomy, monotonous, barren, boring. Imaginary good is boring; real good is always new, marvelous, intoxicating. Therefore 'imaginative literature' is either boring or immoral (or a mixture of both). It only escapes from this alternative if in some way it passes over to the side of reality through the power of art – and only genius can do that.
>
> 1997:120

Robinson achieves this level of genius through the Reverend John Ames. Despite his general goodness, Ames is not boring because of his complex testimony (Wood 2004). He knows from personal experience that life is fraught with suffering. He writes, 'Sorrow seems to me to be a great part of the substance of human life' (Robinson 2004: 104). Nothing makes up for the grief and long years of loneliness he suffers after the loss of his first wife and daughter in childbirth. Ames does not deny the ugliness, sorrow, and suffering in the world, but he focuses his attention on the redemptive power of beauty. Ames appeals to the reader because he teaches us that suffering can be redeemed. Robinson seeks to redeem Ames' suffering by applying to his experience Calvin's theology of aesthetics, whereby he seeks out beauty in the world around him to ameliorate his suffering.

Just as beauty has a sense of entelechy, of wholeness or completion, so too does a well-drawn character. Robinson explains that when she is writing a character, she thinks of them as 'having a palette or music. An aesthetic, in other words' (2018: 104). She admits that this idea seems somewhat constraining as it places limits on the creative choices you can make in relation to writing a character, although paradoxically, these limits liberate a character to be fully themselves (ibid). The important point is that Robinson does not impose these limits on a character before she writes, or even as she writes. Rather, she works from 'a sense of the experience of human presence' (ibid: 105). She tells her students to 'ponder the difference between knowing about someone and knowing him', so that when they choose one or two specific details to share about their character, 'every subsequent choice is disciplined by them' (ibid: 106). In this way, Robinson sees that beauty imposes itself on 'authorial intent' because the fiction resolves in a way that seems inevitable – not in a deterministic sense – but through a sense of entelechy, where a three-dimensional character, with all their particularities, has been carried through a story to a sense of completion (ibid: 107).

Robinson makes a strong correlation between beauty and experience. Through Ames' deep reverence for the sublime, he transcends and redeems his suffering by making room for gratitude, which opens the door to joy. One instance of this is when he pauses from his reflection on the sadness at having disappointed his late father, and the grief that he has nothing to leave his second wife and the son they were blessed with late in his life. He is sitting at his desk, writing his life story for his son, when he pauses to gaze with wonder out his study window and to absorb the beauty of his son blowing bubbles and their cat chasing them; to revel in the laughter shared between his wife and son. Instead of being weighed down with bitterness in his grief, Ames sighs, 'Ah, this life, this world', intimating his deep appreciation of the mystery of existence and of simple joys (Robinson 2004: 10). The fact that Ames is on the hunt for experiences to write down for his son may heighten his attunement to an aesthetic appreciation of life (Kramnick 2018: 14).

Robinson (2004: 280) applies Calvin's theology of aesthetics throughout *Gilead*, as evidenced by Ames' reflection: 'Wherever you turn your eyes the world shines like transfiguration. You don't have to bring a thing to it except a little willingness to see'. That is not to say that Robinson's characters look at life through rose-coloured glasses, but that Robinson's project is focused on the resurrection of the ordinary (Cunning 2022). Robinson (2014: 138) acknowledges the complexity of the human situation as both 'beautiful and strange'. She grants that we are the only creatures given to awe and wonder, but that we are also capable of great evil. She says, 'Our extraordinary complexity is not only our distinction among the animals and our glory but also our tragedy, our capacity to do extraordinary harm' (ibid). Harm which, Grace M. Jantzen (2002) argues, results in the opposite of beauty.

This capacity for harm, resulting in the ugliness of disharmony, disorder, and inter-character tension plays out in the *Gilead* quartet at several levels: the national level, with racial tensions; between intimate friends, through misunderstandings, and among fractured family relationships, through the daily interactions of living in close proximity to one another. However, Robinson complicates the reader's reaction to the harm her characters inflict upon one another by employing Calvin's moral rubric, which places aesthetic demands on ethics, in the sense that you would consider generosity to be a gracious and 'beautiful' gesture. Robinson believes we should judge our characters with the same gracious view of an ethic of aesthetics. In her rendering of the prodigal son, Jack, we most clearly see Robinson find the beauty in a life that, if it were judged simply by a strict moral standard, may seem to have failed (Brown 2009). Just as Robinson applies Calvin's ethic to her characters, we see Ames apply it as he lays aside his moral judgement and disapproval of Jack in favour of an 'aesthetic appreciation' of him (Hinojosa 2015: 135). This moral rubric also complicates the reader's sympathies because most of the harm the characters do to one another is unintended, brought about through gestures that could be considered at best, beautiful, and at worst, benign. It is the kind of unintended harm inflicted through benevolent inaction, best summed up by Ames when he acknowledges in *Gilead*: '[T]here is more beauty than our eyes can bear, that precious things have been put into our hands and to do nothing to honour them is to do great harm' (Robinson 2004: 281).

I offer three examples of this 'harm of benevolence' from *Home* (2008). On the national scale, consider Ames' best friend, old Reverend Boughton's desire for social order, which in and of itself is a good and right desire. Yet, his benign inaction and desire to maintain the status quo, for the sake of avoiding the chaos of social disorder, comes at the cost of social justice, as he ignores the plight of African Americans oppressed by Jim Crow segregation laws: 'The old man said, "I do believe it is necessary to enforce the law. The Apostle Paul says we should do everything 'decently and in order.' You can't have people running around the streets like that"' (Robinson 2008: 98). Andujo (2019: 117) explains that Boughton shows 'antipathy' for the nonviolent direct-action protestors, 'apathy' towards the violence inflicted on them, and is 'relentlessly critical' of the demonstrators, seeing them as the source of unnecessary civil strife and disorder.

At the meso level, consider the unintended jeopardy to the life-long friendship between Ames and Boughton, brought about through the innocuous event of Ames preaching on Hagar and Ishmael, a sermon referred to in *Gilead* and *Home*. His intention was to preach on how, ultimately, we all must relinquish our parenthood and entrust our children to God the father. His motivation was that he would soon be leaving his own son fatherless, and so the text had been on his mind. Lauren F. Winner explains: 'But in church that Sunday two unexpected things happened. Ames, the manuscript preacher, went off text a little more than he typically did, and Jack Boughton was in church. Boughton took Ames' message to be not about Ames, but about his own youthful mistakes' (2019: 90). Jack felt conspicuous sitting in the pew, with the congregants around him well aware that he had abandoned his child in his youth. He told his sister, Glory, that Ames had publicly rebuked him through his sermon. Glory says she will never forgive Ames, and their father is devastated that his dear old friend squandered the opportunity to preach to his godson about the gracious love of God, our true father. Ames and the Boughton family are out of fellowship for days over what would ordinarily be seen as a beautiful act: Ames providing spiritual succour to his flock (Robinson 2008: 206–215).

Finally, at the family level, old Boughton falls asleep, sitting at the dining table in the middle of the night. Jack tenderly picks his father up and carries him upstairs to bed, so he might sleep comfortably. In the morning, Boughton makes clear his offence at the action Jack had intended for his good:

> He said, 'You just picked me up and carried me, didn't you, Jack. Well that's all right. I'm not the father you remember, I know that.'
> Jack put his hand to his brow. 'Of course you are. I didn't – I'm sorry – '
> 'No matter. Never mind. I shouldn't have mentioned it'.
>
> ibid: 74

Despite the many real and varied failings of Robinson's characters, the reader sees them grow in personal insight, or at least make moves toward restoration of relationships. Ames rebukes himself for the town's failure to protect its one-time African American residents. Ames, Glory, and Jack, all contrive to reconcile Ames and Boughton, sharing between them an article of interest that might bring them together to discuss it. And old Boughton 'took instantly to the idea of reconciliation' (ibid: 214). This is evidence of Robinson bringing Calvin's ethics of aesthetics to bear on her characters' interrelating.

Creative Writing Advice

Robinsons novels are lauded far and wide – she is published in twenty-six countries and has won numerous prestigious awards including the National

Humanities Medal, the Pulitzer Prize, the Penn-Hemingway Award, the National Book Critics Award, the Orange Prize, and the Dayton Peace Prize for the grace and intelligence of her writing. Perhaps the reason Robinson's work resonates with millions of people, across so many cultures, is because in her 'loyalty to the absolute beauty in the most ordinary human life', we recognise that she honours and restores our humanity to us through the testimony of her complex characters (Robinson 2017). To heed Robinson's theory of creative writing practice, we need to acknowledge in our characters their subjective experience, which is the human experience of 'love, generosity, regret, and all their interactions' (Robinson 2018a: 37).

At the end of my interview with Robinson, I asked about the writing advice her writing teacher at Brown University, John Hawkes, gave her. She said she was writing in a style that was not characteristic of people of that time and place and was criticised by other students for her departure from the norm. But Hawkes told her to be aware of and loyal to her own voice and to be attentive to the rhythm of language (Hopper and Robinson 2018). This advice emboldened Robinson to keep writing according to her own lights, and echoes in the encouragement she offers her students. She tells them:

> That they have their own testimony to offer, that if they think about what they perceive and what they feel carefully, if they watch other people closely and magnanimously, they will have something new to say, something that's an actual addition to what has been said. That they have no obligation to be derivative or imitative in any way. That is absolutely not the point. I want them to know that if they are thoughtful people, if they have the courage to evaluate things independently and to enjoy the processes of their own thought, then they will give the world something new, something worth having.
>
> Robinson 2009

There remains a resistance to trying to write something beautiful, Robinson says, because people can be fearful that others might claim their work is 'over-wrought'. But at the same time, she says there is incredible enjoyment of language, in capturing experience through analogy and metaphor; there is satisfaction in the attempt to write attuned to the music of language, the palette of the individual character. People deprive themselves of these pleasures because they think, 'Who am I to attempt the beautiful?' (Robinson 2018b). Robinson acknowledges it takes courage to aspire to write something at the very highest levels, and people need reassurance that something is beautiful before they can be at peace with it, as if it's in some way naïve or egotistical to think that they are capable of the higher things that literature has accomplished (ibid). Robinson (2014: 136) does not teach writing technique to her students. Rather, she exhorts them to trust their own intuitions, perception, experience, and thought. She inspires them that through their creative writing practice, through exploring language and telling stories, they participate in 'something so ancient, so pervasive, and so central to human culture that we can assume its significance, even if we cannot readily describe or account for it'. She also believes that every good writer uses beautiful language for emphasis, as it indicates that a level of focus and attention has been achieved (Robinson and Harder 2020). Robinson is aware of the resistance toward writing the beautiful, but she responds: 'And yet the beautiful persists, and so do eloquence and depth of thought, and they belong to all of us because they are the most pregnant evidence we can have of what is possible in us' (Sorensen 2018).

References

Andujo, P. (2019), 'Marilynne Robinson and the African American Experience'. In K. L. Larson and T. Johnson (eds) *Balm in Gilead*, Chicago: IVP Academic, 100–121.

Brown, A. (2009), 'Marilynne Robinson, God and Calvin', *The Guardian*, 4 June. Available online: https://www.theguardian.com/commentisfree/andrewbrown/2009/jun/04/religion-marilynne-robinson (accessed 19 May 2019).

Cunning, A. (2022), *Marilynne Robinson, Theologian of the Ordinary*. New York: Bloomsbury Academic.

Fate, T. M. (2006), 'Seeing The Holy'. *Sojourners*, 35(6): 38.

Fay, S. (2009), 'Marilynne Robinson, The Art of Fiction'. In P. Gourevitch (ed.) *The Paris Review Interviews Vol.IV*, New York: Picador, 438–468.

Gardner, T. (2006), *A Door Ajar*. Oxford: Oxford University Press.

Hinojosa, L. (2015), 'John Ames as Histiographer: Pacificism, Racial Reconciliation, and Agape in Marilynne Robinson's "Gilead"', *Religion & Literature* 47(2): 117–142.

Hopper, B. and Robinson, M. (2018), 'Interview with Marilynne Robinson, Part 2'. Chicago.

Jantzen, G. M. (202), 'Beauty for Ashes: Notes on the Displacement of Beauty', *Literature and Theology*, 16(4): 427–449.

Kramnick, J. (2018), *Paper Minds: Literature and the Ecology of Consciousness*. Chicago: University of Chicago Press.

McGurl, M. (2009), *The Program Era: Postwar Fiction and the Rise of Creative Writing*. Cambridge, MA: Harvard University Press..

McNelly Kearns, C. (2009), 'Religion, Literature, and Theology: Potentials and Problems', *Religion & Literature* 41(2): 62–67.

O'Connor, J. (2011), 'Theological Aesthetics and Beauty as Revelatory: An Interdisciplinary Assessment'. In H. Walton (ed.) *Literature and Theology: New Interdisciplinary Spaces*, Abingdon: Routledge, 111–125.

Pound, E. (n.d.), 'Literary Essays Of Ezra Pound Part 1–3'. Available online: https://archive.org/stream/in.ernet.dli.2015.458777/2015.458777.Literary-Essays_djvu.txt (accessed 20 May 2021).

Robinson, M. (2004), *Gilead*. London: Little, Brown Book Group.

Robinson, M. (2008), *Home*. New York: Farrar, Straus and Giroux.

Robinson, M. (2010), *Absence of Mind*. New Haven, CT: Yale University Press.

Robinson, M. (2012), *When I Was a Child I Read Books*. London: Virago.

Robinson, M. (2014), 'On "Beauty"'. In *The World Split Open*, Oregon: Tin House Books, 121–139.

Robinson, M. (2017), 'Considering the Theological Virtues: Faith, Hope, Love'. In M. Robinson, *What Are we Doing Here?* London: Virago, 205–254.

Robinson, M. (2018a), *What Are We Doing Here?* London: Virago.

Robinson, M. (2018b), 'Writing Faith: A Conversation with Marilynne Robinson'. Notre Dame, IN: University of Notre Dame. Available online: https://www.youtube.com/watch?v=YbEOwAb29i0 (accessed 2 August 2019).

Robinson, M. and Harder, C. (2020), 'Story, Culture, & the Common Good, with Marilynne Robinson'. The Trinity Forum. 24 July. Available online: https://www.ttf.org/portfolios/online-conversation-with-marilynne-robinson/ (accessed 30 July 2020).

Schaub, T. and Robinson, M. (1994), 'An Interview with Marilynne Robinson', *The University of Wisconsin Press Journals Division*, 35(2): 230–251.

Scott, M. S. M. (2016), 'Beauty from Ashes: Aesthetic Transformations of Suffering in Gilead', *CRUX*, 52(3–4): 11–18.

Scruton, R. (2009), *Why Beauty Matters*. London: BBC Two. Available online: https://www.youtube.com/watch?v=bHw4MMEnmpc%0D (accessed 30 April 2019).

Scruton, R. (2011), *Beauty: A Very Short Introduction*. Oxford: Oxford University Press.

Sorensen, R. (2018), 'Book Review: Marilynne Robinson's Wondrous "What Are We Doing Here?"', *Daily Review*. Available online: https://dailyreview.com.au/book-review-what-are-we-doing-here/77457/ (accessed 19 August 2019).

Vogelzang, R. (2018), 'The Likeness of Modernism in Marilynne Robinson's Fiction', *English Studies* 9(7): 744–754. Available online: https://doi.org/10.1080/0013838x.2018.1510625 (accessed 20 August 2019).

Weil, S. (1997), *Gravity and Grace*. Tr. Arthur Wills. Lincoln, NE: University of Nebraska Press.

Winner, L. F. (2019), 'Thinking About Preaching with Marilynne Robinson'. In K. L. Larsen and T. Johnson (eds) *Balm in Gilead*, Chicago: IVP Academic, 85–99.

Wood, J. (2004), 'Acts of Devotion'. *The New York Times*, 28 November. Available online: https://www.nytimes.com/2004/11/28/books/arts/acts-of-devotion.html (accessed 19 August 2019).

10

In Pursuit of the Writer's Life

Despite the Academy

Xu Xi 許素細
with support by research associate Grace Keith, College of the Holy Cross

To write, perchance to publish. Is there any advantage to doing this in the real world vs. in the academy, where many writers end up as teachers of creative writing? What is the measure of success for a writer? To publish, perhaps, but publication doesn't necessarily result in sufficient income or recognition to afford a life. Is it enough to publish enough not to perish, which is all the academy requires because academic publications are not necessarily measured in either sales or literary recognition? Or does it make better sense to pursue the dream of being a writer and take your chances in the real world, which may offer a more expansive life and income, but where literary recognition is even more precarious? After all, if you're hired to teach creative writing in the academy, the real world (that matters to you) might recognise (grudgingly) that this writing thing you do may actually have some merit.

The explosion of creative writing programs in the academy today has redefined the writer's life. When I graduated with my MFA in Fiction in 1985, the first thing I did was leave the university to get a job in the real world where I'd earlier had seven years of business experience in marketing. In total, I worked internationally in the business world for eighteen years while simultaneously pursuing the writing life. My last corporate position was as the Circulation & Special Projects Director at the *Asian Wall Street Journal* in Hong Kong, which I left in 1998. From 2002, I taught mostly graduate-/post-graduate-level creative writing in the academy, and also directed two international low-residency MFA (Masters of Fine Arts) writing programmes based in Asia and America. As of this writing I have two more years in my contract at the College of Holy Cross in Massachusetts as a visiting professor of creative writing, after which I will retire from the academy, probably forever. It therefore seems a fitting moment to reflect on the differences between these two work/life paths in my lifelong pursuit to be a writer.

When in doubt, research. This is a maxim management lives by in business, which is not unlike what happens in the academy. The question foremost in my mind was this: *What obstacles or advantages does the 'real world' vs. the academy present to the writing life?* I compiled a list of approximately seventy writers from around the world whom I personally knew and emailed to ask if they would consent to answering a survey questionnaire and perhaps submit to an interview. The criteria for inclusion on this list was subjectively simple: they had to be published Anglophone authors with books and a reasonably successful record of being regarded as a 'real writer' and I liked them personally and read their work. I left out many American writers I know who fit that criteria because I wanted a geographic spread to mirror my own transnational background. Twenty-four writers (or approximately 35 per cent) completed the survey questionnaire. Here's a snapshot of who they are:

Gender	12 male, 12 female
Nationality	14 USA, 5 Asia-Pacific, 3 UK, 2 Canada
Creative writing degrees	6 none, 18 have MA/MFA/PhDs in creative writing
Other higher degrees	11 hold a variety of other degrees, 13 do not
Genre(s) published	14 lead their list with fiction, 4 with nonfiction, and 6 poetry; 7 published only in one genre (5 fiction, 1 poetry, 1 nonfiction)

Many had done a variety of other work besides teaching creative writing, but only six have never or rarely worked in academia, and generally part-time, as a teacher of creative writing. While this might in part be due to my professional network comprising many who are rooted in academia, the more surprising result was that the majority offered a somewhat conflicted response to the key question in the survey: *Would you prefer to make a living solely from writing?* What I propose to address in this chapter is that conflict, one that I suspect many writers share. Essentially, the question that worries me comes down to this: *Is the so-called 'writer's life' enough of a life for most of us who call ourselves writers?*

Most successfully published writers I've encountered over the years at literary festivals, book signings, conferences, prize ceremonies, workshops, in the academy, and elsewhere tell me roughly the same thing about why they're writers:

it's just something they know they do. Many started young, all were avid readers, and for a significant number, the writer's life was the better alternative or an escape from a less desirable life. 'How did you become a writer?' and 'What inspires your writing?' are the two questions most asked at public fora featuring writers. Being a writer is viewed as something romantic, exciting, desirable, and, judging by the continued growth in creative writing programmes and the numerous workshops offered online and in person, a path in life many aspire to pursue.

My survey's origin questions were more specifically framed: *When did you decide to pursue a career in writing? Briefly describe what inspired you to act on this decision?* A number did not directly respond to the notion of a 'career'. The answers that best sum up the tenor of the responses include one by the Southern-by-way-of-Korea novelist/essayist Sybil Baker: 'I never decided to pursue a career in writing, I started writing in first grade', which is close to my own experience, as well as that of President Obama's second inaugural poet Richard Blanco: 'Wasn't thinking of a career. Just following my creative and intellectual curiosities'. Several cited a combination of factors, notably, the awareness of the possibility of having a writing life, after being steeped in other professions, as Antony Dapiran and Shih-li Kow from Hong Kong and Malaysia respectively indicated in their responses. Several pointed to encouragement by teachers and writing mentors, the way novelist Shawn Wong, who describes himself as a writer/driver/mechanic/human and who edited some of the seminal Asian-American literature anthologies, was encouraged by Kay Boyle. One slightly unusual source of encouragement happened for the Lebanese-Canadian, award-winning novelist Rawi Hage: 'I participated in a visual art execution, I contributed to the catalogue for the show. The curator encouraged me to write more'. Life-changing experiences prompted the decision to be a writer for some respondents: Jee Leong Koh quit teaching in Singapore, moved to the US, came out as a gay man, and wrote; Laurie Alberts worked on fishing boats in Alaska in the early 1970s as a college student, something few women did, after which she switched her concentration to fiction; a family revelation forced Q. M. Zhang to question her academic way of knowing and writing as a social scientist in favour of a more hybrid creative form.

What we seldom get asked publicly about this career path is how much money we make as writers. In fora for business professionals, no one tiptoes around the question of earnings, because a 'career' is supposed to be an upwardly mobile and financially rewarding path. Respondents who had earned a living as journalists were among those who addressed this question more directly. For example, Filipino writer and author of some 42 books Jose Dalisay started college as an engineering major but 'realised that math wasn't for me; I had been writing since grade school and edited my high school paper, so it was easy for me to drop out of college, become a newspaper reporter, work at many jobs before returning to school to pick up my degree'. He did go on to acquire both an MFA and PhD and directed an MFA programme at one of Manila's top universities for years until he retired. Having worked in media myself and met many journalists over the years, I am struck by the difference in their attitude towards writing as a career path compared to those who wish primarily to self-identify as literary writers; I count myself as one of the latter. Those who do publish literary work often treat that writing as an extension of their journalistic career which, in terms of publication, may yield more lucrative publishing contracts and attention by the media world in which they operate. As Dalisay notes of his long career as journalist, literary writer, economist, academic, and commissioned biographer: 'I've lived off my writing all my life (as teaching pays very little where I am). I've never really minded just writing for a living'. His perspective is comparable to other writers I've met from the Philippines and other countries in Asia who write a multitude of different genres, including journalism, as that does seem to typify the writing life more readily than in the US and Anglophone countries where limiting writing to one or two genres appears more common, and where teaching creative writing in a top university can be a reasonably well-paid job, unlike in many Asian nations.

However, many literary writers do make a distinction between their literary work and other forms of writing. Novelist and nonfiction writer Helen Benedict, for example, who teaches journalism in the academy, described her former work as a newspaper reporter as 'writing for a living' but wants her 'writing to be free of having to support me'. By contrast, the English author Jill Dawson, who has published several best-selling novels, said that as a teenager, she 'began pursuing jobs in journalism and trying to make a living as a poet'. This was comparable to the way Eowyn Ivey, a novelist and Pulitzer finalist responded to the question about her work outside of academia: 'Now full-time writer, previously worked as a newspaper journalist'. Journalism is not necessarily perceived as the writer's life, and early in my adult work life, I made the conscious decision not to become a journalist as I knew I wanted to write fiction.

Nguyễn Phan Quế Mai, who wanted to write as a child and did many types of jobs to earn a living before she published her international best-selling debut novel *The Mountains Sing*, says, 'During the beginning stage of my writing career, I had to live from my savings but now I don't have to worry about my finances anymore and feel blessed'. It is significant that her book is part of a new narrative in Anglophone literature about the Vietnam War, or rather, the 'American War' as it was known in Vietnam. Several survey respondents were literary pioneers of hitherto little-published national or transnational narratives in English, or unarticulated political, racial, religious, or gender issues. But what someone writes about often has very little to do with why they choose to become writers, and financial success from publishing is, as Nguyễn suggests, a blessing, which by definition is granted to those fortunate enough to receive this. On earning a living solely from writing, the English novelist James Scudamore, who won many of the important UK literary awards for his books, summed up that dilemma in his 'yes' answer to the question with this caveat: 'as long as I was still free to write what I wanted to write'. Poets, on the other hand, for whom a 'large' print run is rarely above 5,000 or even 1,000, do not expect to earn a living from their books. As the poet/memoirist Natasha Sajé notes, 'The compensation, however, is the freedom of obscurity'.

This image of the writing life as a free and highly independent one is evident in the many comments I've heard from those who live in the 'real world'. A note of envy is unmistakable in the tone of family, friends, or acquaintances who are not in the literary world, because writing is perhaps not fully understood as 'work' as they know it. The long, solitary unpaid hours, squeezed out in between paid work, are totally invisible, while accolades and public appearances are highly visible. It's only among other writers that the conundrum of living that life while trying to earn a living is apparent. The American-Chinese writer Alex Kuo, who has a long career as a published, award-winning author, notes that he has 'never held a position in writing that paid enough income to make a living'. He has chaired academic departments for years, held a position as an academic vice chancellor at a major university, and is regularly invited as a distinguished visiting writer and scholar to universities around the world, as well as been a writer-in-residence for the likes of Mercy Corps. He is also often featured as a writer, speaker, or panellist at literary festivals or conferences. Arguably, these positions are in part dependent on his profile as a writer; he, like many other writers who teach creative writing in academia, does not hold a PhD. Yet years ago, when we were on the same reading bill at some college in the Pacific Northwest after the publication of my third book, he cautioned me against placing too much emphasis on marketing myself and my books. This was shortly after I'd left my business career and was trying to 'succeed' as a writer and hence brought the promotional and PR tactics from my marketing background to this new 'career'. It proved prescient advice, because the longer I've lived the writer's life, the less I've found that courting attention or publicity – what some might consider the 'glamour' of that public life – meaningful, and the more I've craved that 'freedom of obscurity' Sajé expressed.

Notably, it was after I began working in the academy that I became less interested in making a living solely from my writing. In that respect, I am as conflicted as many of the respondents to my survey appear to be. 'Conflicted' is perhaps too strong a description; 'ambiguous', or 'scattered'– the latter term was how my research assistant Grace summarised those responses in her report – might be a more accurate characterisation. Multi-genre, Thai-American writer Ira Sukrungruang, who has been in academia from early in his professional career, responded to the question about the preference for earing a living solely from writing, as did a few others, with 'not entirely'. The novelist and activist Diane Lefer, who has worked various freelance jobs and also taught creative writing at one of the same low-residency MFAs, part time, as I did, observed 'that used to be my dream, but working in social justice is so much a part of my life, I couldn't give it up when it pays or even if it's voluntary'. In fact, she's since given up teaching graduate students in favour of 'offering workshops to marginalized and traumatized populations in the US and abroad'. The noted essayist Brenda Miller, who is a tenured professor in creative writing, also directed graduate studies, edited a major literary journal, and co-authored one of the best-known textbooks for teaching creative nonfiction, declared she had never earned a living through writing, adding an exclamation mark to that declaration. My own feeling is somewhat more mixed, similar to that of Marshall Moore, who is one of the editors of this anthology. Having had a career in social services and taught university courses that were not only in creative writing, he would 'rather not rely solely on one thing for an income', which is much the way I feel. Hedging my bets, as it were.

Of the four respondents who answered 'yes' unequivocally, all were fiction writers and had work experience or career paths less or only partially connected to the academy. Rawi Hage was a photographer, in addition to having held several service jobs. The award-winning Canadian novelist Kim Echlin noted that 'I never supported myself with fiction, only journalism and teaching'. Shih-li Kow, who has never made a living from her writing, was an engineer in consumer goods manufacturing and was also in retail and real estate management until she decided on early retirement. Jill Dawson has been a journalist, taught creative writing, and has a business mentoring writers and running writing retreats; she published her first book at the age of 22 and has been self-employed for about thirty years. Had I stayed out of the academy, as I had earlier chosen to do, would I be less ambiguous or scattered in my focus and thereby more certain about wanting to earn a living solely from my writing?

To be honest, it's ridiculously difficult to be honest about the writing life. Being a writer is so much about adopting and presenting a persona on the page. It's worse in academic writing, as this chapter pretends to be (a useful masquerade), because the most common characteristic of academic discourse is prevarication. At least, that's my observation as someone who previously declared that I never wanted to teach but have since come to enjoy this work as much as, if not more than, work in business which once consumed all my waking hours and more. To be even more honest, now that truth appears to have anchored itself to an ever-elongating, and perhaps infinite spectrum, I have also been known to declare that I am not, in any way, an 'academic' even though my last twenty or so years have comprised earning most of my living in the academy.

I pause to ponder Brenda Miller's pugnaciously poetic punctuation in her response about her writer's life: *I have never earned a living through writing!*

So let me be brutally honest and say, without prevarication, that of course I wished I could have earned my living solely from writing, but the truth is, I didn't. It remains to be seen whether or not I ever will. And yet, despite that, and despite the academy, I have managed to live the writing life, one I wouldn't exchange for all the money in the world.

The most memorable moment in my pursuit of a writer's life had nothing to do with earning a living. It was Just-spring, but the world was not 'mud luscious' as it was in e.e. cummings's poem, because I was in Greece where the world is crisply dry, on the island of Hydra, in the village of Kamini, on the pathway above the Aegean, walking towards the port. It was the year of living in penury because the amount I earned from writing that year was a total of £75, paid to me by the BBC World Service for a piece of fiction broadcast on their Short Story Programme. I was otherwise unemployed, although I worked occasionally, and illegally for Pan, a local bar owner and spear fisherman, until the island's police harassed me into quitting. The year was 1981.

However, it was indeed spring, a Mediterranean one, and poppies, daffodils, and wildflowers bloomed all over the hillsides of white rocks. I had been writing for hours since pre-dawn, working on my first, never-to-be-published novel, although that truth was still a future shock on my time spectrum. Emerging from my writing room, I wandered towards the port, filling my arms with a colourful bouquet of flowers plucked from the hills, and knew that I was finally, truly a writer. The sky was cloudless, a brilliant blue, because the backdrop to such epiphanies must always only be utterly, irrevocably perfect.

That was also the year of throwing away almost seven years of a business career that should have been my lucrative path into management in favour of 'becoming a writer'. Depending on how I tell this story, which I've occasionally done when publicly asked about becoming a writer, I can make it sound adventurous, idealistic, and indescribably romantic so that the mostly younger, aspiring writers in the audience may gasp and murmur in anticipation of their own moments to be. The story I tell less often is about the years of living precariously that followed. Teaching freshman writing as an MFA grad student, wondering why I was acquiring this pointless degree since I had no desire to teach creative writing. Longer years when despair and desperation took hold as my first, second, and third novels never found publishers while I worked increasingly longer hours to afford life in New York City, only to realise that I had fallen far behind former MFA classmates who had published and also had tenure-track academic careers as teachers of creative writing. My eventual return to Hong Kong in the early 1990s, after re-establishing some semblance of a business career, was to find former colleagues had long zipped past me towards far more lucrative and promising management careers. The only thing that kept me going was the knowledge that I was still in pursuit of the writer's life. I was thirty-nine when I finally sold my first book, a novel released after I turned forty. Fifteen books later, the moniker 'writer' is inescapable.

Most of my books have been published by independent or academic presses, and royalties are, at best, a small supplemental income. Yet it was my profile as a 'successfully published author' that did eventually lead to a second career in the academy as a teacher of creative writing.

I began in a tenuous academic space, without tenure, a guaranteed position or any assurance that my semester-to-semester contract would be renewed. In 2002, at the Hong Kong literary festival, Robin Hemley, who has since become my long-time friend and literary business partner, on discovering I did possess an MFA, asked if I wanted to teach at a low-residency programme he chaired. My first response was no, not really. By then I had published five books and had established a dubious reputation as 'a pioneer writer in English' from Asia who now lived in New York City. Or at least, a *New York Times* story on a slow news day said that's who I was. That story appeared on Christmas Day, alongside my PR photograph, which allowed my then-boyfriend-now-husband to prove to his family in New Jersey that his long-distance, dubious girlfriend, who sashayed between New York and Hong Kong, really was the writer she said she was. Even in the era before 'truthiness', if they write and print it, it must be true, regardless.

My hesitation had everything to do with what I still saw as the monocultural nature of the American academy. My own experience in an MFA programme had not been entirely positive. As one of the only students of colour, and a foreign student at that (the three other foreign students were all English, and white), I was not always sure that what I was learning would help me write what I needed to write. None of the faculty or students had ever been to Hong Kong, or anywhere in Asia for that matter, except for one English student who, like me, was older and had a former career as an economist. The focus in fiction was primarily on the short story, usually set in an American suburb, whereas I wanted to write novels that spread themselves all over Asia and partly also in my version of America. But most dauntingly, the pay for entry-level faculty was hideously low for a ridiculous amount of work; I could not see how I would survive teaching five classes of rhetoric and writing to undergraduates each semester until I published well and could, if I were so lucky, get one of those prized positions as a faculty member in an MFA, with the promise of tenure.

Instead, after leaving my business career, I lived frugally with said boyfriend, did some freelance work and traded stocks to grow my savings and the small inheritance I had in order to make the semblance of a living. I applied for and went to every writer's residency that accepted me. All I wanted to do was write as much as possible, without the confines of a full-time job, in between going back to Hong Kong to help care for my mother following my father's sudden and unexpected death.

Robin, a graduate from Iowa who has a well-established academic career, assured me that low-residency teaching was part-time, flexible, and not at all like grad school as we experienced it; Robin is also the most persuasive person I know. Once he confirmed that I could do most of the semester's teaching by email, I agreed to teach one semester. Ten years later, I was still there and even served a term as faculty chair. In 2002, there were few such low-residency MFAs, approximately ten or so nationwide, which generally enrolled older, working professionals, the majority self-funded, instead of the younger graduate students with full-ride fellowships who populate residential programmes such as Iowa or Amherst, Massachusetts where I did my degree. Students only show up on campus twice a year, for ten-day, intensive 'residencies' of workshops, lectures, and readings; and are then paired with a faculty advisor for the semester. When I first started teaching at a private college in Vermont, their low-residency MFA was one of the first such programmes established in the US. Today, there are over fifty and the pedagogical model has broadened to include online teaching, shorter residencies (including international ones), and diversification into varied forms of writing and cross-genre, interdisciplinary creative work. The growth has also meant that many more younger students now enrol because it's possible to work while acquiring the degree, instead of having to move to where the campus is and live there for two or more years as a full-time student, earning peanuts as a teaching fellow. Plus the parallel growth of interest in those wanting to become writers has also meant that residential programmes receive many more applicants. It's not unusual for students to apply to ten or more residential programmes plus backups to low-residency ones. These days, I'm not sure that the writer's life in the world of the MFA is as exclusive or rewarding as it once was. After all, it's not a degree that guarantees either a job or publication or even the assurance of being able to pursue any kind of writer's life.

Ironically, it was this part-time teaching, which pays a supplemental income only slightly better than royalties, depending on where you work, that led to full-time positions for me in the academy. By the time I turn seventy and retire in two years, I will have spent only ten years as a full-time academic, six in one Hong Kong university, three at my current position, and one year as visiting faculty for a semester at two major American universities.

There is no question that the academy at least recognises me as a writer, whereas the business world simply relegates my writing to, at best, an 'avocation' as the boss of one of my bosses described it when she introduced me as a new member of their management team; or at worst, a hobbyist's passion akin to collecting Hello Kitty memorabilia or memorising baseball stats. In the academy, there is less pressure to earn a living solely from my writing, as a position as faculty in creative writing lends credibility to my own work. However, as I come to the end of my second work-for-cash career, I find myself turning back towards the business world to supplement social security in my later years. For one thing, I am an owner and co-owner of two small businesses. Working full-time in the academy, these are necessarily part-time endeavours but later, that could change. Also, I find myself rethinking the potential income from my books. Being published by small, indie presses, I've always participated in the marketing of my work, but my time in academia has made me less proactive on that score. That too can and likely will change. The business of being a writer is something I find intriguing, as I did have to act as my own distributor for some of my earliest works published in Hong Kong to make those books available in the US. Likewise, my publishing contracts are something I actually read, even though I depend on my agent to recommend whatever changes will provide better terms and protect my rights. Having edited several anthologies, I'm often surprised at how many writers barely know the terms of what they've signed.

In my business life, my head would have rolled for such inattention to potential liability.

Perhaps the main problem of academia is that it likes its laurels, probably too much. I soon discovered how important it was for me to learn everyone's accomplishments and disciplines. Academic stars are, after all, blessed with prodigious intellects and the capacity to retain an astonishing number of facts. Business stars, on the other hand, need not be as intellectual, but they do need to know how to get sales or operate profitably, and more important, make their bosses look good. There's also much faster turnover in business as the best way to increase your salary is to get a new job that takes you to the next level, something I learned to do, increasing my pay by as much as 65 per cent in the best scenario. In academia, no one in their right mind surrenders their laurels upon which they rest unless forced to. In the business world, it's also survival of the fittest but it's much easier to walk away because there's no such a thing as tenure, just severance, which can be negotiated to your best advantage as I did, twice; the business world is nothing if not allergic to potential lawsuits.

There is also the problem of efficiency and scale. Even though the working hours in my business career, especially towards the end when I had greater management responsibilities, are far longer than any position I've ever held in academia, you don't have to fill in forms in triplicate to get paid a $200 honorarium. I had a heavy business travel schedule through most of my career – at one job I was away from home 40 per cent of the time – but there was a car to meet me at the airport, business-class travel for longer flights, and expenses covered with minimal fuss. In academia, I'm always filling out expense reports, not to mention obtaining approval for conference travel and sometimes have had to pay out of pocket, something that rarely occurred in business life. Expense reporting was generally far more streamlined, whether in small or large companies; whereas every academic institution I've worked for either full- or part-time appears discombobulated by expense reporting. As for budget planning, which is an ordeal in both academia and business – and I've done both – the minuscule budgets in academia I had to manage took an inordinate amount of time to plan and administer compared to the time taken and systems available for multi-million-dollar budgets I used to manage in business.

The long and short of these differing work experiences for my writer's life is that I was forced to be very focused if I ever wanted to produce any literary work while working in business because there simply wasn't much time for myself. But I was paid well, could afford comforts that made life easier, and writing was the way I would prove to myself that yes, I was indeed a writer. That offered a deeply personal and spiritual challenge that my day job did not, since business is primarily about profitability. I sometimes think that if it hadn't been for those early years of working too hard to afford my writing life, I would not have the writer's life I have now. By the time I moved over to academia, I already had a publishing track record, so it was less about proving myself, and more about progressing and developing artistically as a writer. The academy provides a fulfilling enough job as a teacher of creative writing – my writing students never fail to amuse, entertain, and educate me – and the long holiday breaks and not having to show up in the office daily provide significantly more time to write. Plus reading literature is actually considered 'work' and not a guilty pleasure to be secretly indulged in the 'real world'.

But would I want to earn my income solely from my writing? I can't really answer that now because I haven't done it and I'm not getting younger. When age becomes the excuse for not knowing, the answer (both in academia and business) is to look to those with more years ahead. Evan Fallenberg, a younger former colleague and my co-director at an international low-residency MFA we jointly designed, is a novelist and literary translator and these days an academic department head as well. He gave an admirably centred response to that question: 'I prefer the triumvirate of teaching, writing, translation; the constant move between them keeps me fresh and inspired, never worried about whether any one of them will be enough to sustain me financially and spiritually'.

Just as I would not exchange my writing life for all the money in the world, neither would I exchange any of the experiences my working-for-a-living life has given me. After all, it's who I am, and earning a living comprises much of what I do that has sent me off on this lifelong pursuit of the writer's life. Where else would I go to find my writing inspiration?

Appendix

Survey questionnaire:

1. What advanced creative writing degrees do you hold?
2. What degrees or professional qualifications do you hold in other disciplines?
3. How many books do you have published, and in what genre?
4. Outside of academia, what fields or work professions do you rely on for a source of income?

5. Could you explain your work history? How many years, if any, have you worked in academia?
6. When did you decide to pursue a career in writing and what inspired you to act on this decision?
7. What occupation did you initially pursue before you earned income from writing to provide you with an income?
8. Was writing how you've always earned a living?
9. If you have a primary source of income other than writing, would you prefer to make a living entirely from your writing?

Writers who responded (incl. genres of books published, as self-reported):

1. Helen Benedict, UK/US, novel/nonfiction
2. Marshall Moore, Hong Kong/UK/US, fiction/academic
3. Rawi Hage, Canada/Lebanon, fiction
4. Antony Dapiran, China/Hong Kong/Australia, nonfiction
5. Natasha Sajé, US/Germany, poetry/creative nonfiction/literary criticism
6. Richard Blanco, US/Cuba, poetry/essay
7. James Shea, Hong Kong/US, poetry/literary translation
8. Nguyễn Phan Quế Mai, Vietnam, poetry/zuhitsu/fiction/essay
9. Jose Dalisay, Philippines, fiction/nonfiction/drama
10. Alex Kuo, US/China, poetry/fiction/essays
11. Evan Fallenberg, Israel/US, novel/literary translation
12. Jee Leong Koh, US/Singapore, poetry/essay/novel
13. Eowyn Ivey, US, fiction
14. James Scudamore, UK, novel/literary fiction
15. QM Zhang, US/China, hybrid memoir/fiction/documentary/photography
16. Brenda Miller, US, creative nonfiction/writing instruction/poetry
17. Shawn Wong, US, novel/edited anthologies
18. Laurie Alberts, US/Russia, fiction/memoir/craft of writing
19. Diane Lefer, US, fiction/nonfiction
20. Sybil Baker, US/Korea, fiction/nonfiction
21. Kim Echlin, Canada, novel/nonfiction/translation/children's/edited essay collection
22. Jill Dawson, UK, novel/poetry chapbook/editor anthologies of poetry and stories
23. Ira Sukrungruang, US/Thailand, creative nonfiction/fiction/poetry
24. Shih-Li Kow, Malaysia, short story collection/novel/somewhat literary

11

Writing and Anxiety

What Are Writers When They're Not Writing?

Sam Meekings
Northwestern University in Qatar

When I first entered primary school, each of the students in my class was asked the same question: what do you want to be when you grow up? I was a shy child (and I'm a shy adult) and I struggled with this. I was, by some margin, the shortest boy in the class. I listened as the other kids gave their answers: astronaut, striker for Tottenham Hotspur, ballet dancer, train driver. When it came to be my turn, I gave the only answer that honesty demanded: I wanted to be a dog.

Sadly, this proved impossible. And so I turned instead to my imagination. I started writing stories about our family dog and his adventures. In these stories he could speak to me, of course, though no one else understood. In that sense, the stories I wrote were both an outlet for the anxiety I felt and a way to transform it. By the time I started secondary school, therefore, I had a new ambition. When I grew up, I wanted to be a writer. (There is still a part of me that thinks I should have stuck with trying to become a dog.) I am lucky to have been able to follow this path. But, like many writers, I've come to find that writing for a living (both as a creative writing scholar and practising author) has had the unwelcome side-effect of inviting anxiety into a practice that was once only about joy and play. Writing stories as a child was purely a source of pleasure; however, by aligning my writing with my career and my source of income, I have attached a range of pressures and worries into my writing practice. These undoubtedly affect both my writing habits and approaches, and also the ways in which I interact with the publishing industry.

I am still an anxious person. But I am also a writer. This identity is important to me. The social psychologist Patricia Linville theorised that self-complexity is a function both of the number of an individual's self-aspects (such as the roles an individual might perform as, say, a writer, academic, or teacher) and their separability (Dixon and Baumeister 1991). In other words, identity is bound up with roles and behaviours: people who think of themselves as writers need to be writing in order to maintain that aspect of their self-concept. What happens therefore when this activity is threatened? The career writer and the writing instructor face deadlines and work that both distract and bleed time from writing. The writer may increasingly these days face feedback from their agent or (potential) publisher that their work is difficult to place in a changing market. The short answer, therefore, is that when a writer is not writing there is the risk of an explosion of anxiety and self-doubt. But the longer answer, as this chapter explores, is that writing and anxiety are bound together, and an exploration of how they are intertwined reveals much about the paradoxes at the heart of the writing life.

The relationship between writing and anxiety is a complicated one. In much popular media, writers are represented as tortured geniuses, solitary and antisocial, or at the very least alcoholic or drug-dependant. Throughout the twentieth century, a number of studies were carried out to examine the idea of the 'mad genius' and to propose a scientific link between creativity and mental illness (Jamison 1989; Ludwig 1995). However, more recently there has been a growing argument that these studies represent an oversimplification of an issue that is more far more nuanced and complex than it is often represented (Rothenberg 1995; Schlesinger 2012). The field of study is itself a contentious one, with some scholars asserting a profound interrelation between creativity and psychopathology (Andreason 2008) and others arguing that there is no provable or discernible link (Sawyer 2012). What the debate itself suggests, however, is the complicated correlation between mental health and the creative mind. If the question of whether anxiety and creativity might emerge from the same part of the brain cannot yet be definitively answered by neurologists and neuroanatomists, then nonetheless the question begs several others, among them whether anxiety might itself be a by-product of writing, or alternatively might be the thing that drives or impels the urge to write.

Indeed, there are many ways in which anxiety may be a function of writing. Beyond a sense of unease, worry, and even panic, anxiety can imply a heightened intensity of focus on minute details, which is itself a technique frequently utilised by poetry, fiction, and non-fiction writers alike. Research into anxiety has suggested that it is connected to overactivity in areas of the brain involved in emotions (NHS UK n.d.) and may therefore increase obsession with emotion and behaviours. In other words, anxiety can affect writing habits and subjects. On the flipside, writing may itself trigger changes in the way we react emotionally and mentally to the world. For instance, Keen notes that empirical research has demonstrated that 'fiction writers as a group scored higher than the general population on empathy', and thereby raises the possibility that 'the activity of fiction writing may cultivate novelists' role-taking skills and make them more habitually empathetic' (Keen 2006: 221). In other words, the act of writing itself may have an effect on the way the brain works, and as such influences the ways in which authors interact with the world around them.

In my own writing practice, anxiety both motivates and inhibits, which is another way of saying that it is both fundamental to my writing habits and a barrier to sustained writing. Anxiety produces a heightened awareness of what I am (not) doing and ought to be doing, and triggers a constant reminder of deadlines approaching, projects to be completed, and drafts desperately needing work, and as such sometimes provides the necessary impetus to commit to chaining myself to the chair in front of my laptop for a sustained period in order to tick at least one item off the antagonistic to-do list. However, anxiety also induces a state of mind that is antithetical to the type of creative and critical thinking and reflection that is necessary for the most sustained writing. As medical researchers have pointed out, 'Anxiety modulates the functioning of attention' (Pacheco-Unguetti, Acosta, Callejas, and Lupiáñez 2010: 298) and thereby makes immersed concentration in writing projects difficult. Moreover, it can also serve to blur the critical facilities of the writing and editing (redrafting and revising) process by making an objective reading more fraught since it becomes intertwined with other worries, concerns, and sense of pressure. The internal voice of anxiety is hypercritical and dismissive, and as such is quick to self-judgement and self-doubt. Though this personal experience is purely anecdotal, it nonetheless demonstrates the way that anxiety may drive (some forms of) writing, while at the same time making full engagement with the process more difficult.

Indeed, anxiety's complex relationship with writing illustrates the fact that much about the writing life, and writing practices, processes, and outcomes, are by their very nature paradoxical. This is nowhere more true than in navigating a career path as a working author. One popular career for the writer is, of course, academia. Yet the nature of the modern university is such as to frequently induce further anxiety. Writing is no longer purely pleasurable or immersive: instead it is also suddenly aligned with career expectations and markers. The success of writing endeavours (measured in outcomes and departmental rubrics) is tied to reappointment, tenure, and promotion, and as such is pressurised and thereby further divorced from the play, joy, and experimentation which tends to draw practitioners to creative work in the first place. The university also places several other pressures on the writer, among them a lack of time to write without distractions, since '[a]cademia's never-ending flow of urgent and disparate tasks accelerates the pace of time and creates a constant feeling of time running out' (Gill 2009: 229). This feeling of time running out is, in and of itself, a good working definition of anxiety, and as such suggests something of the complex relationship that writing has with time.

Indeed, the irony is that writing both requires time and facilitates an escape from a regular sense of time. In this way it offers both a trigger for anxiety and an escape from anxiety. Consider some of the language applied to writing habits. Some refer to successful writing as *getting into the groove*; others, *being in the zone*; still others finding *the right headspace*. Whatever terminology is used to describe it, the situation is familiar among writers: as though your fingers barely leave the keyboard, as though words pour from you as fast as water from a bubbling, babbling brook, and as though you've found a shortcut that facilitates an instantaneous translation of ideas straight from the brain to the blank page. This is the platonic ideal of writing, the paragon of what we hope will happen when we manage to clear out enough hours in our schedule to actually sit down and get on with the project that's been lurking at the back of our minds. It is both an escape *from* and an escape *into*, and Joanna Yoo notes that '[c]reative writing enables this sense of timelessness and transcendence by allowing writers to become completely engrossed in their writing encounters' (2019: 152). If writing offers a space beyond anxiety, however, then access to that space is highly fraught.

It is difficult, for instance, to become engrossed in a writing encounter when so much may be dependent on the outcomes of that encounter. It is unlikely to be a surprise to anyone that '[s]tress surveys in U.K. and Australian universities demonstrated high occupational stress levels among faculty' (Catano et al. 2010: p235), and I would assume the case to be broadly comparable in the US and other territories as well. When writing is tied, in the academy, to career expectations and continued employability, then writing becomes inextricably entangled with anxiety and pressure. In the university environment in which so many writing practitioners both write and teach, 'this pressure has turned academia into a rat race, leading to a deep change in the fundamental structure of academic behaviour, and entailing a self-defeating and hence counter-productive pattern' (Landes, Marchman, and Nielsen 2012: 73). This counter-productive pattern means that writing production is inherently loaded with anxiety within the academy, and represents a barrier to immersion in the writing process.

However, it is not only writing within higher education that is bound up with anxiety. All authors, situated within or outside the academy, are having to adapt to changing practices, processes, and forms in the industry. As other chapters in this volume have noted (see in particular Chapter 13 by Marshall Moore), being a writer today means more than just successfully mastering craft, narrative, and composition: it also entails becoming an expert digital marketer, creating and curating your identity-as-brand, and cultivating an audience across social media platforms. It is by now well known that '[o]nline marketing and social media are critical players in book sales and distribution' (Grobman and Ramsey 2020: 42), and as such the role of the writer is no longer limited to the creative act of writing but must extend into the public realm via the continual cultivation of an audience through content creation and dissemination (such as blogging, vlogging, curating email lists, or regular posting on Instagram, Twitter, or others). Such activities not only take time away from writing and so once again play into the anxiety surrounding the loss of that social aspect as a component of identity, but also present several issues. For digital natives (and indeed for extroverts), curating one's life online may often be seen as normal or inevitable; for other generations, however, the sustained pressures of public identity performance can raise a range of issues, especially for the anxiety-plagued writer who is likely to be triggered by the nature of such self-exposure. After all, seriously impaired social functioning is a common component of generalised anxiety disorder (Hoge, Ivkovic, and Fricchione 2012) and so the recent expectation that a successful writer should be a highly social one is problematic. Experiences of authorly anxiety also therefore reveal another paradox about the writing life: many writers are introverted, obsessive, and hyper-critical, yet a common measure of success in the field is based on extroversion (through the garnering of an audience of followers, subscribers, and potential buyers through sustained personal marketing and branding).

The concept of success itself is one that further reveals how anxiety is embedded within the modern writing life. One reason for this is that the writing life is, even for the most esteemed and successful of authors, riddled with rejection. Although as creative writing instructors many of us repeat to our students the mantra that rejection is to be expected as a fundamental part of being a writer, and are likely to be overly familiar with popular anecdotes such as J.K. Rowling's first Harry Potter book being turned down by 12 publishers (Flood 2015), and may feel we have grown the thick skin necessary to dealing with the publishing industry, there is no denying that for most of us each and every rejection still bitterly hurts, and thereby serves to exacerbate anxiety. After all, '[i]t can be daunting to think about having your thoughts, ideas, and/or research critically evaluated by others, and it is infuriating and humbling when your submitted work is rejected' (Brown 2017: 60), and for many writers this is a continuing and regular process. There may be many and varied metrics for success, from the satisfaction of completing a project through to publication itself through to sales figures through to prizes, but this also has a flip side in that each potential stage or goal is loaded with the potential for rejection.

My own experiences are perhaps not atypical. I am lucky to have an agent; but he is frequently not keen on new work I produce and seems to rarely answer emails. I am lucky to have been published by a number of reputable publishers; but this does not seem to help very much in the pitching of new books. I have written more unpublished books than I have ever published, and with each new project I find myself worrying that it will not find a home and that my moment (which in itself feels like hyperbole) has already passed. I am desperately keen to celebrate the publication days and successes of friends, peers, and colleagues, and yet I would be lying if I didn't admit that such news usually prompts an internalised comparison with my own writing and writerly identity, and all the envy and anxiety that provokes. If I can no longer find a publisher or a readership for my works (through traditional or self-publishing) then what does this mean for my self-concept which is reliant on the self-aspect of 'writer' as one function and marker of identity? It means more anxiety.

The writing life is also one in which financial concerns are likely to exacerbate anxiety. A recent survey by the UK's Society of Authors found that 'the average earnings of a full-time writer were just £10,500 even before the health crisis... Meanwhile, most writers need a second job to survive, with just 13.7% of respondents making a living from writing alone without a second job, down from 40% in 2006' (Solomon 2022). These statistics illustrate both the precarious nature of choosing writing as a career, and the anxiety that thereby underpins survival in this field. The fact that the vast majority of writers must rely on a second job also brings us back once again to one other common writerly anxiety: lack of time to write and its ensuing effect on self-concept and identity. Added to this, one must consider the fact that many writers are paying off the costs of student loans for MAs, MFAs, or other creative writing (or writing-adjacent) degrees; that substantial advances for novels are comparatively rare and a thing of the past, while poetry and short-story collections are generally not paid any advances at all; that academia (especially in the age of the adjunct) is rarely a well-paid second job; that freelancing is fraught with uncertainty; and that those authors who choose to self-publish inevitably have to invest their own money in many aspects of the design and publication process. Dogs do not worry about money. But for the rest of us, it is often a source of worry and stress that detracts from (and sometimes makes us question) our vocation.

What then can be done about this complex relationship between writing and anxiety? Are there ways in which anxiety can be countered or minimised so as not to block or threaten the self concept and writerly practice, process, and identity? One potential suggestions is to trade the solitary anxiety of struggling with writing and identity for the support of a writing community: either an online #writingcommunity or a collection of writerly peers. Such communities can alleviate a number of writerly anxieties, as well as inform, influence and motivate writing practices and processes. As Sylvia Gunnery suggests, '[e]specially in the early development of writers, much is gained by learning together and inspiring one another' (2007: 5). Gunnery goes on to note that writing communities provide a wealth of benefits, such as helping members to reflect on writing habits and processes, build self-confidence, reflect on writing styles, generate ideas for writing, make reading-writing connections, develop editorial nuance and skills, explore genre and voice, and provide both a platform and an encouraging environment for sharing works-in-progress (Gunnery 2007). Such communities not only offer a support network that can mitigate some of the effects of anxiety, but also serve to normalise writerly anxieties and concerns, as well as offer a lens through which to reframe success and suggest ways in which the identity of 'writer' extends beyond the writing process and into shared networks and communities.

However, if community offers one way to help process and alleviate some of the anxieties that writers face, it also reflects another paradox at the heart of writing. They can mitigate anxiety by offering support, and strategies for dealing with rejection and time issues, but there is also a comparative and competitive nature underpinning much online (and indeed offline) community that is likely to provoke anxiety. Being inside a community can protect against getting stuck inside one's own head, since writing is so frequently a solitary and solipsistic activity, and yet at the same time many writing communities (from those created by MFAs and other creative writing programs through to those that exist online, such as #writingcommunity on Twitter) run the risk of promoting homogeneity through their groupthink and frequent reiteration of supposed writing lore. Anxiety is often triggered by restrictive norms, and thus community think may have effects on writing habits and processes that hinder rather than help. Once again, the issue of anxiety reveals some of the paradoxes at the heart of the writing life.

Not all paradoxes have to be negative, however. For though committing to a writing life can bring about many stresses and triggers for anxiety, it is also frequently the case that writing itself is in some ways a solution to the issues raised in this chapter. Writing about anxieties, for instance, is one way to regain some control over them. In this case, writing can be the cure as well as the cause, since 'expressive writing [functions] as an alternate low-cost intervention strategy for improving mental health' (Kacewicz, Slatcher, and Pennebaker 2007:

271). Researchers into writing therapies have found that telling stories about ourselves and our past struggles and traumas can help people to 'change the way they view the past and the story they tell about it, which can help to transform this constructed identity' (Dodd 2019: 130), and in this way anxieties and periods of difficulties can be reconstructed and managed. As Dodd continues to point out, '[w]riting and storytelling are ways that we can help people to draw out and explore some of their hidden qualities and re-story their lives' (2019: 138), and it is precisely this re-storying that allows writers to deal with the changes and challenges they face and integrate those into their lives without their entire writerly identity being threatened or destroyed. In addition, writing can be a way to deal with pressures and anxieties that disrupt routines and challenge identities, with a recent study among writers by Whithaus, Alexander, and Lunsford confirming that writing proved particularly useful throughout transitional and difficult moments:

> Given the challenges of the unexpected, which include unanticipated needs to compose in particular genres or to address specific situations, we should not be surprised that some participants spoke of understanding writing as an ongoing form of inquiry, a modality that they use specifically to discover, explore, and generate thinking.
>
> 2022: 10

This reminder that writing is not only limited to the generation of product (a short story, a poem, a novel, or even a chapter in a scholarly volume) is vital, for it foregrounds the fact that writing has many uses and functions that are integral to framing our thoughts about ourselves and the world. Writing about anxiety has, for me, often worked as a way to understand that anxiety and so regain a little control over it.

To sum up, we live in soul-crushing times. Anxiety is not always escapable. As a writer, my practice and habits have frequently been derailed by anxiety, and in this I am certain I am not alone. Experts may still be divided on the links between creativity and mental health, but the pressures of academia, the industry, and audience-building are certain. Anxiety therefore isn't going anywhere. But its presence is also revealing, helping to shine a light on the paradoxes inherent in the writing life. These are key reasons why anxiety needs to be discussed more frankly and explicitly in writing programs and literatures, as an integral part of the world of creative writing. It would also be beneficial to see more courses that focus on writing about the self as a way of understanding, reframing, and strengthening identity, to remind all of us that writing is about more than just the generation of a story, poem, novel, or paper. Meanwhile, the industry should also be mindful of the lore it perpetuates and the conceptions (particularly surrounding branding and social media) that it stokes, since these may very well favour extrovert writers but may be profoundly difficult for introverted or anxiety-prone writers. Now, more than ever, is the time to reject a one-size-fits-all models. Therefore, we must continue to talk – both in literature like this, in online writing communities, and in the classroom – about how we might each individually and communally define success for ourselves beyond the glimmering and envy-inducing classical trajectory of publications, prizes, and legacy. In this way, we might mitigate some of the anxieties surrounding writing careers and rejection.

For myself, I will keep trying to write about my anxiety as a way to generate understanding of it, I will keep talking to students about the anxieties of the writing life, and I will keep trying to normalise discussing the anxieties within writing communities. For now, that is enough. I am a writer who sometimes cannot write. And that's fine, because I have not yet figured out how to become a dog. But I have become a little better at recognising that familiar black dog that traipses behind me, some days a bit closer at my heels than others, and doing all I can not to attempt to outrun him or pretend he is not there, but instead to accept him as a companion that I cannot shake but I can be kinder to.

References

Andreasen, N. C. (2008), 'The Relationship Between Creativity and Mood Disorders', *Dialogues in Clinical Neuroscience*, 10(2): 251–255.

Brown, N. W. (2017). 'In Support of Professional Writing: Response to "Thinking About Our Work: Work"', *Group*, 41(1) (Spring): 59–61.

Catano, V., Francis, L., Haines, T., Kirpalani, H., Shannon, H., Stringer, B., and Lozanzki, L. (2010), 'Occupational Stress in Canadian Universities: A National Survey', *International Journal of Stress Management*, 17(3): 232–258.

Dixon, T. M. and Baumeister, R. F. (1991), 'Escaping the Self: Moderating Effects of Self-complexity', *Personality and Social Psychology Bulletin*, 19: 4–12.

Dodd, L. (2019) 'Re-Storying Lives Using Creative Writing: A Client-Oriented Approach to Overcoming the Health Impacts of Domestic and Family Violence', *Storytelling, Self, Society*, 15(1): 130–140.

Flood, A. (2015), 'JK Rowling Says She Received 'Loads' of Rejections Before Harry Potter Successs', *The Guardian*. 24 March. Available online: https://www.theguardian.com/books/2015/mar/24/jk-rowling-tells-fans-twitter-loads-rejections-before-harry-potter-success (accessed 19 April 2022).

Gill, R. (2009), 'Breaking the Silence: The Hidden Injuries of Neo-Liberal Academia'. In R. Roisin and R. Gill (eds) *Secrecy and Silence in the Research Process: Feminist Reflections*. London: Routledge, 228–244.

Grobman, L. and Ramsey, E. M. (2020), 'Making the Invisible Visible: Careers and the Humanities', *Major Decisions: College, Career, and the Case for the Humanities*. Philadelphia: University of Pennsylvania Press.

Gunnery, S. (2007), *The Writing Circle*. Markham, UK: Pembroke Publishers.

Hoge, E. A., Ivkovic, A., and Fricchione, G. L. (2012), 'Generalized Anxiety Disorder: Diagnosis and Treatment', *BMJ: British Medical Journal*, 345(7885): 37–42.

Kacewicz, E., Slatcher, R. B., and Pennebaker, J. W. (2007), 'Expressive Writing: An Alternative to Traditional Methods', In L. Luciano (ed.) *Low-cost Approaches to Promote Physical and Mental Health: Theory, Research, and Practice*, New York: Springer, 271–284.

Jamison, K. R. (1989), 'Mood Disorders and Patterns of Creativity in British Writers and Artists', *Psychiatry-Interpersonal and Biological Processes*, 52(2): 125–134.

Keen, S. (2006), 'A Theory of Narrative Empathy', *Narrative*, 14(3): 207–236.

Landes, X., Marchman, M., and Nielsen, M. (2012), 'The Academic Rat Race: Dilemmas and Problems in the Structure of Academic Competition', *Learning and Teaching: The International Journal of Higher Education in the Social Sciences*, 5(2): 73–90.

Ludwig, A. M. (1995), *The Price of Greatness: Resolving the Creativity and Madness Controversy*. New York and London: Guilford Press.

NHS UK (n.d.) *Overview – Generalised Anxiety Disorder in Adults.* Available online: https://www.nhs.uk/mental-health/conditions/generalised-anxiety-disorder/overview/#:~:text=Anxiety%20is%20a%20feeling%20of,medical%20test%20or%20job%20interview (accessed 26 April 2022).

Pacheco-Unguetti, A. P., Acosta, A., Callejas, A. and Lupiáñez, J. (2010), 'Anxiety: Different Attentional Functioning Under State and Trait Anxiety', *Psychological Science*, 21(2): 298–304.

Rothenberg, A. (1995), 'Creativity and Affective Illness: An Objection', *Percept Mot Skills*, 80(1): 161–162.

Sawyer, R. K. (2012), 'Creativity and Mental Illness: Is There a Link?' *Huffington Post*, Available online: http://www.huffingtonpost.com/dr-r-keith-sawyer/creativityand-mental-ill_b_2059806.html (accessed 11 April 2022).

Schlesinger, J. (2012), *The Insanity Hoax: Exposing the Myth of the Mad Genius*. Ardsley-on-Hudson, NY: Shrinktunes Media.

Solomon, N. (2022), 'Our Letter to *The Guardian*', *The Society of Authors*. 7 February. Available online: https://societyofauthors.org/News/News/2022/February/Our-letter-to-The-Guardian (accessed 10 April 2022).

Whithaus, C., Alexander, J., and Lunsford, K. (2022), 'When Things Collide: Wayfinding in Professional Writers' Early Career Development', *Literacy in Composition Studies*, 9(1): 1–22.

Yoo, J. (2019), 'Creative Writing and Academic Timelessness', *New Writing*, 16(2): 148–157.

12

The Value in Authors' Writing Self-Reports

Helping Student-Writers Learn the Practice of Writing from Those Who Practice

Tamara Girardi
HACC, Central Pennsylvania's Community College

As we look toward a future in the field of creative writing studies, we should be aware of the social changes and expectations of creative storytelling; the publishing community has been called upon to make space for diverse perspectives and voices. Likewise, our stories must authentically embody the emotion of diverse worlds and life experiences, and finally, through our cognitive processes, writers and the publishing community at large can achieve these tasks identified as critical. Our pedagogy, then, must also evolve to be less exclusive, both in terms of contributing voices and varied rhetorics, so that our learning environments provide the kind of inclusion our student-writers require to thrive in their writing journeys.

Theoretical frameworks serve as foundations for our pedagogy, but what happens when those theories are misguided? The composition and creative writing studies fields are rich with theory and research about how to inspire the best writing in students; since creative writing studies is a relatively young discipline, composition theory has often influenced the burgeoning field and creative writing instructors as well, which is why the connections to composition are included in this chapter. As theories progress and evolve, some pedagogical approaches are lauded, condemned, or both. One case in which this occurred in composition studies was with the expressive and cognitive theories and pedagogy that fuelled the process movement and were later harshly criticised. As scholars such as James Berlin, Patricia Bizzell, and Thomas Kent have urged, composition studies has moved away from process in the aims of developing a new era of post-process approaches, approaches that rely more on social connections than cognition or expressiveness. Berlin's influence is perhaps the strongest in his 1988 essay 'Rhetoric and Ideology in the Writing Class', originally published in *College English* and reprinted in several anthologies (Berlin 2003). The essay reiterates and further illuminates points Berlin made a year earlier in his book *Rhetoric and Reality: Writing Instruction in American Colleges, 1900–1985*. In the essay, Berlin presents cognitive and expressionistic rhetorics as substandard in the writing classroom. Rather, he supports a social epistemic approach as 'a political act involving a dialectical interaction engaging the material, the social, and the individual writer, with language as the agency of mediation' (1987: 730). Berlin's preference for social epistemic is clear in the essay's tone and language. Regarding cognitive and expressionistic rhetorics, he simply points out all the ways in which researchers of each have gotten them wrong.

Similarly, some writing scholars have historically dismissed the value of writers' self-reports. As a developing discipline with burgeoning scholarship, creative writing studies has been sensitive to avoid relying on 'the personal experiences and highly respected "testimony" of the successful novelist or poet who has entered the classroom to profess his or her views of craft and the profession' (Ritter 2011: 92). The intention is to avoid relaying an idealised version of a writer's reality to new writers and to limit the emphasis on 'star' authors who 'teach very little [but] attract attention' (Vanderslice 2008: 70). Such concerns are warranted; however, the research in this chapter proposes an approach that respects *various* voices, not a singular 'star' voice. Likewise, the emphasis is on a variety of authors and their varied experiences, an approach that arguably creates space for all student-writers to identify a personal connection with a published author; the goal is that the personal connection possesses the potential to validate a student-writer's own process and vision. After all, as Bizzaro notes, 'to *not* pay attention to writers' self-reports is to deny the contributions of many of our most important writers' (2011: 132). Thus, previous conversations in composition and creative writing studies regarding appropriate rhetorics and voices in the studying of writing are being explored and challenged here; the exploration of these ideas is relevant because of what we see in *practice*. Authors often question other writers about their cognitive, social, and expressive strategies; in other words, how do writers write? And how can writers learn from other writers by understanding how they write? This chapter asserts that to truly understand writing, especially the act of creative writing in all its forms, creative writing instructors must look to the experts – those who are actively writing and publishing – and incorporate the importance of the cognitive, the expressive, and the social in the writing and publishing experiences of those experts to the benefit of our student-writers.

Writers On Writing

The theory at the foundation of this chapter is that in the act of writing, writers engage a combination of cognitive, expressive, and social dynamics, and how they report on those dynamics is of value to developing writers. To study the validity of this claim, I chose to analyse eighteen interviews with professional writers on writing. The interviews were published in the popular *The Writer* magazine between 2019–2020 under the regular department 'How I Write'. While the fact each interview appeared in the same section of the same magazine and that some of the topic prompts were the same offered some consistency, there are some differences among questions depending on the type of writing the author engages (fiction or nonfiction, for example) and on his or her personal interests or philosophies with writing. Sixty-one percent of the authors interviewed were female, and thirty-nine percent were male. Authors' specialties ranged from historical fiction to memoirs, poetry to short stories, essays to novels. In analysing each of these interviews, I coded the writers' responses as cognitive, expressive, or social using the following definitions:

1. cognitive – the mental steps writers make in the composing process;
2. expressive – the personal or emotional connection between the writer and the text;
3. social – writer interaction with or consideration of society.

Because of the interview form, the research is essentially relying on writer self-reports.

Admittedly, there is somewhat of a disconnect from these writers and the writers we meet in undergraduate creative writing classes. I make no attempt here to compare the writing quality between those two groups. Rather, I am looking to the knowledge of professional writers who engage in the act of writing (most often daily) and have gained an impressive understanding of their processes and how to write well. They are bestsellers, Pulitzer Prize- and other award-winners, Oprah's Book Club selections, columnists, inauguration poets, and university creative writing program directors and faculty; some of their works have been optioned or developed into feature films. They hail from the

United States and from other countries around the world. They represent many backgrounds and ethnicities. Quite simply, they are writers.

Interview Talking Points

The interviews were not published in a traditional question-and-answer format. The topic prompts are simply one-word or shortly phrased talking points. There are some common themes in several of the interviews such as discussions of dialogue, humour, story ideas, writing routines, and why a writer chose a specific genre or age category; however, the pieces studied from the 'How I Write' column highlight a wider array of topics, perhaps those relevant to each writer, although that is not defined as a goal within the text itself. For instance, Gloria Chao's interview includes a section discussing 'Leaving dentistry for writing', Kristen Arnett's highlights taxidermy since it is featured in her book *Mostly Dead Things*, and Lily King's interview discusses her thoughts on 'Writing about the '90s'. Each of those sections are specific to the featured writer's books and backgrounds.

Findings

The first observation to point out from the research is that every interview was coded with each of the three rhetorics. In other words, every one of the eighteen writers references the social, the expressive, and the cognitive as part of their writerly experiences. For some writers, there was a relative balance between the three, but for others perhaps a single sentence was coded with one rhetoric, and then several paragraphs were coded in each of the other two rhetorics. It seemed that some authors' philosophies were more expressive, cognitive, or social than others. One writer might rely on her personal connection to the writing while another believes understanding of cognitive processes is imperative in quality writing. Finally, a historical novelist might have a lot to say about history and society and how it manifests in his or her work. In addition to the balance of each interview possessing some reference to each of the three rhetorics, some authors sparked a balance of the three in individual responses. For instance, under the heading of 'Combining history and creativity', medical historian Lindsey Fitzharris states:

> I call myself a storyteller first and foremost, and a historian second. Being a historian helps to enrich books and guide research, but I'm always looking for the heartbeat of the story. I see my book as a gateway into medical history—by

giving the reader a juicy story to pique their interest. I've always been creative, even going back to when I was a child. I've always had a great imagination and a morbid curiosity. Now I add the element of being a professional historian. I don't want my writing to just be didactic, but [I also want it to be] enjoyable. I want people to fall into the story.

Futterman 2019l

Fitzharris calls on the social when she identifies herself as a historian and addresses her intentions for the reader, giving them 'a juicy story to pique their interest'. She also ended the response by referencing the reader a second time. Her answer also references the emotional aspects of storytelling, noting she is 'always looking for the heartbeat of a story' and that she wants the story to be 'enjoyable', so that readers may 'fall into the story'. Finally, her response highlights cognitive aspects of creating as well when she notes 'I call myself a storyteller', and references the 'great imagination and morbid curiosity' she has always had and how they have informed her writing.

One might argue that the prompt itself created opportunity for all three rhetorics to be present in the response. Therefore, a second example can also be identified in novelist Jami Attenberg's discussion of a rather general concept of writing: setting. Under the heading for 'Setting', Attenberg responds:

I've spent a lot of time thinking about this place [New Orleans], and it's been on my mind. I knew I wanted to set a book here, but I was hesitant because I was new to the area. It took me a couple of years, because I wanted to do it justice. People are protective of this place, and so am I. There are a lot of great writers in New Orleans, but they're not necessarily writing literary commercial fiction about families set in the contemporary era. I was afraid at first to do the thing I'm good at, and then I realised it's my art and my craft – and I became ready. I had to say, 'You can do this'.

Futterman 2020b

The social is easily identified in this example when Attenberg places her concern for her community, the people who are 'protective of this place' ahead of her cognitive beliefs that she can 'do it justice'. Ultimately, the cognitive plays a role when she 'realised it's [her] art and [her] craft'. At the heart of her battle between the social and the cognitive was the expressive. She identifies this by noting, 'I was afraid at first to do the thing I'm good at'. Therefore, the writer incorporates all three rhetorics into her decision to set her novel in New Orleans. Responses like these demonstrate the interconnectedness of social, expressive, and cognitive aspects for successful writers.

Although some writer responses were balanced similarly to the aforementioned examples, many authors' philosophies on writing leaned to one of the three rhetorics. Examples of such responses are shared in the subsections below.

Cognitive Rhetoric

Award-winning and best-selling author, Lily King's responses relied primarily on cognitive references. While she noted that setting her stories in the 1990s 'felt natural' and she 'love[s] reading dialogue', even noting that she bases her decision on revising dialogue on whether it feels right, references to the emotional ended there. Likewise, King identified the growth of dialogue skills as depending on a social process of 'active listening...that comes from years of hearing people talk'. Beyond that, the writers discussed writing about the '90s; starting a new novel; dialogue, revision, and writing routine entirely in cognitive terms. Here are some examples of her cognitive references:

1. 'I think for a lot of writers, we're still taking time to getting used to very modern technology.'
2. 'I usually start with a situation that involves some sort of tension or some uncomfortable situation my character is in. I'm not exactly sure how the character will get out of it or what challenges there will be.'
3. 'Sometimes there's a certain character you didn't think would have a voice, but they wind up having a stronger voice than you can ignore.'
4. 'I think routine is 99.9% of it. I have to write in the morning, and I have to eat before I write—usually eggs. I always have a cup or two of black tea and work for as many hours as I can.' (Futterman 2020f)

Inclusion of a writer self-report such as King's in a creative writing classroom creates a space for students who rely heavily on the cognitive in their own writing processes to experience validation.

One area in the interviews that trended toward the cognitive is in the discussion of writing process. While authors at times expressed a reliance on 'the feel' of an aspect such as whether dialogue, theme, or plot are working, they emphasised the cognitive with such process aspects as: 'If I start with the character, I think about what setting will challenge her most', (Futterman 2020a); 'I always find it is helpful to read dialogue aloud. It's helpful in figuring out which moments we really need to get that close to', (Futterman 2020e); 'Part of the fun is figuring out what's going to happen...I'm a fan of throw it away and start over. I'll outline a draft I've rewritten and make changes I need to, and then rewrite it',

(Futterman 2019j); 'Because I rarely outline, I'm constantly figuring out what's next, what's next; what's my character going to do today? I've learned to recognize when it's working and when it's not' (Futterman 2019k).

These examples demonstrate how authors *think* about their work. Their reliance on the cognitive aspects of writing supports the development of their craft, especially in building routine, a crucial lesson for developing writers to learn to find success. In a creative writing classroom, we might begin a discussion on the cognitive aspects of writing by reading self-reports like those shared in *The Writer* magazine. We can prompt discussion of the cognitive attributes of students' writing with such questions as: How has your thinking about your own process changed over time? What 'thinking' steps do you follow when you begin a new project? What 'thinking' steps do you follow when you draft or revise a project? How much do you rely on 'thinking' rather than feeling or audience expectations when you write? How critical is the cognitive in your storytelling and writing processes? Even for those students who are not yet able to answer the questions, exposure to them may begin that process of embracing how their unique way of thinking contributes to their creation of written works.

Social Rhetoric

Interestingly, while medical historian Lindsey Fitzharris shared the aforementioned response to the prompt of 'Combining history and creativity', otherwise, her responses leaned heavily to the social. Fitzharris referenced the cognitive when she mentioned the need to understand and digest Victorian science and 'be less precious about things', and the expressive when identifying her work to 'become much more comfortable on camera' as part of her writer persona includes creating YouTube videos. That said, her presentation of her writing process and journey is highly focused on the social, specifically both her audience and her collaborators as demonstrated in the following examples:

1. '...[G]etting it down in an engaging way for readers was a challenge... I want them to know what it felt like and smelled like, with strong descriptive elements that readers can envision.'
6. 'If people aren't interested in something, maybe it's not something I should cover in a book.'
7. '[Writing scripts is] done with my friend, filmmaker and editor Alex Anstey. I wrote everything, and he came up with the sagas and special effects.'

8. 'I didn't think of critics when I was writing my first book because I was thinking of the poverty I was facing. I did get some criticism by academics for being too accessible and not nuanced enough. But I know my readers want a fast-paced, interesting story.' (Futterman 2019l)

Perhaps more than ever before, the publishing community places immense emphasis on the social. While literary agents may encourage authors to write stories that resonate with them, the step immediately following creation is placement; to sell a piece of writing, an audience must want to consume it. Additionally, the publishing community is more sensitive than ever to expectations of representation in literature; authors are also appropriately considerate of how a piece might unintentionally harm a community. In other words, writers are thinking about the social aspects of writing perhaps more than they ever have before, a claim that is supported in the data collected for this chapter.

Writers referenced the expectations of their audiences often. Pulitzer Prize-finalist Tommy Tomlinson shared the importance of literary agents and publishers as gatekeeper audiences:

> I sent [my agent] a bunch of book ideas that were terrible. Then I sent him some ideas that he liked. From those, I did four book proposals that didn't make it to a book. He would say, 'This is a good idea, but I can't sell it.' Publishers have to feel strongly that a book will sell before committing to it.
>
> Futterman 2019c

Elizabeth Berg incorporated the expressive and the social in her discussion of audience when she noted, 'I want my work to comfort people...I do have a lot in common with my readers. And that comforts *me*' (Futterman 2019f). Camille Acker identified her audience clearly as, 'black girls and women', but she also noted:

> if I were able to tell a good enough story, it would be able to be more universal. The situations the characters are in are situations that everyone understands— how to move forward in life, things like class and lack of economic empowerment and navigating relationships on every level. I hoped that there would be a larger audience for it but also wanted to make sure that it connected with black girls and women.
>
> Futterman 2019e

Award-winning poet Richard Blanco read his work at President Obama's second inauguration and has set a goal to 'turn metrophobes (people with a fear of poetry) into metromaniacs'. Blanco notes being 'thrust into the public world' following the inauguration, he became more aware of how his work connected with an audience. 'I felt a natural sense of thinking about civic duty as an outgrowth of that. It became not just "me" but "we," and a broader, more pluralistic way of questioning the same things' (Futterman 2020d).

The data was rich with references to audiences and other social connections as well including collaborations with authors and honouring settings that people treasure. Essentially, the social rhetorics of the writing experience recognize that a writer's process and work affects and is affected by the world around them. Developing writers can benefit from this realisation. In our classrooms, we might ask them: How often do you think about your audience when you plan and execute a writing project? How does society influence the content you are writing? How do you want to influence society with your writing? How much influence *should* your audience (agents, editors, publishers, booksellers, readers, librarians, parents of readers, etc.) have on your writerly decisions? How critical is the social in your storytelling and writing processes? All writers intending to publish will encounter interactions with the social in some way, and these questions and discussions have the potential for appropriately preparing them to navigate the interactions successfully.

Expressive Rhetoric

Art is often viewed as having the intention of evoking emotion in readers. While all of the interviews referenced the expressive, short story and essay writer Kristen Arnett's discussion emphasised it (Futterman 2019i). Like the other writers featured in these sections, Arnett references her taxidermy research as relying on the social: 'I don't have any hands-on experience, but I do have a lot of family and friends who've performed taxidermy'. Likewise, her interview highlights the cognitive when she notes, 'I have a question I'm trying to answer, but I don't want to over-structure the plot or narrative. I don't want to know what characters will do because the reader will know, I think'. Nevertheless, the expressive dominates her interview, as demonstrated in the following quotes:

1. 'There are things that happen to all of us that are bad but also kind of funny. When bad things are going on that we have to process, life is still going on around us.'
2. '*Mostly Dead Things* can skew dark: death, family dynamics, grief. That can be overwhelming, and so it was important to me to find the levity in certain situations and make sure there were bright spots with appropriate humour.'

3. 'Usually I feel a short story is complete, but it didn't feel complete with this.'
4. 'I like to be surprised and see what happens.' (Futterman 2019i)

Arnett's expression of emotion, especially humour, in her work and her interest in being surprised as an author prioritises the expressive in her process.

Trends in the data regarding expressive references include the implementation of dialogue. Elizabeth Berg notes, 'I love listening to people talk' (Futterman 2019f). Lily King explains, 'I love reading dialogue but not writing it. I love dialogue in books because I love humans communicating... I write it down, and if it doesn't feel right, I correct it a few days later' (Futterman 2020f). Peter Kispert argues that writing effective dialogue is about 'trusting yourself'. As a commonly discussed craft concept, dialogue was also discussed relative to the social (i.e. listening to others talk) and the cognitive (i.e. strategies for thinking through dialogue choices), a point that further supports the central premise of this chapter.

That said, in keeping with the structure of these subsections, strategies to encourage reflexive thinking for student-writers, creative writing instructors might ask: What aspects of your writing craft do you emotionally connect to? What aspects of craft have you developed strong enough skills in to 'feel' when something you've written is working, or not? Emotionally, what evokes emotion in you as a reader? As a writer, how can you incorporate that strategy to evoke emotion from your own readers? When you write, what emotions do you experience? How critical is the expressive in your storytelling and writing processes? To grow in the expressive aspects of their art is crucial for developing writers. Additionally, when process discussions rely on the cognitive, and student-writers experience pressure of the social, their connection to the expressive, or the emotional relevance of writing and publishing, may empower them to navigate the challenges of the writing life.

Conclusion

Among many publishing professionals the consensus is that writers should write what speaks to them. If they are truly passionate about their work, and the work is good, then it will naturally influence and speak to society as well. The downfall according to many professional writers is if there is no personal or emotional connection between the writer and the text (expressive) or an understanding of the mental steps the writers make in the composing process (cognitive), then the text's interaction with or consideration of society (social) will fail in its attempts to be powerful and influential because the writing just won't be as good as it could be.

As the research here shows, professional writers do embrace all three rhetorics, but just as some professional writers lean toward one rhetoric or another, so will some of our student-writers. Therefore, as their instructors tasked with guiding them through a small part of their writing journey, we must be cognizant first to avoid prioritising one rhetoric over another. Secondly, we must consider, as evidenced in this research, the value in writers' own voices in identifying successful strategies for their writing. An additional takeaway is that approaches to writing and publishing are more varied than we could ever quantify in a chapter of this length, or perhaps any length. By opening our thinking to our student-writers' varied approaches, strategies, interests, and styles, we are making space for them in their own writing journey. A previous criticism of writer-self reports was that writers may not be objectively aware of what they do and how they do it; perhaps a contrary question is: why must they strive for objectivity? Furthermore, isn't their subjective review of their own writing process relevant to the development of new writers? And perhaps most critically, this chapter asserts that creative writing instructors should employ writer self-reports like those analysed in this chapter as models for student-writers to reflect on their own cognitive, social, and expressive encounters with writing.

Interestingly, the claims posited in this chapter could as easily be refuted by another researcher looking to these same 'How I Write' columns; the researcher may identify a sentence coded by this research as social as in fact cognitive. Therein lies the brilliance of the argument: writers' thought processes and craft skillsets vary greatly. What one writer sees as paramount, another writer may dismiss. While one author may emphasise the social in their work, the other may lean more heavily toward the expressive. Although this researcher labelled Lindsey Fitzharris' interview as emphasising the social, a creative writing student might code the interview differently. Perhaps we should offer the student the opportunity to do just that, learning from the writer self-reports in the process.

References

Berlin, J. (2003), 'Rhetoric and Ideology in the Writing Class', in V. Villanueva (ed.) *Cross-Talk in Comp Theory*, 2nd edn, Urbana, IL: NCTE, 717–737.

Berlin, J. (1987), *Rhetoric and Reality: Writing Instruction in American Colleges, 1900–1985*, Carbondale, IL: Southern Illinois University Press.

Bizzaro, P. (2011), 'Writer's Self-Reports, (Com)positioning, and the Recent History of Academic Creative Writing', in P. Bizzaro, A. Culhane, and D. Cook (eds) *Composing Ourselves as Writer-Teacher-Writers: Starting with Wendy Bishop*, New York: Hampton Press, 119–132.
Futterman, A. (2019a), 'How I Write: Nic Stone', *The Writer*, January: 48.
Futterman, A. (2019b), 'How I Write: Stephen McCauley', *The Writer*, February: 48.
Futterman, A. (2019c), 'How I Write: Tommy Tomlinson', *The Writer*, March: 48.
Futterman, A. (2019d), 'How I Write: Craig Morgan Teicher', *The Writer*, April: 48.
Futterman, A. (2019e), 'How I Write: Camille Acker', *The Writer*, May: 48.
Futterman, A. (2019f), 'How I Write: Elizabeth Berg', *The Writer*, June: 48.
Futterman, A. (2019g), 'How I Write: Mesha Maren', *The Writer*, July: 48.
Futterman, A. (2019h), 'How I Write: Gregory Pardlo', *The Writer*, August: 48.
Futterman, A. (2019i), 'How I Write: Kristen Arnett', *The Writer*, September: 48.
Futterman, A. (2019j), 'How I Write: Shaun David Hutchinson', *The Writer*, October: 48.
Futterman, A. (2019k), 'How I Write: Elinor Lipman', *The Writer*, November: 48.
Futterman, A. (2019l), 'How I Write: Lindsey Fitzharris', *The Writer*, December: 48.
Futterman, A. (2020a), 'How I Write: Gloria Chao', *The Writer*, January: 48.
Futterman, A. (2020b), 'How I Write: Jami Attenberg', *The Writer*, February: 48.
Futterman, A. (2020c), 'How I Write: Clare Beams', *The Writer*, March: 48.
Futterman, A. (2020d), 'How I Write: Richard Blanco', *The Writer*, April: 48.
Futterman, A. (2020e), 'How I Write: Peter Kispert', *The Writer*, May: 48.
Futterman, A. (2020f), 'How I Write: Lily King', *The Writer*, June: 48.
Kent, T. (1999), *Post-Process Theory: Beyond the Writing Process Paradigm*, Carbondale, IL: Southern Illinois University Press.
Ritter, K. (2011), '"How the old man does it": The Pedagogy of Emulation in Creative Writing Programs', in P. Bizzaro, A. Culhane, and D. Cook (eds) *Composing Ourselves as Writer-Teacher-Writers: Starting with Wendy Bishop*, New York: Hampton Press, 81–96.
Vanderslice, S. (2008), 'Sleeping with Proust vs. Tinkering Under the Bonnet: The Origins and Consequences of the American and British Approaches to Creative Writing in Higher Education', in G. Harper and J. Kroll (eds) *Creative Writing Studies: Practice, Research and Pedagogy*, Clevedon, UK: Multilingual Matters, 66–74.

13

Author Platform and the Boundaries of Creative Practice

Marshall Moore
Falmouth University, UK

Introduction

It's difficult to say when I first noticed the term 'author platform' being used in the context of writing and publishing. Like many such neologisms, it gained currency insidiously. If one checks trade publications, writing-advice websites, agent websites, and Twitter, 'author platform' is now almost ubiquitous, albeit with a definition that remains difficult to pin down. From a creative practitioner's standpoint, there seems to be a great deal of urgency around it, as if one imperils one's literary career by neglecting one's author platform. A blog post about author platform by Lisa Cooper Ellison – who identifies on her website as a writer, speaker, and writing coach – serves as a good representative example: Ellison admits feelings of 'stress, obligation, fatigue, [and] overwhelm' when she 'neglect[s] her] social media accounts' (Ellison n.d.). But Ellison, like many practitioners, stops short of drawing a cause–effect relationship between author platform and writing success. The existence of this relationship is strongly implied, as if it were a given, yet the mechanics of the process are never spelled out. Taking this near-ubiquity into account, as well as the significance that is attached to author platform, it would seem to be a natural topic for creative-writing scholars to have investigated. Yet at the time of this writing, there remains very little research on the subject. A 2010 paper by Peter Clifton in *Publishing Research Quarterly* looks at various shifts in the industry with respect to how books are marketed and what is therefore expected of authors. Kim Wilkins's paper 'Writing Resilience in the Digital Age' (2014) remains the seminal examination of the subject, however, offering definitions and parameters and flagging up concerns about the toll that expectations around author platform can take on a writer: specifically, that spending hours online focusing on this ambiguous-but-essential task is detrimental to developing the stamina early-career writers need. This paucity of research means that any discussion of author platform and its implications for creative practice will need to draw from a variety of trade publications alongside the extant but limited scholarship.

When I first encountered the term, I understood it intuitively, or thought I did. If asked to define it, however, I would have struggled to articulate its nuances. I think this stems from my initial confusion over the vagueness of the term, the mandate (implicit and explicit) that writers implement it without specific guidance, and the implication that dire consequences would ensue if we were to neglect this aspect of creative practice. One reason for this, I discovered, was a propensity for industry professionals and the authors of writing-advice articles and listicles to discuss it as if it could be assumed the reader already knew what it was. For example, Clifton's 'Teach Them to Fish: Empowering Authors to Market Themselves Online' deploys the term without explaining it (2010). Similarly, in the 2014 book *Build Your Author Platform: The New Rules: A Literary Agent's Guide to Growing Your Audience in 14 Steps*, agents Carole Jellen and Mike McCallister approach the topic in precisely the same way. After a foreword from Jack Canfield, one of the co-creators of the *Chicken Soup for the Soul* franchise, about his early experiences with book promotion, Jelen and McCallister start talking about author platform… again, without actually defining it. In their preface, they largely focus on introducing themselves; in their introduction, they proceed straight to a couple of best-practice examples (on which more later). My point in focusing on these two works is not to impugn Clifton's findings or Jelen and McCallister's guidance but to highlight a problem I find both obvious and surprising: the baseline assumption in these works is that writers are expected to understand what author platform is already, and merely to need help implementing or updating it. In other words, 'it's vitally important, and here's how you do it, but we aren't going to tell you exactly what it is'.

According to publishing consultant Jane Friedman, who curates a well-regarded blog as a long-time industry insider, the term 'author platform' came into circulation during the 1990s, when 'agents and publishers began rejecting nonfiction book proposals and nonfiction manuscripts when the author lacked a "platform"' (2016). In essence, it is – or was – an umbrella term that refers to the way an author can be marketed based on their online presence and public persona. Reader expectations have a great deal to do with this, in the sense that the author is known either for being an expert on a certain subject or for writing in a certain genre. Personal identity may also play a part, in the case of a celebrity author or one who is known to the public as a spokesperson, or when a book is marketed in the pseudo-genres that exist according to the author's race, nationality, gender, sexuality, religion, and so on. My contention, however, is that even this definition is now inadequate. Author platform has, in my view, undergone four stages of evolution in the three decades since its coinage. Each of these has had its own implications for creative practice, with the current iteration being the most concerning to me as an author, publisher, and academic. In this chapter, I will discuss (briefly) my experiences with it as a practitioner, outline the way the definition of author platform has shifted over the years, survey the landscape of creative practice as it exists under the current author-platform regime, and make a few recommendations with regard to how we might manage it.

A Brief but Relevant Autobiographical Interlude

My first impressions of 'author platform' grew out of my anxiety that I'd been assigned one I didn't particularly want. As an out gay man who had written a novel and some short fiction that featured gay characters, I began to feel a certain genre claustrophobia. My editor at Haworth Press (my first publisher), put it bluntly: Haworth's imprint Harrington Park Press was a *gay press*. There would have to be partial nudity on the cover because gay readers, according to this editor (himself also a gay man), were 'just *bovine*'. Ergo, a book with a titillating cover would sell much better than what I would have greatly preferred, something tasteful, something reminiscent of eighties album covers, preferably designed by Peter Saville. Gay fiction as a genre, my editor went on to say, was like the old slogan for insecticidal roach motels in American TV commercials: 'You can check in, but you can't check out!' In essence, once you were identified with the genre, you'd never be able to publish anything else; nor would major commercial presses be interested in future manuscripts.

I had always viewed myself more as a horror writer, or horror-adjacent, occupying a grey area between that genre and literary fiction. I have known I was a writer since early childhood, and much of my self-concept accreted from what I read about the writing life in my early years. Sexual identity may be both fundamental and overarching, but is not the only aspect of a gay person's life, nor of their literary output. Author platform, therefore, seemed to represent a formalisation and perhaps a concretisation of constraints I was afraid of: *This is all that you are. This is all you will be able to write about. You must also write about it in this specific way. Mainstream success will always remain beyond your reach.* This seemed to be an attack on the deepest parts of my identity, a reduction down to one aspect of myself.

Early on in my writing career, I was prone to ranting about not wanting to be pigeonholed, not wanting to hit a glass ceiling. This wasn't unfounded paranoia, either: although the landmark research on the existence of the 'gay glass ceiling' would not be published until 2018 (Aksoy, Carpenter, Frank, and Huffman), it had long been obvious to me that it was an obstacle in publishing as well as in other areas of my professional life. Although I wouldn't go so far as to say I ruined literary cocktail parties, I might have been asked '*That again?*' in a sharp tone of voice more than once. Somewhere along the way, author platform and its attendant imperatives had seeped into my consciousness, and I began to suspect that investing some time and effort in an author-platform upgrade might give my book sales a boost. It is difficult to pinpoint what gave me the idea because the term seemed to be everywhere. Temporarily secure in my delusions of social media as the panacea for writers more people ought to read, I spent months on this endeavour: blogging, tweeting, and offering bits of writing advice. Then reality kicked in: I found the process tiresome, time-consuming, and ultimately unhelpful. Although I didn't realise it at the time, I had – however briefly – fallen into the trap of attempting to work on my author platform without having fully grasped what it was. In the years that followed, usually when I had another book coming out, I made intermittent attempts to be Relevant Online but simply never had the heart for it. Finally, because I was in Hong Kong during the 2019–2020 protests and was concerned (terrified) for my personal safety, I exited Twitter and most other forms of social media, only becoming publicly active again once I moved to the UK in 2020.

An Evolving Definition

The first phase of author platform's evolution appears to be the original usage of the term. As pointed out in Friedman, author platform in its earliest context referred mainly to nonfiction writers who were already in the public eye and would therefore be associated with a certain topic. This could take a number of forms: a thought leader or public figure such as a politician writing about their experiences and views; a celebrity writing a memoir or taking a stand on an issue of public interest; a well-known figure from the business world promoting a book (or pursuing a deal for one) as a part of a larger marketing strategy. Stephen Hawking's *A Brief History of Time*, published by Bantam in 1988, is a good early example: its success as a work of popular science stemmed from a combination of Hawking's credentials as a prominent scientist and his celebrity as a public intellectual with a significant disability. Hawking's identity may not have been the sole basis for his author platform, but it certainly either contributed or became one facet of a wider celebrity status. Jellen and McCallister point to similar examples: the *Chicken Soup for the Soul* books; Malcolm Gladwell's books *Blink*, *Outliers*, and *The Tipping Point*; Steven Levitt and Stephen Dubner's *Freakanomics* (2014: xxxix). Although there is nothing inherently wrong with or problematic about these authors and their books, this is an unattainable standard for most writers. Besides, a key distinction needs to remain clear: this is primarily a *nonfiction* phenomenon, and it predates today's social-media landscape. The salient point is that our hypothetical celebrity, public figure, or blogger already would already have an audience and an established reputation as an expert in a certain field, meaning that publishers could capitalise on (and effectively outsource without compensation) marketing work already done by other people.

Over time, this initial concept of author platform expanded to a second stage that included writers of fiction and other literary forms. There is no way to determine exactly when publishers and agents began applying the new label 'author platform' to the old idea that audiences expected writers to produce only certain types of books. This may be seen as essentially an update of or variation upon the Foucauldian notion of author function: 'the name of an author is a variable that accompanies only certain texts to the exclusion of others' (Foucault 1977: 124), albeit writ large in trade publications such as *Publisher's Weekly* as well as the popular online writing-advice websites. Under the guise of marketing themselves, writers are now encouraged/pressured to produce ancillary work (blog posts, articles, short stories, tweets, and so on) that will further play to the expectations of this hypothetical one-track-minded readership, thereby making it even more difficult to write and publish something different under one's own name due to the amount of time it takes to generate so much content (Wilkins 2014).

The third stage in the evolution – which I now believe is being eclipsed by a fourth, or already has been – differs from the second in terms of scale and predation. It encompasses any and all marketing efforts an author might make, although I perceive a twist in the definition: the term now seems intended to refer to *successful* marketing efforts (or the lure thereof), either *ex post facto* or ongoing, whereas anything that falls short of 'quit your day job' bestsellerdom amounts to little more than aspirational flailing. Clifton (2010) observes the same dynamic: because of what he calls a 'compression of time', author platform is something a writer strives to have already achieved via some arcane combination of strategic tweeting and blogging, a dedicated Facebook page, regular Instagram updates (preferably with cats), or other clever uses of social media, regular literary output, public appearances, and so forth. Thus, the aspirational becomes retroactive. As if it weren't problematic enough that the term is often applied in retrospect rather than at the outset of a writer's publishing and marketing endeavours, or several books into a career, this third version of author platform is troubling in its assumption that authors today have a great deal of time and/or money to spend on these tasks. The peril is exacerbated by the trend of major publishers dropping midlist authors whose books have failed to achieve best-seller status. This phenomenon was first documented over a decade ago (Deahl 2011) and is no less pervasive today.

The fourth, and ongoing, stage of author platform is all-pervasive: I have noticed a trend in book promotion, more on social media than in traditional trade publications, that seems to prioritise representation and online interaction with readers above the stories themselves. Moreover, there is 'a tendency in contemporary literary discourse to equate the author to the literary work produced—that the author is the work and vice versa' (Iyer 2021: 197). As a result of this shift, story and craft sometimes seem to be lower priorities than identity and social justice. This can be seen in the way some writers market their work on Twitter and elsewhere today: via bullet-point lists containing identity-specific data about the author, the characters, and the romantic or erotic aspects of the story. Are they gay, bi, pan, lesbian, straight, queer, questioning, cisgender, trans, nonbinary, genderqueer, masc, femme, monogamous, open, neurodivergent, disabled, sober? Are superpowers involved, or the supernatural? This information is given parity with more traditional basics such as genre and plot. This is not to say that representation, interaction with readers, and participation in online communities are problematic. They aren't, but this mindset posits the creative work as a form of *service*, the existence of which will somehow right social injustices, provide role models for those who lack them in real life, and/or make readers from marginalised communities feel valued and seen. Although there is no doubt creative work *can* serve this purpose over and above its inherent *raisons d'etre* to entertain and inform, this new paradigm seems to treat the potentiality I discuss here as an imperative. Putting the cart before the horse, in other words; or, in academese, a perilous reframing of what creative written work is *for*, as if the process of promotion – perhaps the pursuit of celebrity? – is now the goal and the creative work has been recast as merely one aspect of the content today's creative practitioners may be expected to produce.

The Landscape Is Changing

Creative practice happens at the intersection of what the practitioner imagined the writing (or whatever other art form may be applicable) life would look like and the entangled realities of jobs, families, and other quotidian responsibilities. But where marketing – author platform – is concerned, fiction writers today are still struggling with the standards established by several early successes: E. Lynn Harris famously self-published his first novel *Invisible Life*, sold it out of his car, and took copies to beauty salons and barber shops around Atlanta. The buzz he generated by doing this led, in time, to a publishing deal with Doubleday (Aaron 2021). Amanda Hocking enjoyed remarkable success starting in 2010 with her YA fantasy novels. She made connections with book bloggers, who were becoming a collective force in book marketing then, and she was an early adopter of e-books, charging US$0.99 for first books of the series she would go on to write (Millar 2011). Hugh Howey adopted a similar approach with his novella *Wool*, which went on to sell millions as an e-book and was subsequently acquired (in a paperback deal only; Howey retained his electronic rights) by Simon & Schuster (*Wired* 2013). John Scalzi self-published his early work on his own website and employed a voluntary payment scheme. He has since gone on to a multimillion-dollar book deal with Tor (Liptak 2017). Christopher Paolini penned his debut novel *Eragon* in his teens. His parents, who owned and ran a small press, supported him by financing not only a print run of books but an extensive book tour. As a result of this substantial publicity, the novelist Carl Hiassen's stepson discovered *Eragon* in a bookstore and enjoyed it so much that Hiassen introduced Paolini to his editors at Knopf (Spring 2004).

In each case, these authors set or modified a standard for author marketing in fiction. However, each was in the right place at the right time with the right book in some unique way: Harris was writing about Black gay professionals at a time when major publishers were largely ignoring the Black middle class. Hocking had the benefit of excellent timing, being one of the first to see the potential of (and be championed by) book bloggers. Moreover, she was working in a genre that lent itself well to the e-book format, and her pricing scheme made her work accessible to loyal, story-hungry younger readers. Howey and Scalzi both benefited from similar strategies involving pricing and active engagement online.

Paolini had preternaturally supportive parents with relevant industry experience, then got lucky by meeting an established author who helped him get his big break. Although each of these writers managed to find remarkable success, the conditions under which they did so are not necessarily replicable, a point publishers seem to overlook when they set out their demands for more of the same.

These standards and expectations were very much in place when Wilkins documented them in 2014, writing of being instructed by her publisher to spend hours producing blog posts, reviews, and all manner of other ancillary material to support a new book, and they remain in force today. If anything, the landscape is even more onerous, particularly when an unwary author discovers or is encouraged to adopt the '80/20 model', which Ewan Morrison warns about in an article in *The Guardian* (2012). Adherents of the 80/20 model encourage writers to spend 80 per cent of their time on marketing and only 20 per cent of their time on the writing itself. How is a writer supposed to develop their craft – to say nothing of getting actual books written – while labouring under such a draining, distracting, counterproductive edict? This assumes the author even has time in the first place. According to a 2018 study by CREATe, the UK Copyright & Creative Economy Centre, '[t]he top 10 percent of writers still earn about 70% of total earnings in the profession', but the average annual income for a professional writer is only about £16,000 (Kretschmer, Gavaldon, Miettinen, and Singh 2019). From this, it may be inferred that most working writers have day jobs. There are also family responsibilities to take into account, the burden of which disproportionately affects women. Thus, writers who have long, unbroken stretches of time to work are the exception, not the rule. This is not even the worst version of the writing/marketing balance that can be found online. In a 2016 article in *The Guardian*, Ros Barber warns that '[i]f you self-publish your book, you are not going to be writing for a living. You are going to be marketing for a living. Self-published authors should expect to spend only 10% of their time writing and 90% of their time marketing'. It is as if these so-called marketing experts have either forgotten how much time writing takes, or they have never known in the first place. Experienced writers and writing instructors may know that recommendations such as these are not to be taken completely seriously, but the problem is that they are now part of the mythology that surrounds writing and, as Stephen North has immortalised himself in CW scholarship for pointing out, therefore difficult or impossible to expunge (1987).[1]

I would go so far as to suggest that this packaging of identity with promotion and a constant hustle is partly a response to this pressure from publishers and agents: writers are exhorted to be 'authentic' on social media, to produce content that offers value to potential followers. The self is the only constant. But what is rarely made clear in these exhortations that an author develop their platform is the issue of *focus*. There is, of course, such a thing as tweeting or blogging well. As Gilly Smith puts it,

> In the [I]nternet era, the process of writing has moved from notebooks and post-its scattered on the sitting-room floor to posts on a blog, chronicles of a creative process for anyone to engage with. A modern author needs to be able to test ideas in public, to hold them up for scrutiny and twist and turn them until they make sense. For... would-be writers, the shaping and re-shaping of ideas is an essential skill and involves taking risks if those ideas are to push at the boundaries and spawn original thought.
>
> 2010: 283

But this requires would-be writers to understand what various social-media platforms are actually for, how they work, and how to attract suitable followers/readers/audiences. This kind of thing might be taught in digital marketing programs or modules, but it is not a body of knowledge a typical writer may reasonably be expected to know. It also assumes that having more followers will lead to more sales, which is patently not the case. Certain platforms lend themselves better to certain types of work, but advocates of cultivating an author platform tend either to omit discussing these nuances or appear not to know much about them either. An author who has not done this background layer of research may end up investing countless hours attempting to cultivate an online presence but simply be tweeting, blogging, or posting random images on Instagram to little or no avail. Alternatively, from a pedagogical standpoint, a writing instructor may assume their students are already 'digital natives' and do not need lessons on anything pertaining to the Internet. However, this is an area that is being challenged as well, with 'digital wisdom' having emerged as a theme within education as a suggested approach (Prensky 2009). Ultimately, this unprocessed advocacy of author platform treats all forms of written work as if they are the same. It is disingenuous to imply, even by omission, that a fiction writer who may have sold two short stories and is now searching for a literary agent or shopping their debut novel needs to aspire to the same platform that, say, a prominent politician, scientist, or religious leader already has. I would even argue that it is unethical to do so. Industry professionals ought to understand the difference, as well as the concomitant marketing-related expectations, but purveyors of author-platform advice seem to be operating on the lucrative assumption that writers do not. Both parties create and support a vicious cycle in which writers pressure *themselves* and the publishing industry capitalises on it.

In essence, this incessantly discussed but little-examined mandate around constant promotion and commodification of identity is, in my view, disrupting the very boundaries of creative practice. If a writer is expected to spend upwards of 80 per cent of their time on marketing and promotion, what then is the creative work? The promotion, cultivation, and curation of an online persona; the hustle; or the novel itself? Is the story still a story, or is it first and foremost a vehicle for advocacy and public empathy? Do we need to rethink why creative work exists and what purpose(s) it should serve? Under this regime, is the writer still a writer? Or should we rebrand ourselves as 'content creators' and embrace the nihilism of it all? This is actually not a game of semantics, it's a sincere ontological question for the field.

Conclusions and Recommendations

The notion of author platform is not going to go away. Nor should it; not completely. In this case, the situation is complicated because author platform technically *does* work, at least where specific types of books and writers are concerned. It is not the panacea it has been made out to be, not least because it is such an ambiguous concept, but it is not without worth. What are we to do about it, then? One priority needs to be a sense of clarity around what author platform is and is not. For a nonfiction author who can genuinely claim to have a platform of the first type I described, particularly if some facet of their identity is a key component of the resulting author platform (and they are okay with that), there may not be a problem. Most likely, other aspects of their professional life have created an audience for any book(s) that might result; the marketing work has been done and/or is ongoing; there may well be a robust online presence or a recognisable public persona. For the rest of us, however, the poets and fiction writers and memoirists and playwrights, the way forward is not as obvious because this is a gatekeeping matter: it is the publishers who have shunted marketing responsibilities back onto authors, not a dereliction of duties for which authors ourselves were once primarily responsible. We need to be clear on the fact that there is a difference between being asked to take up a reasonable portion of the marketing duties and being asked to pursue social-media omnipresence as a(nother) full-time job. This is an industry-related issue, and it is more reasonable to suggest that author organisations attempt to push back against publishers than it is for individual authors to make sacrifices in hopes of making progress toward the greater good.

Those of us who teach on creative writing programs need to be clear on these nuances, for ourselves as well as our students. In a workshop-based program, the messages a student is likely to receive are encouragements to focus on craft, to learn to read one's own work, to edit ruthlessly, to read widely, to develop a network of supportive fellow writers. British CW programs typically have an industry-facing mandate and mentality, so matters such as the selection of markets and the etiquette of submission are more likely to be part of the curriculum here than might be the case in their American counterparts (Vanderslice 2011). Conversely, what a hypothetical student will be told *outside* of the classroom (or its online equivalent) is that it is essential to spend more time marketing the work than actually writing it, all in the service of developing this mythical author platform which will then open the doors to literary excellence and undying fame. At best, this makes no sense. At worst, this is where we see author platform becoming detrimental. This is not just a disconnect in the messages that one may encounter in the writing/publishing world: the latter militates against the former; the cart is again being put before the horse. Author platform is offered up almost as a *substitute* for craft, a stance which ought to concern practitioners and educators very much. After all, if students come to believe that the process is actually 80 per cent marketing and only 20 per cent craft and mechanics (or, worse, 90/10!), where is the logic in formally studying writing? What did all those student loans for MAs/MFAs (and, increasingly, PhDs) actually pay for?

Collective action may be part of the solution, whether via networks of writers or professional organisations. The Society of Authors (UK) and the Authors Guild (US) both offer a variety of position papers and advice guides, but their focus is generally on contract terms and the professional ethics of publishing, not on the problems associated with author platform. The Australian Society of Authors leans in and takes a different approach, offering a course via Zoom titled 'Boost Your Author Profile with Google' (Ellison, S. n.d.). A reasonable starting point might be to lobby organisations such as these to develop institutional guidance and recommendations rather than accepting author platform as if it cannot and should not be challenged.

Ultimately, my argument is about resisting some of the groupthink that exists in the writing/publishing world. Author platform has become a popular idea, and why not? Author-services companies have monetised it (or weaponised it, depending on one's budget and perspective), and publishers have benefited, in some cases attempting to mitigate their own financial consequences with clawbacks of advances paid to authors whose books either didn't perform or never appeared (Dugdale 2016). There is little incentive for the industry to change. After all, with lower expenditures on marketing as well as on advances, this arrangement is indisputably advantageous to these parties. At the same time, it creates an untenable double jeopardy for practitioners. Not every writing student will go on to pursue publication, but many will, and these writers will inevitably encounter the scenarios I have discussed. Properly understood and utilised, author platform is a useful way to conceptualise the intersection of author marketing and reader/audience expectations. However, in the longer term, this trend of author platform becoming inextricably interpellated with creative work – or, worse, becoming the end instead of the means – cannot possibly be sustainable.

Notes

1 It should also be pointed out that in *The Making of Knowledge in Composition*, North referred to this body of shared knowledge as lore. In 'Toward a Unified Field: The Complications of Lore and Global Context', however, Stephanie Vanderslice argues that there is a distinction between lore and mythology, the latter being the more problematic of the two (2020). As one of the co-editors of the book in which the Vanderslice chapter was published, I am more than happy to support her view.

References

Aaron, D. (2021), 'E. Lynn Harris & Me: Novelist Rashid Darden Reflects on the Legacy of *Invisible Life* Author', *The Reckoning* (9 February). Available online: https://www.thereckoningmag.com/
the-reckoning-blog/e-lynn-harris-amp-me-novelist-rashid-darden-reflects-on-the-legacy-of-invisible-life-author#gs.dflw32 (accessed 29 September 2022).

Aksoy, C. G., Carpenter, C. S., Frank, J., and Huffman, M. L. (2018), 'Gay Glass Ceilings: Sexual Orientation and Workplace Authority in the UK' IZA Institute of Labor Economics Discussion Paper Series (May). Available online: https://docs.iza.org/dp11574.pdf (accessed 29 September 2022).

Barber, R. (2016), 'For Me, Traditional Publishing Means Poverty. But Self-Publish? No Way', *The Guardian* (21 March). Available online: https://www.theguardian.com/books/booksblog/2016/mar/21/for-me-traditional-publishing-means-poverty-but-self-publish-no-way (accessed 29 September 2022).

Canfield, J. (2014), 'Foreword', *Build Your Author Platform: The New Rules: A Literary Agent's Guide to Growing Your Audience in 14 Steps*. Dallas: BenBella Books: xxv–xxxiii.

Clifton, P. (2010), 'Teach Them to Fish: Empowering Authors to Market Themselves Online', *Publishing Research Quarterly*, 26(2): 106–109.

Deahl, R. (2011), 'Whither the Midlist Publisher?' *Publisher's Weekly* (4 November). Available online: https://www.publishersweekly.com/pw/by-topic/industry-news/publisher-news/article/49398-whither-the-midlist-publisher.html (accessed 29 September 2022).

Dugdale, J. (2016), 'Pay-Back Time for Publishers: Authors Forced to Return Their Advances', *The Guardian Books Blog*, (2 September). Available online: https://www.theguardian.com/books/booksblog/2016/sep/02/pay-back-time-for-publishers-authors-advances (accessed 23 March 2018).

Ellison, L. C. (n.d.), 'Do You Cringe When You Hear the Words "Author Platform?" You're Not Alone'. Available online: https://lisacooperellison.com/do-you-cringe-when-you-hear-the-words-author-platform-youre-not-alone/ (accessed 29 September 2022).

Ellison, S. (n.d.), 'Boost Your Author Profile with Google', Australian Society of Authors. Available online: https://www.asauthors.org/events/category/boost-your-author-profile-with-google-100 (accessed 29 September 2022).

Foucault, M. (1977), 'What Is an Author?' in D. F. Bouchard (ed.) *Language, Counter-Memory, Practice: Selected Essays and Interviews*. Ithaca, NY: Cornell University Press, 113–138.

Friedman, J. (2016), 'A Definition of Author Platform', Jane Friedman Official Website (25 July). Available online: https://www.janefriedman.com/author-platform-definition/ (accessed 29 September 2022).

Gladwell, M. (2000), *The Tipping Point*. Boston: Little, Brown.

Gladwell, M. (2005), *Blink*. Newy York: Little, Brown (Back Bay Books).

Gladwell, M. (2008), *Outliers*. New York: Little, Brown.

Hawking, S. (1988), *A Brief History of Time*. New York: Bantam.

Iyer, S. (2021), 'Cosmopolitan Creative Writing Pedagogies: First-Person Plural and Writing/Teaching Against Offence', in D. Whetter (ed.) *Teaching Creative Writing in Asia*, Abingdon, UK: Routledge, 188–206.

Jelen, C. and McCallister, M. (2014) *Build Your Author Platform: The New Rules: A Literary Agent's Guide to Growing Your Audience in 14 Steps*. Dallas: BenBella Books.

Kretschmer, M., Gavaldon, A.A., Miettinen, J., and Singh, S. (2019), 'UK Authors' Earnings and Contracts 2018: A Survey of 50,000 Writers' CREATe: UK Copyright & Creative Economy Centre. Available online: https://www.create.ac.uk/uk-authors-earnings-and-contracts-2018-a-survey-of-50000-writers/ (accessed 29 September 2022).

Levitt, S. D. and Dubner, S. J. (2005), *Freakanomics: A Rogue Economist Explores the Hidden Side of Everything*. New York: William Morrow.

Liptak, A. (2017), 'Sci-fi Author John Scalzi on the Future of Publishing: "I Aspire to Be a Cockroach"', *The Verge* (22 March). Available online: https://www.theverge.com/2017/3/22/14934064/john-scalzi-the-collapsing-empire-old-mans-war-interview (accessed 29 September 2022).

Millar, S. (2011), 'How a Failed Author Made $2 Million from E-books', *Toronto Star* (3 March). Available online: https://www.thestar.com/entertainment/books/2011/03/03/how_a_failed_author_made_2_million_from_ebooks.html (accessed 29 September 2022).

Morrison, E. (2012), 'Why Social Media Isn't the Magic Bullet for Self-Epublished Authors', *The Guardian* (30 July). Available online: https://www.theguardian.com/books/2012/jul/30/tweet-about-cats-just-write (accessed 29 September 2022).

North, S. (1987), *The Making of Knowledge in Composition: Portrait of an Emerging Field*, Portsmouth, NH: Boynton/Cook Publishers (Heinemann Educational Books, Inc.).

Prensky, M. (2009), 'H. Sapiens Digital: From Digital Immigrants and Digital Natives to Digital Wisdom', *Innovate: Journal of Online Education* 5(3). Available online: https://www.learntechlib.org/p/104264/ (accessed 16 September 2018).

Smith, G. (2010), 'Blogging and the Creative Process', *Journal of Media Practice* 11(3): 281–87

Spring, K. (2004), 'Elf and Efficiency', *The Guardian* (25 January). Available online: https://www.theguardian.com/books/2004/jan/25/booksforchildrenandteenagers.features (accessed 29 September 2022).

Vanderslice, S. (2011), *Rethinking Creative Writing in Higher Education: Programs and Practices That Work*, Wicken, UK: Professional and Higher.

Vanderslice, S. (2020), 'Toward a Unified Field: The Complications of Lore and Global Context', in M. Moore and S. Meekings (eds) *The Place and the Writer: International Intersections of Teacher Lore and Creative Writing Pedagogy*, London: Bloomsbury: 1–14.

Wilkins, K. (2014), 'Writing Resilience in the Digital Age', *New Writing: International Journal for the Practice and Theory of Creative Writing* 11(1): 67–76.

Wired (2013), 'Hugh Howey Goes From Bookstore Clerk to Self-Publishing Superstar', (4 April). Available online: https://www.wired.com/2013/04/geeks-guide-hugh-howey/ (accessed 29 September 2022).

14

Navigating Academia as a Couple, as Parents, as Writers

Stephanie and John Vanderslice
University of Central Arkansas, USA

Anyone who works in the academy knows that, far from the abstracted, lazy professor cliché, college instructors work like dogs. If you are reading this book, chances are you know this better than anyone. It's not just the teaching, of course, but the committee meetings, the academic advising, the task forces, the assessment reports, the thesis advising, and the non-required-but-required night-time events. Trying to fit creative writing on top of all that, God knows, can be very challenging. But raising a family at the same time adds a whole other level of difficulty. We have managed this demanding juggling act – finding and holding tenure-track jobs, writing and publishing books, and finally earning promotions to full professor – but not without challenges along the way, and not without significant help. The good news is this: If you think that your professional or writing life will suffer by either having children or keeping engaged with them, we can assure you that that is the farthest thing from the truth. Or, at least, the farthest thing from our truth. However, it required a lot of strategising and true partnership. For anyone daring to make the same lifestyle choice we did, we offer this how-to list, presented as a discussion, on getting through it all with your sanity and your artistic self intact, and, at least in our case, with no small amount of joy.

But first: why the narrative format? In part, because this is how we roll. John has written scholarship on John Milton, George Herbert, and Walt Whitman as well as creative nonfiction and novels. Stephanie has been writing crossover scholarship since the aughts. We believe that one way creative writer/scholars can influence academic scholarship is by expanding the field's idea of it to include other forms. In fact, Stephanie's book, *Rethinking Creative Writing* alternates chapters between scholarly writing and narrative writing and her earliest piece of scholarship was a critique of the masculinist bias of John Gardner's creative writing how-to books through the lens of Miriam Brody's *Manly Writing: Gender, Rhetoric and the Rise of Composition*. Consequently, she has long believed that, as Elizabeth Flynn notes in 'Composing as a Woman', summarising the research of Belenky et. al., a false dichotomy exists valuing the traditional, abstract, and impersonal as 'male' and personal, interpersonal, and emotional as 'female' (1988). Rather, her crossover scholarship supports Adrienne Rich's recommendation in 'Taking Women Students Seriously' that to 'think like a woman in a man's world means thinking critically, refusing to accept the givens, making connections between facts and ideas which men have left unconnected… and means constantly retesting hypotheses against *lived experience*' (emphasis ours) (Rich 1979).

While Rich speaks to gendered differences in how different people think about a subject critically, a broad framework in which to consider her argument, and a framework that applies to our essay – one written by both a man and a woman – is that of traditional authoritarian/impersonal truth-making, and an individualised, experience-based truth-making, the latter, we are inclined to think, ultimately carrying more credence exactly for being based on life and world and body. Also, hopefully, a truth not just more credible but of more direct use to the reader. Indeed, in providing a narrative of our joint experience as creatives in academia, we believe we can best reflect our particular background as writers and parents and professors in a way that might act as a kind of Ariadne's thread for others navigating their own experiences. As Candace Spiegelman suggests in 'Argument and Evidence in the Case of the Personal', the 'telling of stories can actually serve the same purposes as academic writing', as 'stories and examples have always been woven into successful arguments' (2001). That is, 'all forms of the personal can serve political, social or cultural purposes' (2001). In other words, in a patriarchal/authoritarian society, the personal is political. Politics aside, however, for a window into the efforts of one particular pair of writers/parents to lead productive creative lives (we have 11 published books between us) in the academia of the early twenty-first century, read on for our unsolicited, but we like to think useful, list of life-management strategies.

Lean into your Natural Writing Time – Hard.

JV I've always been an early riser – famously beating my siblings awake by many hours every Christmas morning – but the dual challenges of work and family forced me to make use of the early morning hours such as I never had previously. While I was earning my PhD there were days so loaded with work that I would, on occasion, set my alarm at 4:30am and get a jump on my responsibilities. Notice that I said 'on occasion'. Once our first son came along – and especially after he reached the age of one – what used to be occasional became by necessity completely regular. As he was an early riser himself, the only way I could possibly get any creative writing done, at a time of day when I felt mentally fresh, was to wake up even earlier than he did. He might have been a busy kid, but I was a stubborn adult. I set that alarm, and as soon as I had a cup of coffee in hand, I moved to my writing desk and wrote as best as I could before I heard the tell-tale complaining noises from his crib. I would stop what I was doing and bring him to Stephanie, who would cuddle with him in our bed for a bit, but at that point I knew I only had minutes remaining to get anything done. Very quickly, our son would turn into the smiling and charming but exhausting Energizer Bunny he would stay for the rest of the day, and I would take him back for another hour or two so she could get more sleep. But I knew I was on the clock as soon as I got out of bed. I had frightfully little time to accomplish anything. I think that sense of urgency kept me efficient.

SV So I was the night-time parent and John was the morning parent, and it has been ever thus. As you can see from his description, rising early is his circadian rhythm and rising later – and slowly – is mine. While some might think our circadian differences would be problematic, it's actually made a positive difference in my own life that I was partnered with someone who could hold down the fort while I came to consciousness every day (I am not joking; it has always taken me a good half hour and two cups of coffee to wake up, something that has only gotten worse with age). John also stayed home and taught part time, nights, for several years while our children were young. So when I got home from a day at work, I picked up child duty as I waved goodbye to my partner, setting off for his night class.

I have always done my writing first, before teaching or anything else, in coffee shops or libraries (mostly) and in my office (occasionally – there are usually too many interruptions) during the day, capitalising on this time as the most optimal for writing. I responded to papers and prepped for class at night after my kids were asleep, because I knew that during this time, I was not juiced enough for writing but had enough bandwidth for other tasks. I knew I could still be a good teacher this way – and I have been; ask any of my students. But like John, my first best energy went to my writing. Several of these early years were before the advent of social media, so I really *was* able to concentrate. Since around 2007, however, like a lot of us, I've struggled to stay off the near-narcotic fixes that are whatever is happening on Facebook or Twitter. Fortunately, our kids were older by then and needed us less. So I had more time to struggle through – and to protect. Here is where apps that keep you off social media, like Freedom, can really help. I can't recommend them enough.

More than that though, I cannot stress enough that you must block out and protect your writing time *strategically*, especially from those who love to schedule meetings (usually because meetings help them avoid their own work). I tried hard to advocate in my department that if meetings were to be had, it would be best for all of us if they could be regularly scheduled so that we could block out regular time for our work. For example, in my department, creative writers meet every other Wednesday at 2pm to discuss program business. Beyond these meetings I can plan for, if an impromptu meeting comes up during my writing blocks, unless it is an obvious emergency, I tell the schedulers, 'I'm sorry, I can't come then. I have an appointment.' Get used to saying this when you are asked to do anything during your writing time, either on campus or off. You DO have an appointment. With your work. Unfortunately, you probably don't want to be any more specific than that, because we all know there are plenty of people who don't think writing counts as work, both inside and outside academia.

Choose your Supervisors Carefully

JV That section heading is at least half-facetious because, of course, most of the time you can't choose your own supervisor. So maybe a better heading would be 'Get lucky on your supervisor.' We were very lucky with ours. At least the supervisor we found when we were both freshly minted PhDs, starting our post-doctoral teaching careers. At the time, we had no idea how lucky we were. (But boy did we learn that later on.) Our first department chair was not only an experienced and able administrator – very pro-faculty – but, wonder of wonders, he was also a committed family man who understood and respected the seriousness we brought to this business of parenting. Almost without our asking – in fact, it may very well have been his suggestion – he assigned us alternating class schedules so that one of us could always be home with our children in the early years. Now, for the first two years of our employment at the university, this was not much of a burden for him, because I was teaching part-time as an adjunct and spending most of my waking hours at home (or elsewhere) with our son. Giving me a class or two that did not conflict with Stephanie's schedule as a full-time faculty member was hardly an onerous task. It's a small thing for a department chair to pull off. But not every department chair would. And it paid big dividends for us as a family, both literally and figuratively. For the first two years of our son's life, he did not need to be placed in daycare, which saved us a great deal of money, money that given our paltry salaries we really didn't have. Again, not every administrator would take care of his faculty in this way, but our chair was more than willing. As the years went on, he proved himself to be an excellent chair for many other reasons, but this one favour he bestowed we will forever remember with gratitude.

SV We were lucky, but we also made trade offs. We did not set our sights on working at a Research 1 institution that might have been less family-friendly (but, in retrospect, also compensated us more or provided more release time for research), or to live anywhere near our families on the East Coast, in places where it might have been too costly to get by in terms of not just money but also time. Having spent the early '90s in Northern Virginia, we knew that congested places, where it took an hour to travel five miles from an expensive apartment to campus and find equally expensive parking, were not where we wanted to raise families and have a creative life. There was almost no traffic in our small college town, so trading off kids and going back and forth to work took little out of the day. The cost of living was also substantially lower – including housing, food, and preschool – and the pace of life was slower – which paid great dividends both for our family and our writing lives. This ended up costing something later. We both have higher teaching loads then most of our colleagues elsewhere. And working in the South, we do not enjoy union protections and face the usual stresses of being 'blue in a red state'. But living here did allow us both maximum creativity and family time in the early years.

Think Creatively About Daycare

JV Almost everyone uses daycare. Almost everyone must. And the day finally came when we needed to as well. After two years at the university, I was hired into a full-time position. That was great. No more adjuncting. But it also meant both a higher teaching load and more non-teaching responsibilities. I couldn't avoid meetings anymore! Our chair was still willing to give Stephanie and me opposing schedules, but the idea that one of us could always be home with our son just wasn't practicable. For most of us, the right, in fact only, decision in this situation is to make use of a private full-time daycare facility. And thank heaven for them. (Some colleges and universities actually offer daycare to faculty, but not ours and probably not all that many. At least not in the United States.) We would have done just that, but then we heard about a wonderful and caring woman who looked after kids in her home during the day. This was what we eventually decided on. We enjoyed the flexibility this option allowed. We could send our son there one day a week or five. We could send him for more days one week and less the next. The combination of opposite schedules and an in-home daycare situation meant that as I was moving from a part-time position to a full-time one, I could maximise the time available to be with our son and still tend to the basic responsibilities of my profession and, importantly, my creative work. Best of all was that our son could move from one home to a different home and back again.

By the time our second son came along, this particular woman no longer carried out in-home daycare. But in her place, another opportunity presented itself. We had befriended a young woman who worked for a while as a waitress at a restaurant we frequented who was always especially solicitous towards our children. We knew this young woman was a student at the university and had just quit working at the restaurant. Stephanie tracked down her phone number and called her to ask if she had ever done childcare, and if yes, if she might like to come to our house a few days a week and look after our youngest. Thankfully, she had provided childcare before and was open to the idea (especially the idea that she could do schoolwork during his naps); even better, we found a way to arrange our childcare needs around her class schedule. I don't know if that kind of arrangement can happen everywhere, but it happened for us. By the time the next school year started, when this caregiver had to move on, we learned of another woman – in this case a mother in her early thirties, the daughter-in-law of another faculty member – who took in kids at her house. So that became our son's daycare situation for a few days a week during his third year of life.

That we were able to arrange these varied alternative childcare solutions still strikes me as amazingly fortuitous. We were indeed lucky to have the ability to do that. Most people don't. But, then again, there may be more options out there than appear at first glance. I guess the message here is to think broadly and seek out whatever childcare situation that makes the most sense for your writing and work life. Doing so will go a long way to helping you feel free to advance in your writing and teaching careers. And it will make you feel more at peace as a parent.

I remember something someone told me many years ago: If the parents are less stressed, the kids are less stressed. Keep that as your mantra in regards to daycare. Whatever gives you less stress – whatever that childcare decision that is – is probably the best option for your family and your writing life.

SV   The bottom line is, finding child care is extremely challenging, as is paying for it. But because, as faculty, we were able to juggle our schedules so that we could have more flexible, in-home childcare in the very early years, we saved the cost of full-time 9–5 care, we were individually able to spend more time with our kids, and we were still able to keep to a writing schedule, we all benefited as a family. I'm not going to lie – during the very early years, that is, our youngest's first three years, we might not have been *as* prolific during this circus act. But once the youngest hit preschool our schedules ironed out in ways we could count on from then on. We learned to maximise the time our kids were *in school* as our writing time so we could focus on parenting when they were home (and, for me, prepping for class after they went to bed). We had a certain amount of hours to work and we made the most of it.

Bring the Kids Along!

JV   We learned this one early and by necessity. When our children were young, we lived over a thousand miles from the East Coast, where we were both raised, and where our families still lived. We had no nearby relatives we could call on in a pinch. Thus, when it came to writing conferences and other out-of-town academic activities we faced a drastic choice: either don't go or bring the kids with us. We brought the kids.

Sure, sometimes only one of us participated in the activity, but rather than exclude one parent from the lives of his or her children for three or four days, or strand the other one without help, we chose instead to travel with our children. The number of conferences they 'attended' – being strolled about in the corridors, being walked to nearby play areas or museums, hanging out in hotel rooms, busying themselves in lobbies – are too many to number. On one occasion, when our oldest was just a toddler, we had just moved to the state and knew not a single babysitter, we went to a meeting of the Arkansas Philological Association at which we were on the same panel and explained that we had hoped that one of us could wrangle the toddler in the hall while the other was speaking. Upon hearing this, a kind professor, himself both a father and grandfather, who I would later learn had a state-wide reputation for his generosity, offered to mind our toddler in the hallway outside a meeting room so we both could participate in the session. I guess that might sound like a risky thing to allow, but you will just have to accept that this fellow was, and still is, eminently trustworthy.

We didn't just do this for conferences either. For the summer of 2001, both Stephanie and I were accepted as faculty for a five-week program our university offered in the Netherlands. We eagerly embraced the opportunity and, as usual, brought our boys. It proved to be an unforgettable experience. Not only were we able to explore the Netherlands, but we travelled to Brussels, Paris, and Liège as well. I can't say that travelling overseas with children did not present its own unique challenges – here is an experience of our older son's anxious acting out on a train from Amsterdam to Delft that in the moment had us worried about causing an international incident – but having the kids with us opened up the countries and cities we visited in ways that otherwise we would not have known. And it allowed us to go.

SV I should add, there were, in fact, a few conferences where one of our parents met us in a particular city and helped us out. And I've noticed, more recently, an uptick in grandparents at these conferences which seems like a great idea all around. Certainly, bringing our kids along to conferences had many benefits. Chief among them was that we could still enjoy time as a family in the evenings and our children would come to understand that work was important for *both* of us. So important that we each put in extra effort to help the other parent in making it happen – whether in Disney World (yes, I had a conference in Disney World once) or Milwaukee or in our own hometown.

I was six months pregnant with our second child when we were interviewed for the Netherlands experience. 'You sure you want to do this', the senior faculty interviewing us asked. 'Bring your kids along while you're trying to shepherd college students around Europe?'

'Of course', we told him. We brought our kids everywhere. What was five thousand extra miles?

'Fair enough', he said. 'When my kids were young we were dorm parents. It actually worked out pretty well'.

Sure, there were some hitches in the adventure. The baby, for example, was nine months old but not walking yet – so after we returned, I quickly revised my stance on travelling with children to either travelling with infants or with those who were mobile. Carrying a 25-pound kid around Europe is not for the faint of heart.

But we'd still do it again. First, because it was another chance to bond as a family and as a couple. And second and importantly, the experience opened up worlds to us for our writing. John had an epiphany in the Van Gogh museum that eventually led to a novel on Van Gogh in Arles, years later (and more visits to France, which became a subject in a current novel of mine). I had experiences writing and teaching writing in Europe that I couldn't have had any other way, experiences that wouldn't have happened if I said, 'sorry, we have kids, we can't do that'.

Keep your Perspective

SV I've already pointed out that we both had to protect our best time for writing, leaving the rest, especially evenings, for other work-related tasks. This remains my number one strategy, even now that we are empty nesters. In fact, working on this chapter now is my first task of the day, while a long list of other tasks – course preparation, program administration – awaits. This is not only because writing requires my best energy, but because the other tasks are numerous enough that they could expand to completely take over the day if I let them, crowding out my writing life until there was nothing left. In some ways, it would also be easier to let them take over because it's easier to get bogged down in administrative minutiae that you can check off a list than to do the kind of wool-gathering that creative work requires. And so I remain ever-vigilant against becoming known for how fast I answer an email. I have too much to say across genres: scholarly essays, fiction, creative nonfiction. Finally, I know that if I don't write, my mental health will suffer.

However: Until recently, I protected my writing time by burning the candle at both ends and here mistakes were made. If I wrote 'too much' for one day, or several days, then I would end up doing a lot of extra course prep and administrative work to make up for most of the weekend. Teaching and administrative tasks that were daunting because of those high teaching loads. For years I laboured under the misguided assumption that if I kept churning out the publications in enough volume, eventually my institution would give in and do what others had done: lower the course load a bit for faculty who were more prolific. Maybe a 4/3 or a 3/3? After all, administration had dangled this prospect before us plenty of times, convening committees to investigate workloads, proposing research vs. teaching positions, and even proposing another promotional rung beyond full professor, an endowed professorship that might 'earn' a course release for a few years. Surely, the fact that external evaluations of our MFA program had pointed out that we had an *unusually high* course load for graduate faculty, and that we were *extremely prolific* for these courseloads, might actually mean something to someone. Something would have to give, right?

JV It's worth noting that these administrative tasks, and the temptation to engage constantly in them – including the expectations of some colleagues and various university administrations that we would do so – only became worse the longer we were employed in higher education and the more independent our children became. In some ways, when our kids were young the fact that they were young acted as a kind of natural buffer, one that limited how much time was available to us to delve into minutiae. After your writing time, your family time, and your teaching time, how much time is available, anyway? But as readers of this book know too well, the university is merciless in making time demands upon faculty, and as our kids got older, took on their own lives, and eventually went away to college, the danger of losing time to smaller administrative tasks, meetings, emailing, etc. became more real. As Stephanie has suggested, you have to double down in your resistance.

SV Reader, as it turned out, none of the administration's efforts to review faculty workload meant anything beyond the fact that I was deeply naive to think they ever would. And what gave was the fact that John collapsed in sudden cardiac arrest in October 2021 and was put in a medically induced coma for several days, during which I was not sure if he would live or die.

Suddenly, the amount of writing I had sacrificed sleep and weekends for – the articles, the essays, the stories, the novels, the scholarly books – meant absolutely nothing in the face of losing my life partner. They would not lie beside me at night, breathing so, breathing so, breathing so, or reminisce with me about something our children had done when they were young, or take my hand in a darkened theatre.

Did I regret writing them, or writing at all? Of course not. John and I are both inveterate writers, it's what brought us together, and it's what gives us life. But I came to realise I was doing some of this writing because of a misguided belief that I had something to prove: 'you're not going to give me the course release I deserve – fine, I'll show you, I'll write more!' – and I was doing far too much of it, or rather, giving up too much of my personal life for it. Case in point: when my mother-in-law, a woman I adored, passed away in her late 80s, her large extended family (John is one of eight) gathered for a capacious celebration of her life. It was the first time we'd all been together for years. But I also had a book deadline in two weeks and I was behind. So every night, after my John and my kids went to bed, I stayed up in our Hampton Inn sitting room banging out the last 10,000 words of *The Geek's Guide to the Writing Life*. I regret this now, more for myself than anyone else. No one else knew I was doing it. But I did. Like a lot of things in life (including your children's childhoods), your mother-in-law's funeral only comes along once. I could have just asked for an extension. Put some other things on hold. Taken some time to be more present and reflect on the huge influence she'd had on my life.

JV Looking back, I have to say I am amazed that Stephanie hid these late-night work sessions as well as she did. My recollection is that she participated fully in the events of those days, but what she's saying is that mentally she wasn't as present as she could have been if she hadn't worried so much about getting her book done. And that is a shame, because indeed my mother and Stephanie were quite close. I guess the lesson there is that balancing work and family, making room for work and family, sometimes means putting work completely aside for that family.

SV And for yourself. Here is the part where I say, maybe you don't need to write *too much* and maybe you don't have to almost lose your partner, which brings you right up close to your own mortality, to think about that. Maybe the omnipresence of the pandemic and the spectre of mortality, illness, and disability it has wrought has brought this home for you. Or the great resignation.

I haven't stopped writing. I am not sure I ever will. In the past decades, I have often had numerous writing projects going at once, and sometimes I still do: a scholarly book or article, a novel, a memoir in essays. But I have stopped being in such a hurry about it. In the past, my mantra had been: *so many writing projects, so little time*. I worked as if I might die tomorrow with all the things I wanted to write – novels, memoirs, scholarly books – left unfinished, and that would be itself a great tragedy.

Everyone responds differently to crises. But what our family's health crisis showed me in a way that perhaps nothing else could have, is that, at least to me, the great slate of projects ahead of me didn't really matter. They would still be there or they wouldn't. They would get written or they wouldn't. What did matter was that I wrote when I needed to, about what I needed to. Not that I checked one more publication off my list.

JV Maybe what bears saying is that with your family situation, reader, it might not involve a heart-related health crisis. That may not be what you face. If your kids are still young, it might be a slate of soccer (sorry, football) games that you are faced with. Or days in which they are home sick from school. Or, if they are a bit older, chaperoning them to a variety of orchestra activities. Or hosting a sleepover. Or driving them six hundred miles to a summer camp. In balancing work duties and writing life and family life, you don't want to begin to think of family time as a negative, something carried out only grudgingly, while writing and work time is a pure positive. That's not balance. First of all, family duties are not a negative. They have their own innate value, their own intimate joy. And thinking about your family life as a negative, a time-suck, will make you both an unhappy parent and unhappy employee. Instead, lean into what responsibilities family life demands, and you will be the better person and writer for it. I remember reading an article once by the poet Sydney Lea. I remember Lea saying, with writer-parents in mind, that a writer should be the full person that they are. If your kids are sick, then be the parent who takes care of a sick child. Don't resent it; don't avoid it. Obviously it's better for your children that you do so. But it's not only that. The fullness of the person you are, he said (and I'm paraphrasing), will only be reflected in your writing; it will only make the writing richer.

SV That is definitely true. But I think I want to emphasise something broader: an aversion to busyness in general. Or, rather, a resistance to busyness. My current work in progress is a textbook on teaching creative writing that is, in some ways, my magnum opus, the chance to assemble everything I've thought and researched about the subject over the years. While I am deeply committed to it, for the first time in my life, I asked for an extension on the project, an extension of several months. Not because my annus horribilis had set me back – although that was part of it – but because there was other writing that I needed and wanted to do related to my personal life; and again, for the first time, I realised I didn't want to try to do them both at the same time. Sometimes you can't and sometimes you shouldn't. You really shouldn't, and it's important to make peace with that. You are a whole person. Not just a writing machine.

This knowledge has been hard won but I am glad I have it. I still struggle – shiny new projects constantly appeal to me. I think they always will. But I fight back. I tell myself working through the weekends doesn't help anyone, least of all the most important person: me. I tell myself to rest. To work on one project at a time instead of three. To appreciate my life and my partner and my family and to be present in this moment instead of thinking about the eternal list of accomplishments to check off on a list that will never end *unless I end it*. And so I am working on this chapter on a Friday afternoon at 4:45. In truth, I am a little behind. The old me would go back to it this weekend. The new me won't pick it up again until Monday, three days from the deadline. The new me wants to enjoy her weekend, to rest and restore the energy she will need to get through the next week.

Be like the new me.

References

Brody, M. (1993), *Manly Writing: Gender, Rhetoric and the Rise of Composition*. Carbondale, IL: Southern Illinois University Press.

Flynn, E. A. (1988), 'Composing as a Woman', *College Composition and Communication*, 39(4): 423–435. Available online: https://doi.org/10.2307/357697 (accessed 27 September 2022).

Rich, A. (1979), 'Taking Women Students Seriously', *The Radical Teacher*, 11: 40–43. Available online: http://www.jstor.org/stable/20709173 (accessed 27 September 2022).

Spigelman, C. (2001), 'Argument and Evidence in the Case of the Personal', *College English*, 64(1): 63–87.

www.ingramcontent.com/pod-product-compliance
Lightning Source LLC
Chambersburg PA
CBHW052119300426
44116CB00010B/1725